Innovation in Environmental Leadership

T0270816

Innovation in Environmental Leadership offers innovative approaches to leadership from a post-industrial and ecological vantage point. Chapters in this collection are written by leading scholars and practitioners of environmental leadership from around the globe, and are informed by a variety of critical perspectives, including post-heroic approaches, systems thinking, and the emerging insights of Critical Leadership Studies (CLS).

By taking the natural environment seriously as a foundational context for leadership, *Innovation in Environmental Leadership* offers fresh insights and compelling visions of leadership pertinent to 21st-century environmental and social challenges. Concepts and understandings of leadership emerged as part of an extractive industrial system; this work asks its readers to rethink what leadership looks like in an ecologically sustainable biological system.

This book provides fresh insights and critical perspectives on the vibrant and growing field of environmental leadership. It shows the latest state of knowledge on the topic and will be of interest both to students at an advanced level, academics, and reflective practitioners. It addresses the topics with regard to leadership theory and environmental leadership and will be of interest to researchers, academics, and students in the fields of sustainability, environmental ethics, natural resource management, environmental studies, business management, public policy, and environmental management.

Benjamin W. Redekop is Professor of Leadership Studies at Christopher Newport University, USA.

Deborah Rigling Gallagher is Associate Professor of the Practice of Environmental Policy at Duke University, USA.

Rian Satterwhite is Director of Service Learning and Leadership at the University of Nevada, Las Vegas, USA.

Routledge Studies in Leadership Research

Innovation in Environmental Leadership

Critical Perspectives

Edited by
Benjamin W. Redekop, Deborah Rigling
Gallagher and Rian Satterwhite

LONDON AND NEW YORK

First published 2018
by Routledge

2 Park Square, Milton Park, Abingdon, Oxfordshire OX14 4RN
52 Vanderbilt Avenue, New York, NY 10017

Routledge is an imprint of the Taylor & Francis Group, an informa business

First issued in paperback 2019

Library of Congress Cataloging in Publication Data
A catalog record for this book has been requested

ISBN: 978-1-138-63660-6 (hbk)
ISBN: 978-0-367-25382-0 (pbk)

Typeset in Sabon
by Taylor & Francis Books

We dedicate this book to Seana Lowe Steffen, who left the Earth far too soon. Seana was a bright and visionary spirit who embraced the value of leadership to ensure a sustainable future. Although Seana is no longer with us, she will continue to inspire us.

Contents

List of illustrations

Figures

Table

Boxes

Contributors

Kathleen E. Allen is President of her own consulting firm, Kathleen Allen and Associates. In her consulting practice, she specializes in leadership coaching and organizational change in human service non-profit organizations, foundations, higher educational institutions, businesses, and health care and collaborative networks. Dr. Allen has written and presented widely on topics related to leadership, human development, and organizational development. Currently she is writing a book titled *The Generous Organization: Leadership Lessons Inspired by Nature*. Dr. Allen is a skilled facilitator of organizational change and organizational development. The earmarks of her work are long-term sustainable change and increased capacity in organizations. She has a Doctorate in Leadership from the University of San Diego, CA.

Shawn Andrews is a Mununjali man who currently lives on Wurundjeri country in Melbourne, Australia. As an experienced educator, presenter, and social entrepreneur, Shawn saw an opportunity to teach the world about the importance of connection and how connection can create an inclusive world. Driven by his passion, Shawn created a company called Indigicate. The company, now in its third year, aims to create unity between Indigenous and non-Indigenous Australians by focusing on educating non-Indigenous Australians about connection to self and the environment, and by teaching Indigenous Australian culture and history from an Indigenous perspective.

Jem Bendell is a Professor of Sustainability Leadership at the University of Cumbria and an Adjunct Professor of Management at Griffith University. He founded the Institute for Leadership and Sustainability (IFLAS) in 2012, including the co-development of a successful sustainability-themed international MBA program. He supports senior leaders in business, investment, voluntary organisations, and political parties, on matters of strategy, communications, and professional development. In 2017, he supported the office of the leader of the UK opposition during the general election campaign, including speechwriting. His previous work includes roles at the United Nations and the World Wide Fund for Nature (WWF).

The World Economic Forum appointed him a Young Global Leader for work on sustainable development. He is co-author of *Healing Capitalism* (2014) and volunteers for a grassroots initiative that supports over 300 local currencies around the world with free open source software.

David J. Brown is Professor of Biology and Environmental Science at Marietta College (Ohio). His research focuses on the impacts of environmental pollution. Before becoming a professor, he worked in the biotechnology industry. His current research examines heavy metal pollution in the Mid-Ohio Valley. Dr. Brown has published work in journals such as *Environmental Science and Technology* and *Science of the Total Environment*. He is an affiliated faculty member with the McDonough Center for Leadership and Business at Marietta College, where he teaches courses on leadership and conservation in Central America. Dr. Brown holds a PhD from Duke University.

D. Adam Cletzer is an Assistant Professor in the University of Missouri's Department of Agricultural Education & Leadership, where he supports an undergraduate minor in Leadership Studies. Adam's research interests include ecological and complexity approaches to leadership in community contexts. Adam holds a Bachelor of Science in public relations (2004) and Master of Science in agricultural education and communication (2012), both from the University of Florida. Adam received his Doctor of Philosophy from Virginia Tech in 2016.

Tina Lynn Evans is a Professor of Sustainability Studies at Colorado Mountain College where she teaches in the Bachelor of Arts program in that field. She is also the author of *Occupy Education: Living and Learning Sustainability* (2012, Peter Lang) and the 2016 recipient of the AASHE sustainability research award. Evans teaches permaculture, research methodology and methods, energy issues in society, globalized political economy, beekeeping, and place-centered sustainability praxis. Her recent writings focus on transdisciplinary theory and practice and on generating hope and agency through sustainability education. More information and links to publications can be found online (http://colora domtn.academia.edu/TinaEvans; http://tinalynnevans.com/).

David Forsyth has been studying and working in outdoor and environmental education since 2000. He has worked with school, university, and TAFE students and loves inspiring and equipping young people to make the world a better place. When not teaching, you can find him on wild adventures in the great outdoors or hanging out with family and friends.

Deborah Rigling Gallagher is Associate Professor of the Practice of Environmental Policy at Duke University's Nicholas School of Environment. Her research focuses on business environmental leadership such as corporate engagement in climate policy, carbon pricing leadership, and business engagement in global health. She edited *Environmental Leadership: A Reference Handbook* (Sage, 2012). She received her PhD in Public Policy from UNC Chapel Hill, a Master's Degree in Public Policy from Harvard University's Kennedy School of Government, and a BS in Chemical Engineering from Northwestern University. Dr. Gallagher has also held a series of environmental leadership positions in the public and private sector.

Eric K. Kaufman is an Associate Professor and Extension Specialist in Virginia Tech's Department of Agricultural, Leadership, and Community Education, where he coordinates a graduate certificate program in Collaborative Community Leadership and supports an undergraduate minor of Leadership and Social Change. Eric's research interests include collegiate leadership education and leadership development with adults in community and volunteer settings. Eric holds a Bachelor of Science degree from The Ohio State University (2000); both his Master's and his Doctor of Philosophy degrees are from the University of Florida (2004 and 2007).

Paul Kosempel is currently a Teaching Associate Professor in leadership studies at the University of Denver (DU) as well as Interim Director of the Pioneer Leadership Program. Paul joined the faculty in 2007 and soon after received his doctorate, which explored communication dynamics in mentoring relationships through a relational dialectics lens. His professional experience includes over 20 years in institutions of higher education in various capacities including career development, leadership development, operations, and event management. He is co-convener of the Sustainability Leadership Learning Community of the International Leadership Association. He has presented at multiple conferences of the International Leadership Association and the Association of Leadership Educators. His research interests include leadership and sustainability, assessment of leadership learning outcomes, and mentoring and leadership. He is also part-owner of the Green Bay Packers.

Robert M. McManus is the McCoy Professor of Leadership Studies and Communication at the McDonough Center for Leadership and Business at Marietta College (Ohio). He is the co-author of *Understanding Leadership: An Arts and Humanities Perspective* (Routledge, 2015). His work has appeared in the *Journal of Leadership Studies* and he served as a section editor for the book *Leading in Complex Worlds,* published by Jossey-Bass. His latest work is an edited volume, *Ethical Leadership: A Primer* (forthcoming, Edward Elgar). McManus has also served as the Chair of the Leadership Education Member Interest Group of the International Leadership Association. He holds a PhD in Communication as well as a Master of Business Administration.

Fentahun Mengistu is a PhD fellow in Educational Policy and Leadership at Bahir Dar University, Ethiopia. He earned a BA and MA in Educational

Leadership and Management at Addis Ababa University. In addition, he has been working as a lecturer, researcher, and policy analysis expert both at Wollo University and the Ethiopian Higher Education Strategy Center.

Vachel Miller is an Associate Professor in the Department of Leadership and Educational Studies at Appalachian State University. He currently coordinates the Higher Education Program at Appalachian. In 2015–2016, Vachel lived with his wife Sarah and three children in Bahir Dar, Ethiopia, as a Fulbright Scholar. He holds an EdD in educational policy and leadership from the Center for International Education at the University of Massachusetts Amherst. He is editor of *Apocalyptic Leadership in Education: Facing an Unsustainable World from Where We Stand* (Information Age Publishing, 2017).

Linda G. Olson began teaching at the University of Denver (DU) in 2000 and has spent the past 14 years as Teaching Professor/Director of the Pioneer Leadership Program and Executive Director of Learning Communities and Civic Engagement. Recently, she was appointed Interim Dean of Colorado Women's College at DU. Her research interests include collaborative leadership, leadership development, leadership and sustainability, and leadership ethics. Having led service learning classes throughout the world, Linda brings a vibrant international interest to her teaching and research. In addition, Linda is active in local leadership as an elected City Council Member of the City of Englewood, CO.

Filiberto Penados is Academic Director and indigenous studies and education professor at the Center for Engaged Learning Abroad in Belize. He holds a PhD in education studies from the University of Otago, Dunedin, New Zealand. Dr. Penados has held faculty positions at the University of Belize and Galen University. He is currently affiliated with the University of Toronto, where he is Assistant professor (status-only) at the Center for Aboriginal Initiatives. Dr. Penados was co-founder and director of the Tumul K'in Center of Learning, an indigenous education and development initiative in Southern Belize and president of the Central American Indigenous Council. He currently chairs the board of Julian Cho Society, a Mayan organization, and serves in the advisory committee to the Maya. His current research interests are in indigenous development and education.

Benjamin W. Redekop is Professor of Leadership Studies at Christopher Newport University in Newport News, VA. He teaches courses in the President's Leadership Program at CNU, including Theories and Perspectives on Leadership, Environmental Leadership, and Outdoor Leadership. His books include *Leadership for Environmental Sustainability* (Routledge, 2010), *Power, Authority, and the Anabaptist Tradition* (Johns Hopkins University Press, 2001), and *Enlightenment and Community: Lessing, Abbt, Herder, and the Quest for a German Public*

(McGill-Queen's University Press, 2000). He lives in Newport News with his wife Fran and daughter Katarina.

Rian Satterwhite serves as Director of Service Learning and Leadership at the University of Nevada, Las Vegas, where his office supports academic service learning, a leadership and civic engagement minor, as well as co-curricular service and leadership development. Author of numerous publications exploring topics such as long timescales, complex adaptive systems, critical theory, and peace and sustainability, he is interested in exploring how leadership theory and practice evolve as we increasingly recognize our place within complex natural and social systems.

Girma Shimelis is a Lecturer at Jigjiga University in Ethiopia. He earned his MA in 2011 in Educational Leadership and Management at Addis Ababa University. He is now a PhD student in Educational Policy and Leadership at Bahir Dar University, Ethiopia.

Seana Lowe Steffen (d. 2017) was founder and CEO of the Restorative Leadership Institute, an award-winning certified B Corp. Grassroots to globally, Seana dedicated herself to advancing leadership for collective well-being with her 25 years of experience in leadership and organizational development. A master guide and transformational facilitator, her research and work spanned countries and continents, heads of state, and multinational enterprise teams. Seana's awards include ETown National Public Radio's "E-chievement Award" and Mortar Board's Outstanding Professor. She chaired the World Pulse Global Advisory Network and was a certified UN Climate Change Trainer. Seana was the victim of a tragic automobile accident on September 16, 2017. She touched many lives and was a force for good in the world.

Neil Sutherland After spending his formative years touring across the world in DIY punk bands, Neil has now taken the not-so-obvious career progression of writing and teaching about the theory and practice of organizations. One of his primary interests is the performance of leadership in "alternative" organizations, including radically democratic social movements. Here he draws on Critical Leadership Studies (CLS) to conceptualize leadership as a socially constructed collective process, and is particularly interested in exploring democratic practices and how they facilitate non-hierarchical forms of organization.

Richard Little has worked in the field of leadership development for 35 years: with Impact http://www.impactinternational.com/ and as Visiting Professor at the Institute for Leadership and Sustainability. The organizations that employed Richard as consultant came in every shape, size, and condition and from every sector. "In my consulting work I wish always to offer people alternatives to the seductive fantasies of patriarchal, scopocratic, and dehumanizing managerialism; the goal of my teaching and writing is to contribute to the creation of socially just and sustainable institutions. My ideas about leadership began to take shape when I was expelled from school, a career high-point that I have not since managed to exceed."

Morgan Thomas graduated *magna cum laude* with a BA in History and American Studies, and a minor in Leadership Studies, from Christopher Newport University in May 2015. He is a former Fulbright Scholar and recipient of the Huayu Enrichment Scholarship, and is currently a graduate student in Political Science at the University of British Columbia, focusing on East Asian politics and security.

Simon Western is Adjunct Professor at University College Dublin, Chief Executive of Analytic-Network Coaching, and President of the International Society for the Psychoanalytic Study of Organizations. Simon has international experience as a leadership coach, strategic consultant, and keynote speaker on eco-leadership, delivering "new leadership for the network society." He authored two internationally acclaimed books on leadership and coaching and founded Analytic-Network Coaching Ltd with the purpose of *Coaching leaders to act in "good faith" to create the "good society."*

Introduction

Benjamin W. Redekop, Deborah Rigling Gallagher and Rian Satterwhite

This book offers innovative approaches to leadership from a post-industrial and ecological vantage point. Chapters in this collection are informed by a variety of global and critical perspectives, including post-heroic approaches, systems thinking, and the emerging insights of Critical Leadership Studies (CLS). It builds on previous scholarly work in the growing field of environmental leadership to examine in critical detail the challenges and possibilities of leadership aimed at fostering a more just and sustainable world. By taking the natural environment seriously as a foundational context for leadership, *Innovation in Environmental Leadership* offers fresh insights and compelling visions of leadership pertinent to the post-modern world.

An important aim of this book is to foster understanding and practice of environmental leadership as promoting the flourishing of both the natural environment and humanity within its natural home. Values such as social justice, peace, equality, emancipation, and human rights are thus integral to the discussion (Satterwhite et al., 2015). This collection furthermore reinforces and develops the emerging insight that the biosphere is the ultimate context for all forms of leadership, and that placing leadership into its environmental context transforms and enriches our understanding of leadership in all sectors of human experience. It therefore advances the study and practice of leadership beyond the industrial, managerial, and extractive contexts in which it first took shape while providing direction for those who wish to reconceptualize and redirect leadership for the benefit of all.

Until very recently, the notion that "leadership" as a general construct had anything to do with concern for the natural environment was not widely held in the field of leadership studies (see the literature review in Redekop, 2010, pp. 2–6). This has begun to change, with the recent publication of comprehensive works that situate leadership within its environmental and ecological contexts, including, for example, Western's *Leadership: A Critical Text* (2008/2013 – discussed further below), Gallagher's *Environmental Leadership: A Reference Handbook* (2012), Stober et al.'s *Nature-Centered Leadership* (2013), and a variety of journal articles and book chapters.

The present volume is in some respects a sequel to *Leadership for Environmental Sustainability* (Redekop, 2010), the first multi-disciplinary edited collection to foreground "leadership" as a construct imbued with environmental implications. That work, like *Environmental Leadership: A Reference Handbook*, did not stipulate any particular theoretical or disciplinary perspective, beyond acknowledging the inherent connections and linkages between widely accepted notions of "leadership" and concern for the natural world as the ultimate context for human life and flourishing. The present volume continues the discussion by consciously developing critical, post-heroic, and global perspectives on environmental leadership. In what follows, we briefly highlight the theoretical contours and goals of this book, before introducing individual chapters.

Modern Conceptions of Leadership and the Critical Response

As stated by Western (2013), and echoed by others (e.g. Evans, 2011; Sinclair, 2007; Wilson, 2016), the dominant modern discourses of leadership have taken shape largely from the world of business, industry, and commerce, and are fundamentally "instrumentalist" in orientation, aimed at maximizing profit and efficiency at the expense of all else, including social and environmental well-being (Western, 2013, pp. 7–8). In other words, modern conceptions of leadership arose in concert with what has turned out to be an environmentally unsustainable socio-economic world system, and reflect the weaknesses and vulnerabilities of that system. This is not to say that modern industry is the only context in which the study and practice of leadership have been salient, only that it has been – and continues to be – a highly influential context for the study, practice, and development of "leadership" as a construct.

Since business schools and the larger world of business and industry have been highly active and influential in how we understand and practice leadership, it comes as no surprise that the most stringent criticisms of modern conceptions of leadership have come from the same sector (see for example the literature review in Alvesson & Spicer, 2012). Arising in the wake of Critical Management Studies (CMS), Critical Leadership Studies (CLS) has emerged for the most part out of business schools. According to Collinson (2011), writing in the *SAGE Handbook of Leadership*, CLS denotes "broad, diverse and heterogenous perspectives that share a concern to critique the power relations and identity constructions through which leadership dynamics are often reproduced, frequently rationalized, sometimes resisted and occasionally transformed" (p. 181).

CLS critiques essentialist, heroic, and dualistic understandings of leadership, suggesting instead dialectical approaches that acknowledge follower agency and the realities of power and complexity in human and organizational dynamics (Collinson, 2014; Collinson & Tourish, 2015; Dugan, 2017; Sinclair, 2007; Wilson, 2016). It draws on critical theory (including, importantly, the works of Michel Foucault) to foreground the power/knowledge nexus in social and organizational life, and the hidden and varied ways that those in positions of authority exercise dominance and hegemony, as well as the existence of resistance and nonconformity. It suggests that dominant modern leadership discourses ignore and/or repress the complex power dynamics at play in organizational life, assuming instead consensus and compliance even when they are not present, and ignoring the roles of followers and followership in shaping the leadership process. "Proposing a more nuanced approach to leader and follower power, influence, and agency, critical [leadership] courses re-conceptualise leadership as a co-constructed, asymmetrical and shifting dynamic characterized by complex situated and mutually-reinforcing relations between leaders and followers" (Collinson & Tourish, 2015, p. 577).

A fundamental component of CLS is a strong social/cultural constructivism and critique of essentialism, with CLS scholars holding that "leadership," as a social and cultural construct, is in fact highly dependent upon, and interwoven with, embodied and contextual factors. At the same time, however, what gets mentioned as relevant contexts in these studies normally does not include the natural environment (see for example Collinson, 2011; Collinson, 2014; Collinson & Tourish, 2015; Dugan, 2017; Sinclair, 2007), except occasionally as an afterthought (Wilson, 2016, p. 209). "Context" is often discussed by leadership scholars mainly in reference to cultural context (e.g., Jackson & Parry, 2011, pp. 69–94). Thus, although leadership scholars have for some time been drawing attention to the importance of contextual factors in shaping and conditioning the nature of leadership and the process (e.g., Osborn et al., 2002), even critical theorists and students of the field remain blind to the natural environment as an important – if not the ultimate – context for leadership.

Leadership scholar Barbara Kellerman, in seeking to take context seriously as a factor in leadership (Kellerman, 2015), consigns her discussion of the natural environment to a journalistic chapter on climate change toward the end of her book, and leaves unchallenged the leader-centric focus of the "leadership industry" that she so resolutely criticizes in other texts (e.g., Kellerman, 2012). Kellerman treats "the environment" from within the dominant paradigm of heroic leaders who simply need to be well-informed and well-intentioned in order for positive change to occur, rather than embedding contextual factors like the natural environment into a critique and reconceptualization of "the leadership industry," of which her many works must be counted a part. The result is a repetition of some of the well-known facts and challenges of climate change, combined with boilerplate blandishments for industry leaders to pay more attention to the issue, "manage" others to stop degrading the environment, and plan for the future particularly via the provision of renewable energy (Kellerman, 2015, pp. 223–232).

Thus, both mainstream and critical theorists tend to be myopic when it comes to the foundational role of the natural environment in our lives and leadership. The CLS focus on the socio-cultural construction of leadership ignores the fact that we all inhabit a physical/natural universe that is in the end not a human construction – at least not in its fundamental features. One can certainly argue that our understandings and conceptions of "nature" are at some level social/cultural constructions and that the human–natural system is a "hybrid" of nature and culture; but we do not "construct" the physical world and the laws of nature that govern it any more than we are able to avoid death or change the fact that spewing large quantities of CO_2 into the atmosphere results in global warming.

To take any other view is to succumb to the modern technocratic optimism that has thus far only dug us deeper into ecological crisis, and which has produced unsustainable conceptions of leadership (for discussion of the latter see especially Chapters 1 and 4 in this volume). And to focus solely on human emancipation as the paramount goal of leadership (e.g., Alvesson & Spicer, 2012; Sinclair, 2007), laudable as it may be, is simply to perpetuate the anthropocentrism that is ultimately behind our degradation of the natural world. It should not be a revolutionary statement to say that a normative conception of "leadership" aims not only at human emancipation, but also includes larger and more inclusive ideals about the flourishing of all life on this wondrous and life-filled planet. The causes and effects of human leadership extend to the nonhuman lifeworld; any factory or plantation led by a titan of industry or agriculture that pollutes the biosphere is an example of this proposition.

It is therefore a goal of this collection to broaden CLS to include the natural environment as a fundamental – and neglected – context for thinking critically about leadership. Just as powerful, "heroic" leaders can easily dominate followers and repress healthy resistance and feedback (Collinson, 2011, p. 185; Collinson & Tourish, 2015, pp. 588–589), so can they also dominate the natural world, repressing the important feedback that it has to offer. We suggest that CLS needs to broaden its scope to the wider nonhuman world as a locus for leader domination as well as healthy feedback and resistance. In other words, the "dialectical approach" of CLS (Collinson, 2011, p. 184) needs to include nonhuman actors – and forms of life – in the dialectics of leadership. That such a conclusion logically follows from the CLS critique of leadership as traditionally conceived is demonstrated in that Wilson (2016) belatedly calls for the development of "environmental leadership" at the conclusion to her extended critique of leadership as conceived and taught in business schools (p. 209).

The Eco-Leadership Paradigm: Critical Leadership Studies Meets Ecology

Simon Western is one of the few critical theorists who has advanced a comprehensive social, historical, contextual, and dialectical analysis of the evolution of modern leadership discourse. As such, it takes full account of the natural environment as the ultimate frame, context, and ground for leadership (Western, 2013; see also Western, 2010, and Chapter 3 in this volume). According to Western, there are four historical yet overlapping modern discourses of leadership: Controller (Scientific Management), Therapist (the Human Relations movement), Messiah (Transformational and other forms of "heroic" leadership), and Eco-leadership (Systemic, ethical, distributed leadership models).

Eco-leadership, according to Western, is an emerging discourse that has become salient in the early 21st century in the face of a wide range of emerging trends and dilemmas – the rise of social movements and the quest for environmental sustainability not least among them. The eco-leadership discourse (or "paradigm" – Western uses both terms) is however not simply an "environmental" discourse applicable only to the natural environment, but rather an all-encompassing way of talking and thinking ultimately rooted in ecological and systems-thinking but applicable to all forms of social and organizational life. If the early 20th century era of the "Controller" discourse was rooted in machine metaphors, the 21st century "Eco-leadership" discourse is rooted in ecological metaphors, for obvious reasons: we are being forced to come to terms with the larger ecological system of which we are but a part, which our machines have been steadily altering, impairing, transforming, and destroying.

The emerging eco-leadership discourse "is characterized by new understandings of organizations as ecosystems within ecosystems. The focus is on networks, connectivity, and interdependence, where new forms of distributed leadership occur within organizations, and new connections with stakeholders and wider society takes place. Ethics is at the heart of eco-leadership" (Western, 2013, p. 4). Whether or not we are aware of it, we are increasingly thinking, talking, and acting within the realm of this discourse, since discourses shape and frame what is "thinkable." The various forms and types of leadership thinking that undermine the dominant paradigm of heroic visionary leaders transforming their organizations and followers can be located within this discourse, regardless of any one theorist's ecological concern. The aim of the present work, and others like it, is to bring to the surface the systemic environmental and ecological dimensions and implications of this discourse. According to Western, "'Ecology is not the exclusive domain of the environmentalist' (Hasdell, 2008: 99), and the ecosystems I refer to are not only natural ecosystems, they are also hybrids, made up of nature, technology and the human/social. Eco-leadership therefore is not exclusive to environmental leadership, but applies to all leadership" (2013, pp. 244–245).

Readers who consult Western's work will thus find a fully grounded critical theory, with attention paid to social, political, historical, economic, psychological, and therapeutic elements, in intimate relation and interaction with the ecological systems and processes that sustain and support all life on this earth. Western's contribution has thus been to connect CLS to the natural environment, embedding the insights of CLS within a constructive vision of what leadership can and should look like in the 21st century, and providing a historical and conceptual framework for understanding it and how we got here. As such his work represents one of the most fully-developed critical theories of environmental leadership currently available, and it informs the present collection.

However, to highlight Western's work does not mean that a variety of other thinkers have not also begun to explore the deep connections between post-heroic, critical conceptions of leadership and ecological concerns and perspectives; and this volume is offered as a state-of-the-art collection of some of the best recent thinking on this topic. Readers will find a series of stimulating, readable chapters that range across the spectrum of scholarly disciplines, devoted to critical exploration of relationships and connections between "leadership" and the natural world. In addition, readers will notice different emphases and perspectives at work: for example, some contributors focus more on leadership, while others focus more on followership; some are highly theoretical, others more praxis-oriented. Some chapters are more personal and oriented toward individual consciousness and self-development, while others are more sociological and outward-looking. A number of the chapters have an international/global dimension, and many of the chapters weave empirical data into their analyses. The chapter sequence flows from more overtly critical/theoretical pieces to more praxis-oriented and empirical studies, culminating in chapters that emphasize more personal and spiritual/philosophical perspectives. We suggest that reading the chapters in order will provide a rich and unfolding sequence of ideas, data, and reflections on environmental leadership.

Finally, it is our contention that while critical perspectives can help illuminate the contours of post-heroic forms of leadership that are attuned not only to social but also environmental justice, it would be naïve to dismiss the role of powerful positional leaders in all walks of life, and thus a critically informed pragmatism is in order: there is unlikely to be one single form or conception of "leadership" that is "the" answer. The best critical theory is not simply deconstructive but also reconstructive, leveling the playing field so that new and diverse perspectives and understandings can emerge alongside – and perhaps help transform – existing ones, and it is our hope that this volume can play a constructive role in this process.

Chapter Descriptions

In Chapter 1, "The Seven Unsustainabilities of Mainstream Leadership," Jem Bendell, Richard Little, and Neil Sutherland argue that the prevailing leadership imaginary, so far from supporting the transition to a sustainable society and economy, may actually hinder it and be itself unsustainable. This is because it depends on the discoursal maintenance of power relations and a narrow range of organizing possibilities, and may thus discourage or disable more collective, collaborative, or distributed forms of leadership, deliberation, organizing, and problem-solving. Drawing on the field of

Critical Leadership Studies (CLS), the authors integrate these critiques by outlining "seven unsustainabilities" of mainstream leadership thinking, and the antidotes that are relevant to sustainability, before offering a definition of sustainable leadership and outlining some potential implications for the future of research, practice and education.

Chapter 2, "A Case for Universal Contexts: Intersections of the Biosphere, Systems, and Justice Using a Critical Constructionist Lens," by Rian Satterwhite, examines the natural intersections between the biosphere, systems, and justice, and their role as universal contexts for leadership. Utilizing critical theory and constructionist perspectives, Satterwhite suggests that leadership theory and practice need common ground to stand upon and that acknowledging these universal contexts helps to achieve this. They are descriptive rather than prescriptive in nature, meaning that acknowledging their reality shapes our discourse and practice while still allowing space for the myriad of cultural and organizational realities that spring from this common ground. Satterwhite argues that this approach does not lead to a grand unified theory of leadership; rather, it provides a common language and a common set of overarching goals across the diversity of leadership theory, research, and practice.

In "The Eco-Leadership Paradox" (Chapter 3), Simon Western examines some of the challenges and paradoxes faced by those desiring to introduce Eco-leadership into their organizations. For example, leaders can revert to "Messiah" or "Controller" leadership in seeking to bring Eco-leadership into an organization. In response to this paradox, Western develops the idea that Eco-leadership is a "Meta-Discourse" that allows us to understand and deploy previously dominant leadership discourses in a useful fashion, and he explores the deep ideological underpinnings of prevailing leadership discourses – which he characterizes as "Individualism-More" – and the need for the development of a new ideology of "Network-Ethics." Doing so helps to productively engage with the paradoxes that can arise when an attempt is made to move from "Controller," "Therapist," and "Messiah" discourses to Eco-leadership, a radically different approach to leadership.

In Chapter 4, "Sustainable Leadership: Toward Restoring the Human and Natural Worlds," Tina Lynn Evans asks: "Can we develop leadership today that is not inherently corrupt and manipulative? Can we organize people effectively within systems of leadership and participation in order to (re)cast societies into forms that nurture and justly serve people and nature simultaneously?" In answering these and other questions, Evans argues that sustainability cannot be achieved in the absence of social justice because social injustice derives from the same mindset – the same narrow instrumentalist orientation to the world and others – that fuels environmental destruction. To pursue sustainability through manipulative and exploitive means would entail creating new systems of domination that would feed the creation of new, unsustainable systems. Rather, Evans makes several claims: 1) sustainable leadership is centrally defined by the purposes it serves; 2) sustainable leadership embodies a fitting response to the socio-ecological challenges implicated in the decisions and actions taken; 3) sustainable leadership is integrative and ultimately place-centered; 4) everyone must have access to serve as a leader; 5) leadership must be actively developed in everyone in a sustainable society; and 6) sustainable leadership engages imperfectly in processes of long-term cultural change.

Heretofore, there have been few, if any, empirical studies linking an ecological approach to leadership with organizational success. In "Eco-Leadership, Complexity Science, and 21st-Century Organizations: A Theoretical and Empirical Analysis" (Chapter 5), D. Adam Cletzer and Eric K. Kaufman address this gap by offering empirical findings, informed by complexity science and systems theory, supporting the claim that an ecological approach will lead to more adaptive organizations that have greater success over time. They first discuss the promise of complexity science in leadership studies and the 21st century organization as an ecological system, before turning to their empirical findings and discussion of what an eco-leader might do to help their organization to become truly ecological in form and function.

In Chapter 6, "Toward an Understanding of the Relationship Between the Study of Leadership and the Natural World," Robert M. McManus proposes that leadership scholars must more fully incorporate the natural world into their understanding of leadership if we are to better understand the leadership process. Building upon the Five Components of Leadership Model advanced by McManus and Perruci in *Understanding Leadership: An arts and humanities Perspective* (2015), McManus proposes that the natural world be conceived as playing a role equal to the other five components of the model, resulting in a more capacious definition of leadership: "Leadership is the process by which leaders and followers develop a relationship and work together toward a goal (or goals) within a context shaped by cultural values and norms, *and functions within and is constrained by the natural world.*" Echoing the biologist E.O. Wilson, McManus concludes that "Perhaps the time has also come to cease calling the incorporation of the natural world into the process of leadership simply 'environmental leadership' and start calling it real-world leadership."

Chapter 7, "The Unseen Revolution: Leadership for Sustainability in the Tropical Biosphere," by Paul Kosempel, Linda G. Olson, and Filiberto Penados, explores sustainability leadership efforts that are quietly taking place in the tropical biosphere in Belize. The authors answer the call to examine leadership efforts in the "majority world," and to understand how these leadership efforts reflect the concerns and perspectives of critical approaches to leadership studies. Friends for Conservation and Development, Long Caye at Lighthouse Reef Atoll, and The Nature Conservancy-Belize are three such efforts that make significant contributions to sustainable development within the tropical biosphere. Their work is largely unseen by the larger world, but is essential to their nation and our world, and provides examples of eco-leadership in practice.

The following three chapters turn our attention to leadership in the context of climate change. In Chapter 8, "Heroes No More: Businesses Practice Collaborative Leadership to Confront Climate Change," Deborah Rigling Gallagher details the efforts of United Nations Global Compact (UNGC) members to perform *collaborative environmental leadership* and engage in climate policy development at the global level under the auspices of the UNGC's Caring for Climate (C4C) platform. The author attended a series of UNGC meetings from 2013–2015, interacting with attendees to uncover the ways in which environmental leadership practice evolved and to knit together a working theory of collaborative environmental leadership. The chapter begins with an overview of the history and structure of the United Nations Global Compact as a transnational public–private partnership and agent of environmental leadership. The Caring for Climate platform is then detailed. This sets the stage for a larger consideration of how UNGC members engaged collaboratively in two C4C initiatives, Responsible Corporate Engagement in Climate Policy and Carbon Pricing Leadership, and were thereby instrumental in facilitating the landmark 2015 Paris Climate Agreement.

In "Climate Change Leadership: From Tragic to Comic Discourse" (Chapter 9), Benjamin W. Redekop and Morgan Thomas begin their analysis with an overview of the first-generation climate leadership of Al Gore, James Hansen, and Bill McKibben, whom they characterize as propounding a "tragic" and "catastrophizing" discourse. It then moves to analysis of interviews with 14 second-generation climate leaders from the US, Canada, Mexico, the Philippines, Hungary, South Africa, Taiwan, and Australia, contextualized by recent academic research on this topic. The authors suggest that this second generation of climate leaders offers a more "comic" discourse that acknowledges the tragic consequences of inaction but tends to avoid catastrophizing rhetoric, appealing to a sense of hope and possibility despite limited progress on this issue. They show that despite significant variations in approach and emphasis, interviewees generally lend credence to Western's conception of an emerging eco-leadership discourse (discussed above, and at greater length in Chapter 3).

In "Followers' Self-Perception of Their Role in Addressing Climate Change: A Cultural Comparison" (Chapter 10), David J. Brown and Robert M. McManus report on survey data collected over the past four years as part of a travel class they have taught on conservation and leadership in Central America. While traveling, the class administered surveys in Costa Rica and Belize based upon a survey that was conducted in the United States in 2007 (Yale Environmental Poll, 2007). The authors first examine three portions of the survey that are directly linked to followership and the role followers play in understanding and addressing the problem of climate change, before putting the findings into cultural, educational, economic, and media context. The relevance of climate change to followers, and the role of followers in addressing climate change, are then discussed, followed by the authors' conclusions. Throughout the chapter, survey data from Costa Rica, Belize, and the United States is analyzed in a comparative fashion, and provisional explanations for differences between the three countries are advanced. This comparative perspective allows for a broader understanding of why climate change in the United States is more controversial and not as well understood as in most other countries in the world. Here, as in other chapters in this volume, there is much to be learned about environmental leadership and followership from people in the "majority world" (Kosempel et al., Chapter 7).

In Chapter 11, "Ending the Drought: Nurturing Environmental Leadership in Ethiopia," Fentahun Mengistu, Girma Shimelis, and Vachel Miller argue that the intensified severity of environmental problems and their social justice implications call for a new kind of leadership attuned to the interconnections of ecology and social equity as integral to national development. In a country like Ethiopia where rapid economic growth has become a coveted (and often unchallenged) prize, they suggest that leadership across the institutional landscape should be reoriented toward concern for ecological responsibility and social justice. As such, they favor a locally-grounded approach to environmental leadership, anchored in the economic, social, cultural, political, and religious limitations and possibilities of particular places. Their analysis challenges a sometimes assumed ideal in environmentally oriented leadership discourse of an "eco-champion" leader who can operate fluidly in an unbounded (or undefined) cultural/geographic space.

"We Don't Conquer Mountains, We Understand Them: Embedding Indigenous Education in Australian Outdoor Education" (Chapter 12), by Shawn Andrews, provides a compelling personal narrative demonstrating how Andrews embeds lessons about Indigenous Australian history and culture into outdoor experiences run by the company he founded, Indigicate. Andrews highlights the importance of forging "connection" between leaders and participants as they tell their stories in outdoor settings. By doing so, participants are linked to each other, the natural environment, and the history of aboriginal peoples who were on the land long before the arrival of European colonists. Andrews suggests that when leaders share their story and lead from a position of connection to self, community, and the environment, they are able to immerse groups in that connection. Their connection-driven leadership opens the senses and provides a platform for the individual to engage in new sights, sounds, and feelings.

In Chapter 13, "Critical Internal Shifts for Sustainable Leadership," Kathleen E. Allen explores the "interior work" of environmental leadership, examining critical internal shifts to value systems and deep motivations for integrating sustainable leadership practices into our personal and organizational lives. She identifies four "worldview shifts" needed for environmental leaders: 1) from seeing our organizations and communities as closed systems to seeing them as open systems; 2) from a worldview of separation to one that recognizes our connection and interdependence with other beings; 3) from short-term to long-term thinking; and 4) from seeing our organizations and our environment as inert systems to seeing them as living systems. The chapter draws out the implications of these shifts and concludes with a discussion of strategies that can be used to help an individual shift their worldviews.

The final chapter, "From Peril to Possibility: Restorative Leadership for a Sustainable Future" (Chapter 14), by Seana Lowe Steffen, suggests that achieving a sustainable and peaceful coexistence of all living beings in the biosphere will require that we answer this ultimate leadership question: *How do we bring out the best of our diverse humanity to ensure a sustainable future?* For Steffen, the emergence of "restorative leadership" offers a response. This chapter draws on research and interview data showcasing underrepresented voices across a range of geographic and sector engagement. In addition to the international women's coalition WECAN and its members such as Amazon Watch (an indigenous rights advocacy organization), insights are illustrated by a rural community in the United States (Greensburg, Kansas), scientific leadership representing the voiceless interests of nature (biologist Janine Benyus and oceanographer Sylvia Earle), and the INGO Tostan. Findings illuminate the paradigm of restorative leadership and highlight practices that translate to remarkable outcomes including the establishment of marine protected areas, arresting deforestation, evolving sustainable design innovation, and thriving out of natural disaster. As such, the chapter provides a hopeful and inspiring valediction to this collection.

The Conclusion briefly reviews and synthesizes some of the main themes and ideas presented in this collection. However, we expect that readers will come to their own conclusions as well, and that this collection will foster continued discussion, debate, reflection, and action that helps to build a more just and sustainable world for all of its inhabitants.

The Editors

References

Alvesson, M., & Spicer, A. (2012). Critical Leadership Studies: The Case for Critical Performativity. *Human Relations*, 65(3), pp. 367–390.

Collinson, D. (2011). Critical Leadership Studies. In A. Bryman, D. Collinson, K. Grint, B. Jackson, & M. Uhl-Bien (Eds), *The SAGE Handbook of Leadership* (pp. 181–194). Thousand Oaks, CA: SAGE Publications Inc.

Collinson, D. (2014). Dichotomies, Dialectics, and Dilemmas: New Directions for Critical Leadership Studies? *Leadership*, 10(1), pp. 36–55.

Collinson, D., & Tourish, D. (2015). Teaching Leadership Critically: New Directions for Leadership Pedagogy. *Academy of Management Learning & Education*, 14(4), pp. 576–594.

Dugan, J. (2017). *Leadership Theory: Cultivating Critical Perspectives*. San Francisco, CA: Jossey-Bass.

Evans, T. (2011). Leadership Without Domination? Toward Restoring the Human and Natural World. *Journal of Sustainability Education*, 2(March), pp. 1–16. www.jsedimensions.org/wordpress/wp-content/uploads/2011/03/Evans2011.pdf.

Gallagher, D. (2012). *Environmental Leadership: A Reference Handbook* (2 vols.). Los Angeles, CA & London: Sage Publications, Inc.

Jackson, B., & Parry, K. (2011). *A Very Short, Fairly Interesting and Reasonably Cheap Book about Studying Leadership (2nd ed.)*. Los Angeles, CA & London: SAGE Publications, Inc.

Kellerman, B. (2012). *The End of Leadership*. New York: HarperCollins.

Kellerman, B. (2015). *Hard Times: Leadership in America*. Stanford, CA: Stanford Business Books.

McManus, R. M., & Perruci, G. (2015). *Understanding Leadership: An Arts and Humanities Perspective*. Abingdon: Routledge.

Osborn, R., Hunt, J., & Jauch, L. (2002). Toward a Contextual Theory of Leadership. *The Leadership Quarterly*, 13, 797–837.

Redekop, B. (2010). *Leadership for Environmental Sustainability*. New York & London: Routledge.

Satterwhite, R., McIntyre Miller, W., & Sheridan, K. (2015). Leadership for Sustainability and Peace: Responding to the Wicked Challenges of the Future. In M. Sowcik et al. (Eds), *Leadership 2050: Critical Challenges, Key Contexts, and Emerging Trends* (pp. 59–74). Bingley: Emerald Group Publishing.

Sinclair, S. (2007). *Leadership for the Disillusioned: Moving Beyond Myths and Heroes to Leading that Liberates*. Crows News, NSW: Allen & Unwin.

Stober, S., Brown, T., & Cullen, S. (2013). *Nature-Centered Leadership: An Aspirational Narrative*. Champaign, IL: Common Ground Publishing LLC.

Western, S. (2010). Eco-Leadership: Towards the Development of a New Paradigm. In B. Redekop (Ed.), *Leadership for Environmental Sustainability* (pp. 36–54). New York & London: Routledge.

Western, S. (2013). *Leadership: A critical text* (2nd ed.) London & Thousand Oaks, CA: SAGE Publications, Inc.

Wilson, S. (2016). *Thinking Differently About Leadership: A Critical History of Leadership Studies*. Cheltenham & Northampton, MA: Edward Elgar.

Yale Environmental Poll. (2007). Yale Center for Environmental Law and Policy (undertaken by Global Strategy Group). In the authors' possession. For a summary, see: http://climatecommunication.yale.edu/publications/american-opinions-on-global-warming/.

1 The Seven Unsustainabilities of Mainstream Leadership

Jem Bendell, Richard Little and Neil Sutherland

Introduction

In the face of limited progress on a range of social and environmental issues, many proponents and analysts of corporate action on sustainable development issues are calling for more *leadership for sustainability* – a call to which this book responds (Redekop, 2010; Adams et al., 2011; Evans, 2011; Gallagher, 2012; Metcalf & Benn, 2013; Shriberg & MacDonald, 2013). Such calls for leadership reflect a desire for greater and swifter change. In that context, researchers and educators can explore what is useful knowledge to enable such change. In this chapter, we suggest that some assumptions about the meaning of the term "leadership" may hinder, not help, that process of change.

We demonstrate this limiting effect by placing the concept of leadership under the scope of an analysis based on the primacy of discourse. We draw upon Critical Discourse Analysis (CDA), which starts from an awareness that the abuse, dominance, and inequality of power relations can be enacted, reproduced, and, ultimately, resisted by text and talk (Fairclough, 1995). We argue that the prevailing leadership imaginary, so far from supporting the transition to a sustainable society and economy, may actually hinder it and be itself unsustainable, in the sense that it depends on the discoursal maintenance of power relations and a narrow range of organizing possibilities (Gemmil & Oakley, 1992). Further, we suggest that it may thus discourage or disable more collective, collaborative, or distributed forms of leadership, deliberation, organizing, and problem-solving (Hurlow, 2008; Denis et al., 2012). If this is the case, more of the same "leadership" will not help the goal of sustainability.

We share with Evans (2011) and Western (2008) the view that dominant paradigms of leadership are part of the cause of the current crisis of unsustainability and will develop that argument in this chapter. Therefore, precisely because we are interested in sustainability, we address leadership *per se* rather than limit analysis to leadership on environmental or social topics. Though scholarship in this field may be expected to focus on those persons who have responsibility for topics explicitly to do with "sustainability," given the state of conceptual development, we think that doing so could leave untenable concepts to be imported from those who analyze and promote conventional approaches to leadership. For instance, in much of the still scarce scholarship on leadership for sustainability, some of which is cited in our opening sentence, leaders and leadership have sometimes been described in terms that emphasize exceptionalism, personal "authenticity," an individual locus of action, and a generalized other that is the object of leadership. There is also evidence of sustainability-infused leadership development programs uncritically incorporating assumptions about leadership (see for instance Peterlin, 2016).

Even those theorists who propose to break with mainstream notions of leadership may still repeat what Bolden and Gosling (2006) call the "refrain" of the mainstream competency approach to leadership. For example, the following statement may seem at first to reflect an inclusive and collectivist approach, but on another reading, may be thought to identify leadership with a special individual who acts upon an unreflecting group: "[leadership is] a form of community praxis in which one coalesces and directs the energies of the group" (Evans, 2011, p. 2). Impressive and helpful people do exist, but with this chapter we wish to show that the prevailing discourse on leadership can limit our understanding of the potential for creating the greater change that inspires the calls for more "environmental leadership" or "leadership for sustainability."

Therefore, rather than a detailed deconstruction of existing texts on leadership for sustainability, in this chapter we offer a broad synthesis of relevant literatures that either use, or can inform, a more critical approach, drawing on the field of "Critical Leadership Studies" (CLS). We integrate these critiques by outlining "seven unsustainabilities" of mainstream leadership thinking, and the antidotes that are relevant to sustainability. At that point we offer a definition of "sustainable leadership" and conclude by outlining some potential implications for the future of research, practice, and education.

Our definition will be purposely tentative. Rather than offer a systematic construction of a new concept of "sustainable leadership," we are placing existing concepts of leadership in the context of dominant narratives of "managerialism" (Enteman, 1993) that limit an assessment of the potential types and locations of action on sustainability. This process of tilling the conceptual earth will allow new ideas to bloom, including those that deploy structured approaches to define "sustainable leadership" or "sustainability leadership" concepts and theories. Without such insights from CDA, attempts at rigorous concept development in the organizational sciences (Podsakoff et al., 2016) may be limited by assumptions that reflect dominant discourse.

While we are reticent to suggest that it is unnecessary to focus on the behavior of senior role holders, such as chief executives or politicians, we argue that the assumptions that leadership is theirs *alone* to express and that leadership by special individuals is the most salient matter in organizational or social change are both unhelpful and yet widely promoted, with major implications for sustainable development.

Defining Leadership and Sustainability

"Sustainability" is often used as a shorthand for the term Sustainable Development. Since the adoption of the Brundtland Report by the UN General Assembly in 1987, "sustainable development" has been promoted by many as an integrated way to address diverse dilemmas, such as poverty, illiteracy, unemployment, disease, discrimination, environmental degradation, crime, conflict, and limited human rights or justice (WCED, 1987). That "sustainable development" seems to offer all good things to all people has been one reason for its popularity and, some say, a reason for it leading to largely ineffectual activities on those dilemmas (Perez-Carmona, 2013).

Such an "ambiguous compromise" (Purvis & Grainger, 2004, p. 6) has proven to be a resilient one. The adoption of 17 Sustainable Development Goals (SDGs) by the United Nations in 2015 marks a renewed interest in the hope that governments, cities, firms, and other organizations can achieve progress on social and economic factors while not degrading the environment.

In this chapter, we term the sustainability issues that people are working on as shared "dilemmas," rather than challenges or problems, to reflect both their complexity and a growing worldview that no longer regards them as problems to solve but situations to cope with. We call them "shared" because they involve collective causation, affect the many (albeit differentially), and will need collective action to address or adapt to them.

Just as the terms "sustainability" and "sustainable development" are deployed in quite different contexts and with different implied exclusions and inclusions, so the word "leadership" is used to mean or imply quite different things (Jackson & Parry, 2008) while seeming to represent a common, monolithic, understanding. Unpacking such usages may not have direct value in deliberation or action, but can help prepare the ground for people to navigate the plurality of possibilities for leadership and sustainability. Among the many definitions of leadership in management studies, we will use the following to begin our discussion: "Leadership is any behavior that has the effect of helping groups of people achieve something that the majority of them are pleased with and which [observers] assess as significant and what they would not have otherwise achieved" (Bendell & Little, 2015, p. 15).

The notion of leadership being a *behavior* rather than a position of authority is inherent in this definition. In addition, it reflects the relational quality of leadership so that acts need to be welcomed by a majority of those in a group. Moreover, the external observer plays a key role when categorising acts as leadership. Specifically:

> Leadership involves the ascription of significance to an act by us, the observer, where significance usually involves our assumptions or propositions about values and theories of change. If our theory of change is that the CEO has freedom of action and can impose change, then we would naturally look for leadership to be exhibited at that level. If our

values are that profit-maximising for shareholders in the near term is a good goal, then we would not question a CEO's "leadership" in achieving such goals. We should note that these are rather big "Ifs."

(ibid.)

Utilizing this definition allows us to break free from some of the mainstream assumptions in management and leadership scholarship and training, including the idea that leadership is a individualistic quality. In this chapter, we explore how deep the criticisms go and the implications for enabling action on sustainable development.

Insights from Critical Leadership Studies

While mainstream approaches to leadership and management continue to permeate academic and practitioner interest, the last decade has seen a counter-trend of scholars who seek to unpack what they consider unhelpful assumptions and directions in "mainstream" approaches to leadership. While it is difficult to summarize all of the work conducted in this field, Collinson notes that the aim of Critical Leadership Studies (CLS) is to investigate "what is neglected, absent or deficient in mainstream leadership research" (2011, p. 181). This involves understanding and exposing the negative consequences of leadership by examining patterns of power and domination enabled by overly hierarchical social relations, questioning these "exclusionary and privileged" discourses, and investigating the problematic effects that this has on organizational functioning and individual well-being (Ford, 2010).

"Critical Theory" has a significant part to play here – a motivation toward emancipatory projects and empowering grassroots and oppressed groups against dominant discourses promoted by elites. Such research challenges the field of management and leadership that may be distorted in favor of capital and the owners of capital, gender exclusion and other forms of social violence, and unsustainable forms of commerce and industry (Blunt & Jones, 1996; Nkomo, 2011). A key theme in such work is the critique of a set of ideas called "Managerialism," which value professional managers and their forms of analysis, authority, and control, and their tendency to bring ever more aspects of life into the orbit of management (Enteman, 1993; Parker, 2002). There are parallels here with some critiques of international "development" that influence approaches to sustainability, which we will return to below. Before that, we next summarize some of the main elements of the critique made by CLS – converging around a problematization of an overly individualistic understanding of leadership. We then outline some implications for leadership scholarship and leadership development work that is motivated by concern for various shared dilemmas.

The Individualist Mistake

Mainstream approaches to leadership are keenly focussed on the development of permanent, stable, and hierarchically positioned individuals, rather than to the development of collective, relational, or dialogical leadership. Leaders are routinely described as needing to be authentic, visionary, driven, and emotionally intelligent. The image of the leader that emerges from what Gosling and Bolden (2006) call the "repeating refrain" of leadership competencies is of a deracinated superman (or, in a feminized variant that emphasizes collaboration, intuition, and nurturing, a superwoman). This "hero-focus" has received criticism over the past 15 years from mainstream management literature (Palus et al., 2012). However, even explicitly "post-heroic" or egalitarian accounts of leadership as bottom-up or, variously, as distributed (Woods et al., 2004), transformational (Bass, 1998), or "servant" (Greenleaf, 1977) may not fully address the degree to which these ideas are undermined by lingering positional metaphors of hierarchy, or by their failure to address questions of gender or, worse, are co-opted by hierarchical, instrumentalist managerialism (Fletcher, 2004). The CLS analysis of the implicit hero focus of leadership studies provides a deeper critique in at least four key areas.

First, the "dark side" of leadership practice is a key interest. Thus, various CLS theorists have explored issues such as domination, conformity, abuse of power, blind commitment, over-dependence, and seduction (Khoo & Burch, 2007; Schyns & Schilling, 2013; Sheard et al., 2013). They have coined terms including "toxic leadership" (Benson & Hogan, 2008; Lipman-Blumen, 2006); "destructive leadership" (Einarsen et al., 2007); "leadership derailment" (Tepper, 2000); and, "aversive leadership" (Bligh et al., 2007). Other scholars have discovered tendencies for narcissism and psychopathy amongst senior role holders and how that can be encouraged by popular discourses about leaders being special and powerful (de Vries & Miller, 1985; Gudmundsson & Southey, 2011). Evans (2011) characterizes the prevailing model as "exploitive leadership" and argues that such masculinized, hierarchical leadership reproduces the domination of nature by humanity. For scholars interested in the social dimension of sustainability, including matters of fairness, rights, and well-being, these dark sides will be of concern.

Rather than responding through a deepened critique, mainstream leadership scholars proclaim problems can be solved through mitigating qualities like humility, authenticity, emotional intelligence, or self-knowledge, while leaving unchallenged the assumption that "leaders" pursue exclusively corporate goals by largely instrumental means (Kouzes & Posner, 2003). Characteristically, this literature keeps up the search for an ideal trait description of the leader: lists of qualities, propensities, behaviors and habits proliferate, often including "character" and "authenticity" (Gardner et al., 2011).

The second turn in CLS aims in part to reveal the flaws of this traits focus, and of secondary efforts to promote values and authenticity among leaders. We do not have space here to rehearse this argument in detail, but in summary: leadership trait lists tend merely to describe competent human beings, emphasizing, for example, honesty and intelligence (Zingheim et al., 1996). The effort to identify traits might itself be seen as serving the very bureaucratic impulse to which leadership, with its implied freedom of moral action, is the remedy. The reliability, stability, and predictive value of trait descriptions are all in any case contested. The most telling critique of traits suggests that their pursuit is a circular process in which socially constructed discourses of leadership are interrogated from within the constraining assumptions of those same discourses (Burr, 1995). Indeed, it is not unreasonable to argue that leadership is idiographic, episodic, and situationally inflected, to the extent that no imaginable set of descriptors could apply to all potential leaders (Fairhurst & Grant, 2010). Traits are, from this view, not internal personal structures but "social processes realised on the site of the personal" (Gergen, 1994, p. 210).

Rather than focusing directly on traits, another response has been to help senior individuals to reflect upon, clarify, articulate, and live by their most important values, and, ostensibly, to help legitimize values-based behavior in professional life. Courses under the heading "Authentic Leadership" pursue that aim. Executives are encouraged to seek coherence between their life story and their seeking or holding a senior organizational role; and congruence between their thoughts and deeds (George, et al., 2007). Potential benefits may include greater self-confidence, appearing more authentic in one's job, enhanced oratorical skill and higher levels of motivation from colleagues (Gardner et al., 2011). Typically, participants in authentic leadership programs are offered opportunities for systematic self-exploration; these processes, however, could be characterized as opportunities for self-justification, as exploration of self is framed by the aim of constructing narratives that explain one's right to seniority within a corporation – an almost "divine" right to lead. Self-realizations that might undermine one's ability to work for certain firms, or transform the basis of one's self-worth, or challenge one's assumption of self-efficacy, do not appear to be encouraged (Bendell & Little, 2015). For scholars interested in transforming organizations so they reduce their harm on the environment and society, or increase their positive contributions, the exploration of values in authentic leadership may seem like a start, but it could be unhelpfully limited.

Indeed, insights from critical sociology are ignored or obscured in Authentic Leadership scholarship and action, as is commentary on how our perspectives and sense of self are shaped by language and discourse (Fairclough, 1995; Gergen, 1994). Such insights challenge the view that we can achieve depths of "self-awareness" by reflecting on our experiences and feelings without the benefit of perspectives from social theory. Authentic leadership builds on assumptions about the nature of the individual, including the assumption that our worth comes from our distinctiveness.[1] Adorno (1973) argues that this idea of authenticity is characteristic of a nostalgic post-Christian impulse to replace the "authority of the absolute" (such as a God) with "absolutized authority" (whether that is from an organization, law, or the rectitude of a leader).

A third set of analyses shows how a focus on a leader's values, charisma, and other attributes serves to distract from and de-problematize issues of the legitimacy, or not, of power-wielding roles in organizations and societies. When we consider leadership, we are considering how groups of people decide how to act: addressing ancient questions of socio-political organization with diverse intellectual traditions. They are investigated today in fields of political philosophy, public policy studies, civil society studies, and international development studies. We cannot delve into these areas in this chapter, but note that a recurring theme is that matters of decision making involve reflection on processes that support the rights, dignity, and contribution of all individuals in groups. Yet studies of leadership often render unproblematic modes of decision making and patterns of power (see Gemmill & Oakley, 1992; Western, 2008). Given that good governance is such a central question for Sustainable Development, this subtle sidelining of questions of accountable governance is a concern.

A fourth set of analyses in CLS revolves around questioning the "romance" of leadership – whereby mainstream perspectives ignore contextual factors and disproportionately attribute responsibility for outcomes to individuals occupying hierarchical positions. Psychological research since the 1980s has demonstrated that people, across cultures, tend to exaggerate the significance of the actions of individuals when compared to other factors shaping outcomes (Meindl et al., 1985). This concludes that we are susceptible to seeing "leadership" when it isn't necessarily there or important – a collectively constructed "romantic discourse." Their work reflects the "false attribution effect," widely reported by social psychologists, as people's tendency to place an undue emphasis on internal characteristics to explain someone's behavior, rather than considering external factors (Jones & Harris, 1967). Perhaps our susceptibility to this effect arises because we are brought up with stories of great leaders shaping history, and this myth is perpetuated in our business media (Bendell & Little, 2015).

Furthering this line of inquiry, leadership itself has also been framed as a "social myth" – one which creates and reinforces the illusion that individual leaders are in control of events and organizational performance (Gemmill & Oakley, 1992). That is, the existence and valorization of leaders serves to repress uncomfortable needs, emotions, and wishes that emerge when people work collaboratively (Gastil, 1994; Gemmill, 1986); and subsequently, individuals are able to project their worries and anxieties onto individual leaders, who are seen as omniscient and all-powerful. Members therefore perceive themselves as free from anxiety, fears, struggles, and the responsibility of autonomy (Bion, 1961), but also induce their own learned helplessness and passivity: that is, they "willingly submit themselves to spoon feeding, preferring safe and easy security to the possible pains and uncertainty of learning by their own effort and mistakes" (Gemmill & Oakley,

1992, p. 98). For Gemmill and Oakley therefore, leadership – in the form widely assumed today – is dangerous and inherently unsustainable, leading to infantilization and mass deskilling. They stress the need to denaturalize taken-for-granted assumptions in order to develop new theories of leadership that "reskill" organizational members, encourage collaborative working environments, and do not rely on superhuman individuals.

Similar commentary has been made by other theorists. For example, Ashforth (1994) argues that authoritative leaders often engage in behaviors such as belittling of followers, self-aggrandizement, coercive conflict resolution, unnecessary punishments, and the undermining of organizational goals. Schilling (2009) and Higgs (2009) reported that leaders often exhibit behaviors that aim at obtaining purely personal (not organizational) goals, and may inflict damage on others through abuses of power. Finally, a number of theorists (Conger, 1990; Padilla et al., 2007) proposed that the behavior of "followers" may also contribute to destructive practices – especially in regard to self-esteem issues, the playing of power games, and treating the leader as an idol.[2] As many scholars of sustainability in general, and "leadership for sustainability" in particular, are interested in enhancing change, these disempowering effects of dominant assumptions about leadership should be a concern.

Taken together, the four CLS critiques outlined above converge around challenging a form of "methodological individualism" – where single individuals are seen to bear extraordinary powers (Basu, 2008). Their research has shown how focusing on an individual leader can enforce an *acontextual* and short-termist view; one which pays little attention to broader socio-economic processes, planetary concerns, or collective well-being. While differences exist between the aims and objectives of the critical scholars cited thus far, at the heart of these debates is the notion that a reliance on overly hierarchical conceptualizations of leadership may have problematic impacts on organizational effectiveness, well-being, and broader social change: they are irreconcilable with creating sustainable societies (Alvesson & Spicer, 2012; Evans, 2011; Sutherland et al., 2014; Western, 2008). That is, for all their focus on attempting to achieve economically effective outcomes, hierarchical conceptions of leadership fail to acknowledge the importance of long-term socially sustainable, efficacious, and humane relationships between and among organizational actors.

Assuming Purpose

Inherent in our discussions so far is the idea that a focus on consequentialism runs strong throughout mainstream leadership discourse. That is, it is taken as natural that the primary purpose of organizations is to achieve economic goals, rather than goals associated with equity, democracy, and environmental sustainability (Jackson & Parry, 2008). A review of the assumed outcomes of leadership within 25 years showed that all types of outcome exist within an instrumentalist and consequentialist approach that concerns improving organizational performance, rather than considering the purpose of the organization, the performance issue concerned, or the impact on stakeholders (Hiller, et al., 2011). This mainstream corporate view is typically expressed in "econophonic" and "potensiphonic" terms – the taken-for-granted language that prioritizes economic outcomes over all others and potency, power, and performance over other human modalities (Giacalone & Promislo, 2013). There has been little room for doubt and reflection on the purpose of business, work, and economic progress within that leadership discourse. Thus, the challenging of econophonic and potensiphonic language in leadership studies can be an emancipatory activity, and key to nurturing "reciprocal, sustaining relationships among people and between humans and nature" (Evans, 2011, p. 2).

Some theorists demand that we see this issue through an imperialist economic context – pointing toward the idea that under modern capitalist society, centralization, hierarchy, domination, exploitation, manipulation, oppression, and scapegoating are inherent features of life (Barker, 1997; Bhabha, 1994). If this is the context for one's analysis, then the "social myth" of leadership can be regarded as one of many nodal points in a discoursal web of ideas and practices whose effect is to infantilize and prepare mass audiences for compliance in their own exploitation. Indeed, despite our earlier criticisms of the assumptions and approaches within "authentic leadership," its focus on self-development could provide an opening for work on the deeper personal transformations that might allow for different types of purpose to be clarified and pursued through leadership acts.[3] In addition, the importance of purpose to leadership is receiving greater attention from leadership scholars, without that purpose being assumed to be congruent with narrowly defined corporate goals (Kempster, et al., 2011). Growing interest in sustainability leadership or sustainable leadership can be seen in that context: an effort to plug the purpose gap in contemporary corporate life. A business rationale for corporate leaders to be clear on a purpose beyond narrow corporate goals is also developing, with some researchers arguing that firms with a clear public purpose do better financially over the longer term (Big Innovation Centre, 2016).

However, the concept of sustainability that emerges through these initiatives is often limited and problematic – as we will discuss below. Therefore, unless the interest in purposeful business and purposeful leadership allows for a deeper exploration of sustainability than that which aligns simply with existing corporate interests, it is unlikely to address this limitation to mainstream leadership approaches.

Beyond Critical Analysis

In order to counteract the various problems generated through mainstream leadership discourse, some CLS scholars have pointed toward the value of a more emergent, episodic, and collective understanding of leadership – involving acts that go beyond the realm of single individuals, and toward a more pluralistic practice (Bendell & Little, 2015; Western, 2008). Indeed, in recent years the term "collective leadership" has emerged as "an umbrella concept that includes studies … applying the core insight of relationality to the key problems in [organization and society. … Relationality reveals the individual as a node where multiple relationships intersect: people are relational beings" (Ospina & Foldy, 2015, p. 492). Some use the term to include distributed, shared, and co-leadership, due to an assessment that they all focus more on complex relations between individuals. Research on "distributed leadership," for example, has shown how leadership actors can emerge anywhere in an organization and leadership becomes a cultural trope around which motivated action accretes, a position supported theoretically by sensemaking theory (Weick, 1995), activity theory (Bedny, et al., 2000), communities of practice theory (Lave & Wenger, 1991), and practice theory (Nicolini, 2012). Ospina and Foldy continue by noting:

> Collective leadership shifts attention from formal leaders and their influence on followers to the relational processes that produce leadership in a group, organization or system. Relationality motivates attention to the embeddedness of the leader–follower relationship in a broader system of relationships and to the meaning-making, communicative and organizing processes that help define and constitute these relationships.
>
> (2015, p. 492)

Further than this, various scholars note the potential of more collective forms of leadership as a "sustainable" organizational practice, given that it allows for empowerment, reduces alienation, and increases democracy and participation (Evans, 2011; Western, 2008).

Understood like this, it may seem that more distributed forms of leadership could remedy the problems raised by CLS scholars in regard to mainstream discourse. However, many recommendations described as "collective leadership" *nevertheless* retain a reliance on special individuals as leaders, whether by role or by act. In addition, some studies have found that "collective leadership" is used rhetorically by managers who pursue individual aims within inefficient bureaucracies (Davis & Jones, 2014). For example, when it is presented as a practice that mitigates hierarchical power, especially in business organizations, distributed leadership sometimes becomes little more than a way of rhetorically extending employees' freedom of action (and weight of responsibility) while maintaining circumscriptive rules (Dainty, et al., 2005). Thus, we conclude that the absence of a critical framework to deconstruct assumptions about leaders, goals, and legitimacy can hamper post-heroic and distributed forms of leadership. It is the more radical approaches within the collective leadership field, particularly concerning the nonprofit sector, that resonate with the insights of CLS and could therefore be used in a new conception, theory, and practice of sustainable leadership.

Implications for Sustainable Leadership

Thus far, we have noted how Critical Discourse Analysis can reveal and denaturalize limiting assumptions in the field of leadership, and in what follows we demonstrate how it can also aid the field of Sustainable Development. As described earlier, Sustainable Development and its related activities became established in the late 1980s, when offered as a coherent agenda for governments around the post-Cold War world. It also coincided with the rise of another idea for public policy, called New Public Management (NPM), which regarded citizens as users of services and incorporated practices from the private sector (Schachter, 2014). Looking back, NPM and its closely related tropes of leadership and entrepreneurialism can be seen to have colonized the process of sustainability, reducing it to a problem that can be solved by individualistic leadership in a process dominated by capital (Bessant, et al., 2015; Perez-Carmona, 2013; Steurer, 2007). Intentional or not, this colonization was aided by the growth of voluntary corporate engagement with sustainability that then influenced the understandings of policy makers, experts, and campaigners on how to approach social and environmental problems (Ball & Bebbington, 2008). A counter process was also occurring with the transfer of concepts of environmentalists and social justice campaigners into the private sector, thus leading to what Anderson & Mungal (2015) describe, albeit in a different sector, as the inter-sectoral transfer of discourses.

CDA invites us to question how a phrase can ideologically encourage certain perspectives and not others – including "collocation." The term "Sustainable Development" is a collocation; that is, two words that are likely to co-occur with greater than average frequency. Most collocations ("two peas in a pod") are unproblematic, but when both terms are in any way contested, or liable to hypostatization, each word can have the effect of de-problematizing the other, thus doubling and redoubling the potential ideological loading of the phrase. One risk is that important questions of what is development is displaced by a focus instead on what might be distinctly "sustainable." Thus, when considering sustainability, we should attempt to uncover assumptions about development, including assumptions about "social" progress. There is a long tradition of this fundamental questioning of progress in the anti-development or post-development fields, which typically argue that the development concept is an extension of colonialist and imperialist power relations in the global economy (Sachs, 2015; Rahnema & Bawtree, 1997). These critical perspectives need to be drawn upon in the future, for "sustainable leadership" to be a rigorously developed concept and a meaningful practice (Bendell et al., forthcoming).

In order to illuminate the insights from CLS, and make them more accessible for future research and practice, we have developed a synthesis of seven main "unsustainabilities" in mainstream leadership. We hope this will prepare the conceptual ground for the development of new approaches to sustainable leadership research, practice, and education.

The Seven Unsustainabilities of Leadership

1   *Ignoring purpose, or assuming the primary purpose to be the benefit of an employer;*
2   *Assuming or believing a senior role holder to be most salient to organizational or social change;*
3   *Ignoring the political and moral aspects of an exclusive focus on enhancing the agency of senior role holders;*
4   *Assuming that "leader" is a continuing quality of a person rather than a label;*
5   *Assuming that the value of an individual lies mostly in their confidence in their distinctiveness;*
6   *Assuming that leadership development is about learning more rather than about unlearning;*
7   *Believing that material progress is always possible and best.*

However, we recognize that critique alone is not a sufficient contribution. Western (2008: 21), for example, suggests that "critical theorists must go beyond identifying 'bad leadership practice' and aim to create and support successful ethical frameworks for leadership," and Sutherland et al. argue that attention should be paid to understanding "how organizational alternatives *to* mainstream understandings of leadership might be constituted" (2014, p. 16). Therefore, we can flip the seven criticisms into the following seven recommendations for more sustainable leadership:

Seven Recommendations for More Sustainable Leadership

1   *Explore purpose and meaning as central to personal and professional action. By doing so, enable individuals to clarify their provisional understanding of personal aims and how they may, or may not, relate to existing organizational aims, to support a more holistic assessment of personal and organizational performance.*
2   *Recognize that organizational or social change is affected by people at all levels and through social processes, so knowledge about collective action is key. By doing so, encourage people to learn more about how groups can function more effectively through enhanced collaboration.*
3   *Consider the political and moral aspects of authority and bases for legitimacy of leadership acts, thus encouraging a focus on how one's*

potential actions relate to the needs of the collective, stakeholders, and wider society.

4   *Recognize that "leader" is a label and people can take acts of leadership without it meaning they are permanent "leaders." Understanding this provides a valuable opportunity for developing overall leadership capacity within organizations, rather than mistakenly seeing it as the domain of a chosen, or emergent, few.*

5   *Appreciate the value of an individual is as much through their similarities and connectedness to others and all life, as through their distinctiveness. Doing so allows a move away from seeing organizations as hierarchies, toward pluralistic sites characterized by ongoing debate, discussion, and deliberation.*

6   *Understand that leadership development is about both learning new ideas and unlearning existing ones. In this regard, practitioners can be encouraged to let go of limiting assumptions as they develop critical consciousness, and therefore simultaneously oppose practices as well as propose new approaches.*

7   *Realize that personal purpose and meaning can ultimately transcend notions of material progress in any form or the associated means of control. Doing so challenges the consequentialist, means-end philosophies of contemporary business and organization, and instead promotes an ideology centered on compassion and creating a new world in the shell of the old* (Gordon, 2010).

While the above recommendations relate to leadership more generally, we stress the importance of going beyond the narrow focus on individual leaders' abilities, skills, attributes, and behaviors, and toward developing *all* organizational actors' critical thinking skills (Brookfield, 1987), and creating spaces in which to discuss future possibilities for sustainability (Evans, 2011). In social studies, we appreciate how theoretical development can take many forms and does not require making predictions based on a theory (Abend, 2008). Instead, our contribution is providing a framework for interpretation of claims about leadership for sustainability. Affecting people by revealing limiting assumptions embedded in leadership discourse has been documented in areas beyond sustainability (Alvesson & Spicer, 2012). Therefore, our work has practical implication in that synthesizing critiques and making them available to people and scholars engaged in sustainability may reduce the influence of limiting concepts. We limit our predictions to this process of consciousness-raising. We contend that professionals who avoid the seven unsustainabilities of leadership will enable more positive (or less negative) change; that organizations will witness more positive (or less negative) change; and designers or commissioners of leadership development will encourage more effective change-enabling capabilities from their participants.

At this point we can offer a tentative definition of "sustainable leadership": *Sustainable leadership is any ethical behavior that has the intention and effect of helping groups of people address shared dilemmas in significant ways not otherwise achieved.*

Our conceptualization of sustainable leadership includes the seven necessary conditions (Podsakoff et al., 2016). First, that leadership involves a behavior, or act, which can also include an intentional non-action. Second, that the act is ethical according to a framework held by the person and capable of being understood by observers. Third, that the behavior helps groups of people achieve something. Fourth, that the achievement relates to addressing shared dilemmas, such as economic, social, environmental, or cultural problems that affect many people. Fifth, that the change is significant according to both the group affected and the observers, including people who wish to describe leadership, like ourselves. This recognizes the subjective nature of ascribing leadership. Sixth, that the behavior created an effect that was additional, whereby if it had not occurred, then the outcome would not likely have been achieved. We recognize this element is based on our theories of change and is a difficult element to assess. Seventh, that the person exhibiting the behavior intended to pursue positive change on the dilemma. We hope that the definition of sustainable leadership serves to remind us that leadership is about change involving acts rather than positional power, sustainability is about dilemmas that might not be solved, that both intention and effect are important to consider, and that the significance of acts will be attributed by observers based on their own values and assumptions.

Conclusions

Throughout this chapter, we have argued that prevalent notions of these concepts can be unhelpful to practitioner and/or researcher engagement with the shared dilemmas of our time. We have drawn upon sociologically-informed critiques of leadership and sustainability and explained how the idea of leadership, as a myth of potent individual action, has been deployed in the service of unsustainable growth and exploitation. Those who suggest that the world needs leadership in the transition to a just and sustainable world must ask whether or not the leadership they imagine is the product of wishful thinking fed by an infantilizing managerial *dispositif* (Gemmill & Oakley, 1992). Instead, we have argued that the idea of leadership must be disentangled in its discoursal function in the service of oppression before it can be reconfigured as a modality of democracy and placed in the service of justice and sustainability. We integrated and summarized these critiques by stating *Seven Unsustainabilities of Leadership* and therefore made seven recommendations for more sustainable leadership. We choose the term sustainable leadership due to it emphasizing that dominant notions of leadership are unsustainable as well as our current planetary predicament.

Notes

1 Vedic philosophies provide critiques of, and explanations for, why we might enjoy a process of self-construction via self-reflection exercises. An emphasis on the "authentic self" might be regarded as an effort to find a "rock of safety against the cosmic and the infinite" (Aurobindo, 1972, p. 229). Aurobindo further argues that an aspect of our consciousness is "not concerned with self-knowledge but with self-affirmation, desire, ego. It is therefore constantly acting on mind to build for it a mental structure of apparent self that will serve these purposes; our mind is persuaded to present to us and to others a partly fictitious representative figure of ourselves which supports our self-affirmation, justifies our desires and actions, nourishes our ego" (ibid.).

2 We must note that many scholars assume the word "follower" as little more than the inverse of the word "leader," a form of hypostatization that tends to support the naturalization of hierarchy, rather than its questioning.

3 It is worthy of note that authentic leadership and other approaches that focus on values have begun to be criticized from another perspective altogether: that they don't help managers' careers (Pfeffer, 2015). Such criticisms may provoke more debate in mainstream scholarship but are not aligned with the deeper questioning of purpose we explore here.

References

Abend, G. (2008). The Meaning of "Theory." *Sociological Theory*, 26(2), 173–199.

Adams, C., Heijltjes, M.G., Jack, G., Marjoribanks, T., & Powell, M. (2011). The Development of Leaders Able to Respond to Climate Change and Sustainability Challenges: The role of business schools. *Sustainability Accounting, Management and Policy Journal*, 2(1), 165–171.

Adorno, T. (1973). *The Jargon of Authenticity*. London: Routledge & Kegan Paul.

Alvesson, M., & Spicer, A. (2012). Critical Leadership Studies: The case for critical performativity. *Human Relations*, 65(3), 367–390.

Anderson, G., & Mungal, A.S. (2015). Discourse Analysis and the Study of Educational Leadership. *International Journal of Educational Management*, 29(7), 807–818.

Ashforth, B. (1994). Petty Tyranny in Organisations. *Human Relations*, 47(7), 755–778.

Avery, G.C., & Bergsteiner, H. (2011). Sustainable Leadership Practices for Enhancing Business Resilience and Performance. *Strategy and Leadership*, 39(3), 5–15.

Aurobindo, S. (1972). *The Life Divine*. Centenary Library (Vol. 18, Book 1). Pondicherry, India: Sri Aurobindo Ashram.

Ball, A., & Bebbington, J. (2008). Editorial: Accounting and Reporting for Sustainable Development in Public Service Organizations. *Public Money & Management*, 28(6).

Bass, B. (1998). *Transformational Leadership: Industry, military and educational impact*. Mahwah, NJ: Erlbaum.

Barker, R. (1997). How Can We Train Leaders If We Do Not Know What Leadership Is? *Human Relations*, 50(4), 343–362.

Basu, K. (2008). Methodological Individualism. In S.N. Durlauf & L.E. Blume (Eds) *The New Palgrave Dictionary of Economics* (2nd ed.). New York: Palgrave Macmillan.

Bedny, G.Z., Seglin, M.H., & Meister, D. (2000). Activity Theory: History, research and application. *Theoretical Issues in Ergonomics Science*, 1(2), 168–206.

Bendell, J., & Little, R. (2015). Seeking Sustainability Leadership. *Journal of Corporate Citizenship*, 60, 13–26.

Bendell, J., Little, R., & Sutherland, N. (forthcoming). Beyond Unsustainable Leadership: Critical social theory for sustainable leadership. *Sustainability Accounting Management and Policy Journal*, 8(3).

Benson, M., & Hogan, R. (2008). How Dark Side Leadership Personality Destroys Trust and Degrades Organisational Effectiveness. *Organisations and People*, 15(3), 10–18.

Bessant, S.E.F., Robinson, Z.P., & Ormerod, R.M. (2015). Neoliberalism, New Public Management and the Sustainable Development Agenda of Higher Education: History, contradictions and synergies. *Environmental Education Research*, 21 (3), 417–432.

Bhabha, H.K. (1994). The Postcolonial and Postmodern: The question of agency. In H. Bhabha, *The Location of Culture* (pp. 245–282). London: Routledge.

Big Innovation Centre. (2016). The Purposeful Company Interim Report, 15th May. www.biginnovationcentre.com/media/uploads/pdf/The%20Purposeful%20Company%20Interim%20Report.pdf.

Bion, W. (1961). *Experiences in Groups*. London: Tavistock Publications.

Bligh, M., Pillai, R., & Uhl-Bien, M. (2007). The Social Construction of a Legacy: Summarising and extending follower-centred perspectives on leadership. In B. Shamir, R. Pillai, & M. Bligh (Eds), *Follower-centred Perspectives on Leadership: A tribute to the memory of James R. Meindl* (pp. 265–277). Charlotte, NC: Information Age Publishing, Inc.

Blunt, P., & Jones, M.L. (1996). Exploring the Limits of Western Leadership Theory in East Asia and Africa. *Personnel Review*, 26(1/2), 6–23.

Bolden, R., & Gosling, J. (2006). Leadership Competencies: Time to change the tune? *Leadership*, 2(2), 147–163.

Brookfield, S. (1987). *Developing Critical Thinkers: Challenging adults to explore alternative ways of thinking and acting*. San Francisco, CA: Jossey-Bass.

Burr, V. (1995). *Social Constructionism*. Hove & New York: Routledge.

Collinson, D. (2011). Critical Leadership Studies. In A. Bryman, D. Collinson, K. Grint, B. Jackson, & M. Uhl-Bien (Eds), *The SAGE Handbook of Leadership* (pp. 181–194). Thousand Oaks, CA: SAGE Publications Ltd.

Conger, J. (1990). The Dark Side of Leadership. *Organizational Dynamics*, 19(2), 44–55.

Dainty, A., Bryman, A., Price, A., Greasley, K., Soetanto, R., & King, N. (2005). Project Affinity: The role of emotional attachment in construction projects. *Construction Management and Economics*, 23(3), 241–244.

Davis, H., & Jones, S. (2014). The Work of Leadership in Higher Education Management. *Journal of Higher Education Policy & Management*, 36(4), 367–370.

Denis, J-L., Langley, A., & Sergi, V. (2012). Leadership in the Plural. *Academy of Management Annals*, 6(1), 211–283.

Einarsen, S., Aasland, M., & Skogstad, A. (2007). Destructive Leadership Behaviour: A definition and conceptual model. *The Leadership Quarterly*, 18(3), 207–216.

Enteman, W.F. (1993). *Managerialism: The emergence of a new ideology*. Madison: University of Wisconsin Press.

Evans, T. (2011). Leadership Without Domination? Toward restoring the human and natural world. *Journal of Sustainability Education*, 2(March), 1–16. Available at: www.jsedimensions.org/wordpress/wp-content/uploads/2011/03/Evans2011.pdf.

Fairclough, N. (1995). *Critical Discourse Analysis: The critical study of language*. London: Longman.

Fairhurst, G., & Grant, D. (2010). The Social Construction of Leadership: A sailing guide. *Management Communication Quarterly*, 24(2), 171–210.

Fletcher, J. (2004). The Paradox of Postheroic Leadership: An essay on gender, power, and transformational change. *The Leadership Quarterly*, 15(5), 647–661.

Ford, J. (2010). Studying Leadership Critically: A psychosocial lens on leadership identities. *Leadership*, 6(1), 1–19.

Foster, J. (2015). *After Sustainability*. Abingdon: Earthscan.

Gallagher, D.R. (Ed.) (2012). *Environmental Leadership: A reference handbook* (2 vols.). Los Angeles, CA & London: Sage Publications, Inc.

Gardner, W.L., Cogliser, C.C., Davis, K.M., & Dickens, M.P. (2011). Authentic Leadership: A review of the literature and research agenda. *The Leadership Quarterly*, 22(6), 1120–1145.

Gastil, J. (1994). A Definition and Illustration of Democratic Leadership. *Human Relations*, 47(8), 953–975.

Gemmill, G. (1986). The Mythology of the Leader Role in Small Groups. *Small Group Behaviour*, 17(1), 41–50.

Gemmill, G., & Oakley, J. (1992). Leadership: An alienating social myth? *Human Relations*, 45(2), 113–129.

George, B., Sims, P., McLean, A., & Mayer, D. (2007). Discovering Your Authentic Leadership. *Harvard Business Review*, 85(February), 129–138.

Gergen, K.J. (1994). *Realities and Relationships: Soundings in social construction*. Cambridge, MA: Harvard University Press.

Giacalone, R.A., & Promislo, M.D. (2013). Broken When Entering: The stigmatization of goodness and business ethics education. *Academy of Management Learning & Education*, 12(1), 86–101.

Gordon, U. (2010). *Anarchy Alive! Anti-authoritarian politics from practice to theory*. London: Pluto Press.

Greenleaf, R. (1977). *Servant Leadership: A journey into the nature of legitimate power and Greatness*. Mahwah, NJ: Paulist Press.

Gudmundsson, A., & Southey, G. (2011). Leadership and the Rise of the Corporate Psychopath: What can business schools do about the "snakes inside"? QUT Business School, Queensland University of Technology, Queensland.

Higgs, M. (2009). The Good, the Bad and the Ugly: Leadership and narcissism. *Journal of Change Management*, 9(2), 165–178.

Hiller, N.J., DeChurch, L.A., Murase, T., & Doty, D. (2011). Searching for Outcomes of Leadership: A 25-year review. *Journal of Management*, 37(4), 1137–1177.

Hurlow, S. (2008). *Language of Leadership*, PhD Thesis, Cardiff University.

Jackson, B., & Parry, K. (2008). *A Very Short, Fairly Interesting and Reasonably Cheap Book About Studying Leadership*. London & Thousand Oaks, CA: SAGE Publications, Inc.

Jones, E.E., & Harris, V.A. (1967). The Attribution of Attitudes. *Journal of Experimental Social Psychology*, 3(1), 1–24.

Kempster, S., Jackson, B., & Conroy, M. (2011). Leadership as Purpose: Exploring the role of purpose in leadership practice. *Leadership*, 7(3), 317–334.

Khoo, H., & Burch, G. (2007). The "Dark Side" of Leadership Personality and Transformational Leadership: An exploratory study. *Personality and Individual Differences*, 44(January), 86–97.

Kouzes, J., & Posner, B. (2003). *Exemplary Leadership*. San Francisco, CA: Jossey-Bass.

Lave, J., & Wenger, E. (1991). *Situated Learning*. Cambridge: Cambridge University Press.

Lipman-Blumen, J. (2006). *The Allure of Toxic Leaders: Why we follow destructive bosses and corrupt politicians – and how we can survive them*. Oxford: Oxford University Press.

Meindl, J., Sanford, B., Ehrlich, B., & Dukerich, J. (1985). The Romance of Leadership. *Administrative Science Quarterly*, 30(1), 78–102.

Metcalf, L., & Benn, S. (2013). Leadership for Sustainability: An evolution of leadership ability. *Journal of Business Ethics*, 112(3), 369–384.

Nicolini, D. (2012). *Practice Theory, Work, and Organization: An introduction*. Oxford: Oxford University Press.

Nkomo, S. M. (2011). A Postcolonial and Anti-Colonial Reading of "African" Leadership and Management in Organization Studies: Tensions, contradictions and possibilities. *Organization*, 18(3), 365–386.

Ospina, S., & Foldy, E.G. (2015). Enacting Collective Leadership in a Shared-Power World. In J. Perry & R.K. Christensen (Eds), *Handbook of Public Administration* (pp. 489–507). San Francisco, CA: Jossey-Bass.

Padilla, A., Hogan, R., & Kaiser, R. (2007). The Toxic Triangle: Destructive leaders, susceptible followers, and conducive environments. *The Leadership Quarterly*, 18, 176–194.

Palus, C.J., McGuire, J.B., & Ernst, C. (2012). Developing Interdependent Leadership. In S. Snook, N. Nohria, & R. Khurana (Eds.), *The Handbook for Teaching Leadership: Knowing, doing, and being* (pp. 467–492). Thousand Oaks, CA: SAGE Publications.

Parker, M. (2002). *Against Management*. Cambridge: Polity Press.

Peterlin, J. (2016). Incorporation of Sustainability into Leadership Development. *Economic and Business Review*, 18(1), 31–53.

Perez-Carmona, A. (2013). Growth: A discussion of the margins of economic and ecological thought. In L. Meuleman (Ed.), *Transgovernance: Advancing sustainability governance* (pp. 83–162). Heidelberg, Germany: Springer.

Pfeffer, J. (2015). *Leadership BS: Fixing workplaces and careers one truth at a time*. New York: Harper Business.

Podsakoff, P.M., MacKenzie, S.B., & Podsakoff, N.P. (2016). Recommendations for Creating Better Concept Definitions in the Organizational, Behavioral, and Social Sciences. *Organizational Research Methods*, 19(2), 159–203.

Purvis, M., & Grainger, A. (Eds) (2004). *Exploring Sustainable Development: Geographical Perspectives*. London: Earthscan.

Rahnema, M., & Bawtree, V. (Eds) (1997). *The Post-Development Reader*. London: Zed Books.

Redekop, B.W. (Ed.) (2010). *Leadership for Environmental Sustainability*. London & New York: Routledge.

Sachs, J. (2015). *The Age of Sustainable Development*. New York: Columbia University Press.

Schachter, H. (2014). New Public Management and Principals' Roles in Organizational Governance: What can a corporate issue tell us about public sector management? *Public Organization Review*, 14(4), 517–531.

Schilling, J. (2009). From Ineffectiveness to Destruction: A qualitative study on the meaning of negative leadership. *Leadership*, 5(1), 102–128.

Schyns, B., & Schilling, J. (2013). How Bad are the Effects of Bad Leaders? A meta-analysis of destructive leadership and its outcomes. *Leadership Quarterly*, 24(1), 138–158.

Sheard, G., Kakabadse, N., & Kakabadse, A. (2013). Visceral Behaviours and Leadership: A dark side of boardroom life? *Journal of Management Development*, 32(1), 18–35.

Shriberg, M., & MacDonald, L. (2013). Sustainability Leadership Programs: Emerging goals, methods & best practices. *Journal of Sustainability Education*, 5(May), 1–21.

Steurer, R. (2007). From Government Strategies to Strategic Public Management: An exploratory outlook on the pursuit of cross-sectoral policy integration. *Environmental Policy and Governance*, 17(3), 201–214.

Sutherland, N., Land, C., & Bohm, S. (2014). Anti-leaders(hip) in Social Movement Organisations: The case of autonomous grassroots groups. *Organisation*, 21(6), 759–781.

Tepper, B. (2000). Consequences of Abusive Supervision. *Academy of Management Journal*, 43(2), 178–190.

WCED. (1987). *Our Common Future*. World Commission on Environment and Development. Available at: www.un-documents.net/our-common-future.pdf.

Weick, K.E. (1995). *Sensemaking in Organisations*. Thousand Oaks, CA: SAGE Publications, Inc.

Western, S. (2008). *Leadership: A Critical Text*. London & Thousand Oaks, CA: SAGE Publications, Inc.

Woods, P.A., Bennett, N., Harvey, J.A., & Wise, C. (2004). Variabilities and Dualities in Distributed Leadership: Findings from a systematic literature review. *Educational Management Administration Leadership*, 32(4), 439–457.

Zingheim, P.K., Ledford, G., & Schuster, J. (1996). Competencies and Competency Models: Does one size fit all? *ACA Journal*, 5(1), 56–65.

2 A Case for Universal Context

Intersections of the biosphere, systems, and justice using a critical constructionist lens

Rian Satterwhite

Introduction

Leadership is a socially constructed phenomenon, situated in context, place, and time. This book makes the case that 1) the biosphere is a predominant and pervasive context of leadership theory and practice, and that 2) critical and constructionist perspectives are important tools in exploring what leadership does – and can – look like when the biosphere is an acknowledged context of leadership practice.

This chapter makes explicit the natural intersections between the biosphere, systems, and justice utilizing a critical constructionist lens. These topics are threads throughout the book, but it is worth more fully exploring their intersection at the outset. While each is yet a niche topic in leadership studies literature, their union creates a powerful tool that serves to refocus leadership – an otherwise amorphous concept – toward purposes of justice, shared responsibility, and more intentionally shaping the interwoven systems that form the warp and weft of our biological and social lives. This framework is also consistent with the call for more complex and inclusive ways of understanding the world (Kegan, 1994), and by extension, leadership.

Drath (2001) observes that "… leadership is in fact changing in ways determined by changes in our way of life, in our ways of understanding, and especially in our ways of interrelating" (p. xiv). In other words, the context of leadership continues to evolve and our understanding of it must keep pace. One of the challenges of situating leadership in context is the associated presumption that it then becomes problematic to translate lessons learned to other contexts, each of which is seen as essentially unique. The dominant thought seems to be that we must adapt ourselves and our behavior repeatedly; navigating new waters, new priorities, new values, and new relationships with each new leadership challenge. The fractured landscape of the field itself is reflective of this thinking. Business leadership. Nonprofit leadership. Public leadership. Youth leadership. Followership. Leadership for social change. Leadership development. Leadership education. Executive coaching. Organizational consulting. It is possible to identify sub-genres, industries, and consulting practices so numerous as to be nearly limitless. Our ability to parse leadership into infinitesimally discrete domains is astonishing. The implicit message in all of this is that while there may be translatable lessons, the context in each scenario or environment is different enough to warrant disparate and sometimes competing studies, methods, purposes, and philosophies.

Further, efforts in the literature to ground leadership in something more substantial that will apply across contexts have either been anchored in a problematic reductionism or largely amount to personal values and identity clarification. Stop me if you've heard this before: bringing our authentic selves to each context is the only way to ensure any consistency and trans-latable lessons from experience to experience. After all, *we* are the only constants from context to context, correct? If so, leadership development simply becomes personal development … an awfully slippery (and worry-ingly narcissistic) slope. In this narrative, we are assumed to be the only mobile and consistent thread woven throughout our varied leadership experiences and, even more concerningly, our values are frequently pre-sumed to be natural unto themselves, having been born from within through little to no external influence. The unfortunate effect of this focus on inter-nal, personal development is that it blinds us to several truths that have become increasingly apparent, but with which we continue to struggle: 1) we are not alone, nor have we arrived "here" on our own; 2) discrete otherness is a falsehood except at a microbiological level; 3) our inherent and fundamental interconnectedness is frequently uncomfortable because it conveys weight – and responsibility – to seemingly intractable challenges that can easily overwhelm our sense of self-efficacy and agency. The result is too often a vicious spiral of willful blindness and valued ignorance. The alternative – the picture that the biosphere, systems, and justice together paint – is uncomfortable for many to contemplate: a shared responsibility for challenges, timelines, systems, species, and generations that span far beyond our normal perceived sphere of influence (or concern).

Donella Meadows, in sharing her wisdom on systems thinking, has a great deal to say about our state of willful ignorance. She writes that:

> We rarely see the full range of possibilities before us. We often don't foresee (or choose to ignore) the impacts of our actions on the whole system. So instead of finding a long-term optimum, we discover within our limited purview a choice we can live with for now, and we stick to it, changing our behavior only when forced to … we misperceive risk … we live in an exaggerated present … we discount the future … We don't give all incoming signals their appropriate weights. We don't let in all news we don't like, or information that doesn't fit our mental models. Which is to say, we don't even make decisions that optimize our own individual good, much less the good of the system as a whole.
>
> (2008, pp. 106–107)

One of the fundamental lessons of systems thinking is that we create the boundaries that define a system; that, in truth, most of these boundaries are permeable, as systems are connected to other systems in an intricate and beautiful tapestry. Creating these boundaries is an important exercise in filtering a potentially overwhelming set of information and has proven to be a powerful analytical tool, but mistaking the tool for an immutable truth is equivalent to not seeing the forest for the trees. Unfortunately, this is a mistake we make repeatedly and often.

Margaret Heffernan (2011) offers related research on willful blindness, arguing that despite genuine utility (greasing social interactions, limiting the debilitating stress of major traumatic events, etc.), "the mechanisms that make us blind to the world also put us in peril … And all the time that these perils go unacknowledged, they grow more powerful and more dangerous" (p. 4). Continuing, Heffernan alerts us to "a central truth about willful blindness: We may think being blind makes us safer, when in fact it leaves us crippled, vulnerable, and powerless. But when we confront facts and fears, we achieve real power and unleash our capacity for change" (ibid.). It is my hope to better illuminate some of these facts and fears in examining the biosphere, systems, and justice as universal contexts and critical constructionism as an important lens to employ in leadership in the 21st century. First, let's explore critical and constructionist approaches, and then we can make the case for the three universal contexts.

Critical Theory

Critical theory questions "the hidden assumptions and purposes of competing theories and existing forms of practice … [insisting] that thought must respond to the new problems and the new possibilities for liberation that arise from changing historical circumstances" (Bronner, 2011, p. 1). Most importantly, it concerns itself not "merely with how things were but how they might be and should be" (ibid, pp. 1–2). Brookfield (2005) clarifies that "critical theory is normatively grounded in a vision of a society in which people live collectively in ways that encourage the free exercise of their creativity without foreclosing that of others. In such a society people see their individual well-being as integrally bound up with that of the collective" (p. 39). Brookfield proceeds to articulate a set of seven "learning tasks" that must be undertaken to create such a society: challenging ideology, contesting hegemony, unmasking power, overcoming alienation, learning liberation, reclaiming reason, and learning democracy (ibid).

Owen (2015) adapts these generalized learning tasks to leadership studies, calling on leadership educators to "interrogate their own biases, beliefs, and practices" in order to "develop critical consciousness" (p. 14). Adapting Brookfield's learning tasks referenced above, Owen poses difficult and thought-provoking reflective prompts for leadership educators including

How/where are leadership educators learning forms of reasoning and action that challenge social, cultural, and political ideologies? How are we modeling these processes for students? How are leadership educators learning about hegemony ... and their own complicity in its continued existence? How might leadership itself intentionally or unintentionally support hegemonic processes? To what extent do leadership educators challenge notions of groupthink or the dominance of the collective? Where do leadership learners experience individualized learning and support so that they can foster "rebellious subjectivity"?

(p. 15)

These and other questions challenge us to more effectively and critically examine our own role in advancing hegemonic and normative ideology in the theory and practice of leadership.

The unapologetic future orientation found within critical theory is consistent with how leadership studies *should* function as well as how it *needs* to function in our present times. There is insight to be gained from studying history and present-day practices, but I worry that the field is too timid in boldly envisioning how leadership *ought* to be, even if that is different from how it is currently perceived and enacted. We have the opportunity to shape what future leadership looks like. Critical theory points us strongly in this bold new direction with its liberatory purpose.

Employing a critical lens in leadership studies is not simply an exercise in wishful optimism. It demands a willingness to wrestle with fundamental questions, unearth hidden assumptions, participate in a difficult process of deconstruction/reconstruction, and to more critically analyze our social location as leadership scholars, trainers, educators, practitioners, and students. Criticality provides a moral direction to leadership, focusing as it does on emancipation and unearthing unequal power relations. Western (2013) writes that "The task of critical theory is to study power and knowledge relations, to challenge dominating structures, and also to prevent leadership becoming another instrumental project, serving only to promote greater efficiency, productivity, profit, with little reflection on its wider impact on society" (p. 8). Much of the dissonance within the field itself can be seen as a reflection of this struggle: contributions to the field either shaping leadership as an instrumental tool for unequal power relations and historical systems of oppression, or seeking to reframe, challenge, and ground the concept in emancipatory goals like social justice and sustainability.

It is important to recognize that much of leadership studies itself is thoroughly situated in what Dugan (2017) calls "the story most often told;" in other words, awash in a particular and dominant ideology, shaped by hegemonic norms and assumptions, and generally driven by a belief (sometimes implicit, sometimes explicit) in the power of reductionist analysis. Dugan reminds us that:

Given leadership is a socially constructed phenomenon, society naturally plays an enormous role in how it is framed. That framing, however, is through the lens of dominant stocks of knowledge, ideology/hegemony, and social location. Without intervention and the application of critical perspectives, leadership theory inherently reflects a "story most often told." We have the power and agency to disrupt this, but doing so requires critical learning.

(2017, p. 327)

By becoming more critical learners and actively disrupting these processes, we may shape leadership theory and practice to be an affirming place of reclamation and social change. Further, I will argue that adopting this critical perspective is complemented by a constructionist paradigm that expands our capacity to see these shared contexts and effectively co-construct our future, guided by the universal contexts of the biosphere, systems, and justice.

A Critical Constructionist Lens

Critical theory is a powerful analytical perspective that, despite an established history in what is called Critical Management Studies (Alvesson & Willmott, 1992, 1996; Alvesson & Spicer, 2012; Collinson, 2011, 2014; Collinson & Tourish, 2015; Fulop & Linstead, 1999; Klikauer, 2015), has yet to be broadly embraced in the field of leadership studies. Constructionist perspectives have also been slow to be explored fully in the field. In one of the most notable examples of a constructionist approach to leadership, Ospina & Sorenson (2006) write that,

A constructionist lens suggests that leadership happens when a community develops and uses, over time, shared agreements to create results that have collective value. Grounded in culture and embedded in social structures such as power and stratification, these agreements influence and give meaning to members' actions, interactions and relationships, and help people mobilize to make change happen.

(p. 188)

This perspective pushes us further toward a collective approach to leadership where leadership is the property of the group/community/organization, and is consistent with other efforts in the field to disentangle the work of leadership from the heroic individual. Bringing critical and constructionist lenses together reinforces the strengths of each and yields powerful insights about meaning making, power, and the structures that shape our perceptions. Here, I advocate for utilizing a critical constructionist approach when examining the three universal contexts of leadership: the biosphere, systems, and justice.

Ospina & Sorenson (2006) further explore a constructionist lens on leadership:

> The generation of meaning is always a social, rather than an individual process, because to engage in meaning-making human beings draw from existing previous meanings in their culture, and the latter, in turn, is embedded in historically grounded social structures ... A constructionist view presumes that our understanding of leadership is socially constructed over time, as individual interact with one another, rather than being something embodied in individuals or possessed by them.
>
> (pp. 189–190)

Thus, if meaning (and, for these purposes, our understanding of leadership) is socially constructed over time and necessarily shaped (and limited) by ideas already established, then these previously established ideas take on critical importance. Drath (2001) argues that "leadership effectiveness is related more to the sharing of meaning in a community than it is to any particular style or approach to leadership" (p. 28). If, as a constructionist lens suggests, we are working with the tools – the meaning – that those before us have built, we must be mindful of the limitations of those tools. Critical theory allows just such a stance as it examines ideology/hegemony, and offers the ability to, as Dugan (2017) deftly demonstrates, deconstruct and reconstruct concepts in ways that are more inclusive and equitable. A constructionist approach, then, further illuminates the consequences of ideology/hegemony and the hidden constraints on our thinking and being that critical theory unearths, while critical theory deepens the implications of the social construction of reality that constructionism explores.

Importantly, constructionism and critical theory are also to some extent in tension with one another. By this I mean that constructionism runs the danger of being overly constrictive; too focused on what is rather than on what might be. The previously discussed future orientation of critical theory and its inherently hopeful orientation (see the discussion of "critical hope" in Preskill & Brookfield, 2009, p. 171) challenges us to learn from and interrogate – but not be trapped by – what has existed in the past. At the same time, the analysis of shared and historically situated meaning in constructionism serves to ground critical theory in practice and lived experience. The tension in time orientation between the two frameworks (present and future versus present and past) serves to strengthen both when brought together and may even contribute to expanding our relationship to multiple time scales as Satterwhite, Sheridan, and McIntyre Miller (2016) call for.

Successfully bridging theory and practice is also particularly important here. Critical theory and constructionist perspectives are highly active, recognizing the power of our interaction with the world and with one another in shaping meaning and purpose. Martin & Te Riele (2011) argue that "An urgent need exists for educational work that is situated, reflexive, and hopeful. This will require a new relation between theory and practice where critical pedagogy is responsive to the generative possibilities of place-based struggles and politics" (p. 24). The same holds true for leadership and leadership education. A critical constructionist lens is a powerful analytical tool that yields significant and challenging insights for the field, not the least of which is a valuing of lived experience and local context. However, an equally true but seemingly opposite insight – dialectical in nature – is that these same local contexts are shaped, to one extent or another, by universal ones.

The Case for Universal Contexts of Leadership

What is the meaning of leadership? What is the purpose of leadership? What are we to make of a concept so vexing that the greatest scholars of the topic cannot agree on a basic definition? Every field of study thrives and innovates from its contested approaches and philosophies, but most mature fields tend to have some basic building blocks from which to begin. A vigorous and active dialogue about fundamental truths is vital for any field, but so too is the seeking of common ground, of building bridges and generating shared meaning. I suggest that in leadership we can, in fact, find common ground from which to begin.

A comprehensive literature review of the field of leadership studies is beyond the scope of this chapter. My assertion is simply this: despite any number of earnest attempts to wrestle with these core questions (e.g. Burns, 1978; Drath, 2001; Drath, et al., 2008; Goethals & Sorenson, 2007; Rost, 1991), the field finds itself in an all-too familiar place of patchwork narratives that function to disprove and contend with one another more often than integrate and build. My hope, here, is to provide a platform from which we can more successfully integrate and build, to identify threads that are or should be woven throughout all leadership theory and practice. I wish to deconstruct the story most often told about leadership – that of heroic individuals generating novel visions independently of their contexts and communities – and reconstruct it in such a way as to recognize our universal contexts.

One approach is to analyze the ideology of the field. Are there ideologies so entrenched that other voices have been constrained, concepts so dominant (hegemonic) as to crowd out the possibilities of alternative pathways? Senge (2006; Senge et al., 2008) has strongly made the case for both systems and sustainability, eventually integrating the two and calling "systems citizenship" (in the context of sustainability) the "leadership mandate for this millennium" (2006). Heifetz (1994, 2006), too, has contributed significantly to these emerging areas of focus, to the point that the concept of adaptive leadership was noted as central in *Leadership for Environmental Sustainability* (Redekop, 2010, p. 243), the first full multidisciplinary treatment of the concept. Others, including Wheatley (2006) and Uhl-Bien & Marion (2008), have received praise but still find general disengagement with their important conceptual contributions in the literature. The point here is not to call attention to all overlooked thinkers and authors (that list is indeed long), but simply to establish that there are dominant and nondominant narratives, concepts, and perspectives within leadership studies, and that critical constructionism is an important tool for generating and analyzing this map of power and ideology in the field. Applying a critical construc-tionist lens helps us break down the barriers that we have built – challen-ging our willful blindness – and just as importantly offers meaningful pathways to reconstruct more inclusive and holistic perspectives. We must better nurture the ability to unearth, question, critique, and ultimately reshape fundamental assumptions.

With the background on critical and constructionist approaches in place, let's now attempt to establish the case for the three universal contexts: the biosphere, systems, and justice (Figure 2.1).

No matter our individual background, I assert that we share these common contexts. Even as we continually learn to more genuinely value and engage our differences, we should also become more adept at acknowledging our commonalities. This is not born out of a reductionist universalism, but

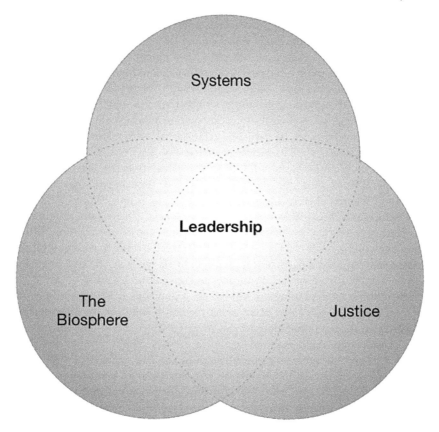

Figure 2.1 Universal Contexts of Leadership

instead a truth that clearly emerges when examining the biosphere, systems, and justice.

Universal Context: The Biosphere

We are, at a fundamental level, biological beings composed of numerous complex systems, interacting with our environment in the reproduction of self (Capra & Luisi, 2014; Maturana & Varela, 1987; Satterwhite, 2010). We are also highly complex beings possessing consciousness and wrestling with questions of purpose and meaning and value. We do this in community. We are taught by, learn from, rail against, and seek out the company of others. But we are not alone as a species; we are dominant but not solitary, uniquely-powerful yet strangely susceptible. We are surrounded by, embedded in, made from, and reliant upon natural systems of both organic and inorganic processes. We are deeply interconnected in ways that are fractal in nature; this interconnectedness repeated and present at deeper and deeper levels of analysis. To be clear, this interconnection is dynamic and changeable, but it is also unavoidable.

If we share these starting places, then leadership (which for this purpose is essentially how people come together and do coordinated work in order to achieve a mutually beneficial outcome), as a human activity, is necessarily built upon this common biological and interdependent foundation. Aside from any moral arguments that could – and *should* – be made about our larger responsibility to multiple generations or other species, our biological reality necessitates that we tend to the natural systems of which we are a part.

The responsibility to tend to our relationship with nature is as fundamental as it is shared. This idea is of course not new, but it has yet to fully seep into daily consciousness let alone the calculations of our constructed systems. Writers and thinkers calling for this fundamental reorientation abound: Wendell Berry, Henry David Thoreau, Ralph Waldo Emerson, Rachel Carson, E.O. Wilson, and countless others. Those calls are difficult to heed because they so fundamentally challenge not necessarily our beliefs, but our comfort. Our social systems and therefore our lives are typically constructed around a particular willful blindness: ignoring the true costs and unsustainable nature of our decisions and consumption habits.

In addition to the biological and ethical arguments to be made, there are also practical ones in favor of situating the study and practice of leadership squarely in its biospheric context. Shriberg (2012) makes a convincing case that "leadership skills required for sustainability closely mirror the skills needed to address other major challenges of the 21st century" (p. 469). He continues, arguing that "This shift is necessary not only because it would be good for the planet and, therefore, for the natural capital that underlies all wealth but also because this form of leadership would create fundamentally different and higher functioning organizations" (p. 477). In other words, leadership that acknowledges the biosphere as the ultimate frame in which we operate has the potential to transcend environmental sustainability and positively influence other important leadership goals that we might share.

At first glance, responsibility to natural systems may appear to be localized, but systems thinking (and modern ecological studies) teach us that we are not so separate from natural systems located at a geographical distance. Everything is connected; it is simply a matter of degree and time. This is an idea whose time has come, a reality we must now embrace and integrate. Kuenkel (2016), writes that:

> The times of paralysis are over. There is a larger goal everybody can tap into. Sustainability leadership is on the agenda, yet many are afraid to make a move that pushes the comfort zone. Today, ten [or more] years farther along in our global discussion on sustainability, the answer is there: If we want to learn to lead better, we can place our leadership in the context of sustainability. Sustainability is a leadership task. It creates meaning. It creates a better world.
>
> (p. 220)

While this book examines environmental leadership – and thereby participates in the discourse of environmental sustainability – the concept necessarily extends beyond what usually comes to mind when thinking of environmental sustainability. Edwards (2005) succinctly expands the discourse of sustainability to include the "four Es:" environment, equity, education, and economy. In doing so, many complex global (and local) challenges are linked together, helping us to better understand them as common facets of broader systems.

For these reasons, we arrive at the natural world – the biosphere – as the ultimate context within which all leadership challenges occur. Some localized leadership challenges will more explicitly incorporate the sustainability of human/natural systems as a goal than others, but to ignore the biosphere entirely is to ignore both our long-term good and a shared biological reality. With this context, I reissue a challenge in reframing leadership: "Leadership's purpose, in any capacity, becomes nothing less than the pursuit of a just relationship with one another and the world around us" (Satterwhite, 2012, p. 582).

Universal Context: Systems

Systems are a second universal context. Meadows (2008) offers a clear starting point in defining a system: "A system is an interconnected set of elements that is coherently organized in a way that achieves something" (p. 11). The term complex systems is, in essence, simply a recognition of the interconnectedness of any particular system that we might identify with others around it (and the complex behavior of systems as a result of their interconnectedness). Our primary challenge related to this context is to reframe (i.e., expand) the way we see the world while nurturing an ability to see, read, influence, and shape systems. Toward that end and explicitly building upon Meadow's definition referenced above, Stroh (2015) defines systems thinking as "the ability to understand these interconnections in such a way as to achieve a desired purpose" (p. 16). This, I suggest, is a fundamental challenge of leadership education and development.

One of the best starting places for seeing systems is looking inward and locally. We are surrounded by – and reliant upon – systems. We are, inescapably, made of systems ourselves (Burn, 2013; Meadows, 2008; Satterwhite, 2010). What's more, we actively construct systems (and are frequently confounded by them) as a means to deal with complex realities. In order to move beyond this hopeless cycle of being surprised by the actions and consequences of the systems that we have created, we must learn to think and see differently, more expansively. Stroh (2015) offers important insights emerging from systems thinking that are eminently relevant to sustainability leadership: 1) The relationship between problems and their causes is indirect and not obvious. 2) We unwittingly create many of our own problems but have the ability to address them through our own behavior. 3) Most quick fixes generate unintended consequences, ultimately distancing us from our goals. 4) In order to optimize the whole, we must improve relationships among the parts. 5) Only a few key coordinated changes sustained over time will produce large systems change (p. 15). Stroh continues, suggesting that "People's good intentions to improve social systems are often undermined when they apply conventional thinking to chronic, complex social problems" (2015, p. 16).

We live in a world shaped and defined by systems and their interplay – their interdependence – with one another. This is the second universal context of leadership and we must strive to better see and shape these systems. Any leadership that does not start here will inevitably make the mistakes of conventional thinking that Stroh warns against.

In her reflection on the development of systems thinking, Meadows (2008) writes that:

> What was unique about our search was not our answers, or even our questions, but the fact that the tool of systems thinking, born out of engineering and mathematics, implemented in computers, drawn from a mechanistic mind-set and a quest for prediction and control, leads its practitioners, inexorably I believe, to confront the most deeply human mysteries ... the future can't be predicted, but it can be envisioned and brought lovingly into being.
>
> (pp. 167–169)

Further, she writes that "Living successfully in a world of complex systems means expanding not only time horizons and thought horizons; above all, it means expanding the horizons of caring" (2008, p. 184). Systems shape our lives, and adopting a systems perspective allows us to see these systems, ultimately challenging us to expand our spheres of concern. Systems thinking is akin to falling down the rabbit hole in Alice In Wonderland: once we begin to see these systems and our interconnection/interdependencies, we cannot see the world in the same way as before.

Universal Context: Justice

As has already been named, critical theory has "progressive intentions" and, when applied to leadership, it "aims to create a better society by rethinking, rediscovering and reinventing leadership" (Western, 2013, p. 3). Western's use of critical theory in leadership theory and practice is the same as my own: "to situate leadership within an ethical and emancipatory framework" (ibid.). He notes that "the lens of emancipation is concerned with promoting justice, equality, ethics, a sustainable environment, liberation and autonomy" (Western, 2013, p. 11). Here one can see how the universal contexts begin to weave together: using critical theory (also holding true for a critical constructionist lens) recasts the purpose of leadership to the enactment of justice and sustainability while uncovering and reshaping systems of power that hinder these goals.

Justice, of course, is not only the domain of critical theory and has been a discourse present in leadership studies for some time. The social change model of leadership (Higher Education Research Institute, 1996) is often cited as one of the most commonly used leadership models with college students both in programming and research, and it may be seen as orienting learners toward a social justice perspective. Additionally, Ospina et al. (2012) offer a strategic social change leadership model utilizing a constructionist framework and grounded humanism as the foundation. The model aims for long-term outcomes of changed structures, policies, and thinking (p. 256). Importantly, this model also clearly defines social justice as "a call for fairness and equality of opportunity for all human beings. It encompasses particular values of inclusion, social solidarity, transparency and accountability, democracy, and equity" (p. 271). Justice discourse in leadership theory can be found elsewhere as well, but it is typically treated as a special case as opposed to a universal or shared purpose.

To whatever extent the discourse of justice is present in the field, it is almost always limited to the human frame. It must now be expanded to include the biospheric level, to the non-human realm. This bridge between social and environmental justice has already been constructed using Schlosberg and Carruthers' (2010) "pluralistic discourse of justice" and Amartya Sen's capabilities theory approach (Satterwhite et al., 2015). It is increasingly apparent that the pursuit of justice in the human realm requires the pursuit of justice in the natural realm, and vice versa. This insight further emphasizes the interconnected nature of our three universal contexts, but it also signals a dramatic shift in the perceived contexts and purposes of leadership.

Conclusion

Paulo Freire (1970) notes that, "Knowledge emerges only through invention and re-invention, through the restless, impatient, continuing, hopeful inquiry human beings pursue in the world, with the world, and with each other" (p. 72). This chapter is a call to recognize that as we restlessly pursue knowledge about the world, with the world, with each other, we do so *in* the world, shaped by shared contexts and unequal power relations. Adopting a critical constructionist lens begins to unearth the ways in which leadership theory and practice have, at times overtly but often unintentionally, served the interests of the few and advanced normative ideology inconsistent with progressive goals such as shared liberation, environmental sustainability, and justice. Systems thinking helps us to expand our spheres of concern and see the ways in which we participate in – and, for some, benefit from – systems of oppression. Ultimately, I believe leadership theory and practice needs common ground to stand on and the universal contexts help us to achieve this. They are descriptive, rather than prescriptive in nature, meaning that acknowledging this reality shapes our discourse and practice while still allowing for the myriad of cultural and organizational realities that spring from this common ground.

I have made the case that the biosphere, systems, and justice are universal contexts that must be acknowledged in leadership theory and practice. These are backdrops against which we must see and measure ourselves, but they must also increasingly be foregrounded in our purpose and practice. They do not lead to a grand unified theory of leadership; rather, they provide a common language and perhaps a common set of overarching goals across the diversity of leadership theory and research. They are threads by which we might weave a more integrative tapestry of leadership. Throughout this book, you will find examples from around the world of people actively framing leadership in similar ways, throughout a variety of environments and fields of work.

Kenny Ausubel (2012), referencing David Orr's work around ecological literacy, writes, "What all education is finally about is how we are to live in this interdependent world" (p. 189). Leadership theory and practice has the potential to help us achieve that end, but only if we are brave enough to surface and question the hidden assumptions and constraints of our cultural and discipline-based perspectives.

One caution I should offer is this: acknowledging universal contexts is not the same as leaping to a "we are all human and therefore the same" stance. If anything, the constructionist framework used here emphasizes the uniqueness inherent in each of our experiences as we interact with the world and those around us. Layer on top of that the socialization of group and cultural norms that critical theory helps unearth, and it becomes quite clear that our experiences and perspectives have not all been shaped in the same ways. Nonetheless, we have been socialized and lived our lives within these three universal contexts. Our richness and diversity springs from this common ground. My intent in making the case for universal contexts of leadership is that doing so provides a foundation from which to more effectively explore our differences while arriving at shared meaning and purpose. bell hooks (2003) notes that

> Creating trust usually means finding out what it is we have in common as well as what separates us and makes us different. Lots of people fear encountering difference because they think that honestly naming it will lead to conflict ... it will always be vital, necessary for us to know that we are more than our differences, that it is not just what we organically share that can connect us but what we come to have in common because we have done the work of creating community, the unity within diversity, that requires solidarity within a structure of values, beliefs, yearnings that are always beyond the body, yearning that have to do with universal spirit.
>
> (pp. 109–110)

Much of the hard work remains in nurturing the "unity within diversity," building shared meaning and purpose over time. In doing so, we are well served in coming to recognize our shared contexts of the biosphere, systems, and justice while adopting a critical constructionist lens. Doing so holds transformative potential for leadership theory and practice. This chapter has barely scratched the surface in exploring the full implications of these contexts; they run deep and will require our collective investment to explore, engage, and adjust our thinking and systems accordingly.

References

Alvesson, M., & Spicer, A. (2012). Critical Leadership Studies: The case for critical performativity. *Human Relations*, 65(3), 367–390.

Alvesson, M., & Willmott, H. (1992). *Critical Management Studies*. London: SAGE Publications, Inc.

Alvesson, M., & Willmott, H. (1996). *Making Sense of Management: A critical introduction*. London, UK: SAGE Publications, Inc.

Ausubel, K. (2012). *Dreaming the Future: Reimagining civilization in the age of nature*. White River Junction, VT: Chelsea Green.

Bronner, S. E. (2011). *Critical Theory: A very short introduction*. Oxford: Oxford University Press.

Brookfield, S. (2005). *The Power of Critical Theory: Liberating adult learning and teaching*. San Francisco, CA: Jossey-Bass.

Burn, S. (2013). Seeking Alignment in the World Body: The art of embodiment. In Melina, L., Burgess, G., Falkman, L., & Marturano, A. (Eds), *The Embodiment of Leadership* (pp. 65–83). San Francisco, CA: Jossey-Bass.

Burns, J.M. (1978). *Leadership*. New York: Harper & Row.

Capra, F., & Luisi, P.L. (2014). *The Systems View of Life: A unifying vision*. Cambridge: Cambridge University Press.

Collinson, D. (2011). Critical Leadership Studies. In A. Bryman, D. Collinson, K. Grint, B. Jackson, & M. Uhl-Bien (Eds), *The SAGE Handbook of Leadership* (pp. 181–194). Thousand Oaks, CA: SAGE Publications, Inc.

Collinson, D. (2014). Dichotomies, Dialectics and Dilemmas: New directions for critical leadership studies? *Leadership*, 10(1), 36–55.

Collinson, D., & Tourish, D. (2015). Teaching Leadership Critically: New directions for leadership pedagogy. *Academy of Management Learning & Education*, 14(4), 576–594.

Drath, W. (2001). *The Deep Blue Sea: Rethinking the source of leadership*. San Francisco, CA: Jossey-Bass.

Drath, W.H., McCauley, C.D., Palus, C.J., Van Velsor, E., O'Connor, P.M.G., & McGuire, J.B. (2008). Direction, Alignment, Commitment: Toward a more integrative ontology of leadership. *The Leadership Quarterly*, 19, 635–653.

Dugan, J. (2017). *Leadership Theory: Cultivating critical perspectives*. San Francisco, CA: Jossey-Bass.

Edwards, A.R. (2005). *The Sustainability Revolution: Portrait of a paradigm shift*. Gabriola Island, BC: New Society Publishers.

Freire, P. (1970). *Pedagogy of the Oppressed*. New York: Continuum.

Fulop, L., & Linstead, S. (1999). *Management: A critical text*. London: Macmillan.

Goethals, G., & Sorenson, G. (Eds) (2007). *The Quest for a General Theory of Leadership*. Cheltenham: Edward Elgar.

Heffernan, M. (2011). *Willful Blindness: Why we ignore the obvious at our peril*. New York: Bloomsbury.

Heifetz, R. (1994). *Leadership Without Easy Answers*. Cambridge, MA: Harvard University Press.

Heifetz, R. (2006). Anchoring Leadership in the Work of Adaptive Progress. In F. Hesselbein, & M. Goldsmith (Eds), *The Leader of the Future 2: Visions, strategies, and practices for the new era* (pp. 73–84). San Francisco, CA: Jossey-Bass.

Higher Education Research Institute. (1996). *A Social Change Model of Leadership Development: Guidebook* (Version three). Los Angeles, CA: Higher Education Research Institute.

hooks, bell. (2003). *Teaching Community: A pedagogy of hope*. New York: Routledge.

Kegan, R. (1994). *In Over Our Heads: The mental demands of modern life*. Cambridge, MA: Harvard University Press.

Klikauer, T. (2015). Critical Management Studies and Critical Theory: A review. *Capital & Class*, 39(2), 197–220.

Kuenkel, P. (2016). *The Art of Leading Collectively: Co-creating a sustainable, socially just future*. White River Junction, VT: Chelsea Green Publishing.

Martin, G., & Te Riele, K. (2011). A Place-based Critical Pedagogy in Turbulent Times: Restoring hope for alternative futures. In C.S. Malott and B. Porfilio (Eds), *Critical Pedagogy in the Twenty-first Century: A new generation of scholars*. Charlotte, NC: Information Age Publishing.

Maturana, H., & Varela, F. (1987). *The Tree of Knowledge: The biological roots of human understanding*. Boston, MA: Shambhala Publications.

Meadows, D. (2008). *Thinking in Systems: A Primer*. White River Junction, VT: Chelsea Green.

Ospina, S., Foldy, E.G., El Hadidy, W., Dodge, J., Hofmann-Pinilla, A., & Su, C. (2012). Social Change Leadership as Relational Leadership. In M. Uhl-Bien & S. Ospina (Eds), *Advancing Relational Leadership Research: A dialogue among perspectives* (pp. 255–302). Charlotte, NC: Information Age Publishing.

Ospina, S., & Sorenson, G.L.J. (2006). A Constructivist Lens on Leadership: Charting new territory. In G. Goethals & G. Sorenson (Eds), *The Quest for a General Theory of Leadership* (pp. 188–204). Northhampton, MA: Edward Elgar.

Owen, J. (2015). Transforming Leadership Development for Significant Learning. *New Directions for Student Leadership*, 145, 7–17.

Preskill, S., & Brookfield, S.D. (2009). *Learning as a Way of Leading: Lessons from the struggle for social justice*. San Francisco, CA: Jossey-Bass.

Redekop, B. (Ed.). (2010). *Leadership for Environmental Sustainability*. New York & London: Routledge.

Rost, J. (1991). *Leadership for the Twenty-First Century*. New York: Praeger.

Satterwhite, R. (2010). Deep Systems Leadership: A model for the 21st century. In B. Redekop (Ed.), *Leadership for Environmental Sustainability* (pp. 230–247). New York & London: Routledge.

Satterwhite, R. (2012). Halting the Decline: How leadership theory and practice can address global biodiversity loss. In D. Gallagher (Ed.), *Environmental Leadership: A reference handbook* (pp. 577–585). Los Angeles, CA: SAGE Publications, Inc.

Satterwhite, R., McIntyre Miller, W., & Sheridan, K. (2015). Leadership for Sustainability and Peace: Responding to the wicked challenges of the future. In M. Sowcik, A. Andenoro, M. McNutt, & S.E. Murphy (Eds), *Leadership 2050: Critical challenges, key contexts, and emerging trends* (pp. 59–74). Bingley: Emerald.

Satterwhite, R., Sheridan, K., & McIntyre Miller, W. (2016). Rediscovering Deep Time: Sustainability and the need to re-engage with multiple dimensions of time in leadership studies. *Journal of Leadership Studies*, 9(4), 47–53.

Schlosberg, D., & Carruthers, D. (2010). Indigenous Struggles, Environmental Justice, and Community Capabilities. *Global Environmental Politics*, 10(4), 12–35.

Senge, P. (2006). Systems Citizenship: The leadership mandate for this millennium. In F. Hesselbein & M. Goldsmith (Eds), *The Leader of the Future 2: Visions, strategies, and practices for the new era* (pp. 31–46). San Francisco, CA: Jossey-Bass.

Senge, P., Smith, B., Kruschwitz, N., Laur, J., & Schley, L. (2008). *The Necessary Revolution: How individuals and organizations are working together to create a sustainable world*. New York: Doubleday.

Shriberg, M. (2012). Sustainability Leadership as 21st Century Leadership. In D. Gallagher (Ed.), *Environmental Leadership: A reference handbook* (pp. 469–478). Los Angeles, CA: Sage Publications, Inc.

Stroh, D.P. (2015). *Systems Thinking for Social Change: A practical guide to solving complex problems, avoiding unintended consequences, and achieving lasting results*. White River Junction, VT: Chelsea Green Publishing.

Uhl-Bien, M., & Marion, R. (Eds) (2008). *Complexity Leadership Part 1: Conceptual foundations*. Charlotte, NC: Information Age Publishing.

Western, S. (2013). *Leadership: A critical text* (2nd ed.) London & Thousand Oaks, CA: SAGE Publications, Inc.

Wheatley, M. (2006). *Leadership and the New Science*. San Francisco, CA: Berrett-Koheler.

3   The Eco-Leadership Paradox

Simon Western

Introduction

This chapter examines the new paradigm of Eco-leadership and the paradox that arises for many leaders when trying to implement it. Eco-leadership refers to an emergent leadership discourse found within organizations at the beginning of the 21st century. Eco-leaders conceptualize organizations as *"eco-systems within eco-systems,"* departing from the organizational machine metaphors of the 21st century. They focus on distributed and net-worked forms of leadership within organizational eco-systems in order to ensure the inter-dependent parts of the whole are connected (Western, 2008/2013; Western, 2010).

Eco-leaders also take an ethical stance on the environment and social issues, both within and beyond their organizations. *"Eco-systems within eco-systems"* highlights how organizations function like an eco-system internally, but are not closed systems and are impacted by external eco-systems, which are economic, political, technological, social, and environmental. Meta- and micro-structures and diverse cultures are constantly interacting and co-creating what we imagine to be an organization. Organizations like eco-systems have interconnected parts, systems, and sub-systems and have living networks consisting of people, technology, and nature. An organization is a fluid and changing entity rather than a fixed object. Some organizations are more stable than others, but in today's networked society, however stable they appear, each is vulnerable to disruption from other parts of the eco-system, hence the need for Eco-leadership. The Arab Spring revolutions, 2008 financial meltdown, and recent political and business shocks signify the levels of disruption in today's increasingly networked and interconnected society.

Organizations have a cultural climate across the whole, with micro-climates in different parts. The cultural climate is made up of dynamic human and non-human interactions within organizational architectures and nature itself (Latour, 2005). Imagine a small family carpet business high in the Hima-layas, or a large factory in the suburbs of a huge polluted mega-city. Both of these organizations consist of human and non-human actors, relying on technologies and people working together, both consist of architectures where "form ever follows function" (Sullivan, 1896) designed to fit the local and specific production requirements, and both are connected and impacted by local and global natural environmental issues including water supplies, air quality impacting on worker health and well-being, climate change, etc.

Together these conditions create cultures; the organization as a body has a holistic cultural climate that is pervasive but not completely dominant, because within organizations micro-climates also exist and the whole can be impacted by micro-climates changing quickly. Something happens in one part of the organization and emotions can go viral – they are contagious. Conscious and unconscious dynamics are inspired by hope, fear, dis-illusionment, and melancholy (Western, 2013, pp. 107–119). Collective states of mind emerge from illusions and disillusions, from customers, clients, service users, suppliers, downstream workforces, or middle managers. If senior leaders at the center do not have distributed leaders everywhere, picking up nuances and changes, the contagious and viral impacts of dis-ruptive changes take hold before adaptive leadership can act. This is why Eco-leadership is a meta-discourse for our times, not replacing other dis-courses, but embracing them and utilizing them in a generative way while taking a strategic overview of the whole. Eco-leadership means a radical re-imagining of how organizations function. It requires a rethinking of purpose and of how value is measured. A belief in "emancipatory ethics" (Western, 2013, pp. 11–13) feeds the organizational libido, which becomes the drive that ignites and sustains this reimagining.

Eco-Leadership in Context

Eco-leadership is the most recent of four dominant leadership discourses.[1] This conceptual model emerged from doctoral research that focused on a critical discourse analysis of leadership in the West over the past century (Western, 2005). This research has been widely cited and informs the present volume (see the Introduction). The four dominant discourses that I identified are set out in Figure 3.1 and Box 3.1 below.

Box 3.1 The Four Discourses of Leadership:

1 *The Controller leadership discourse*: Controller leadership is under-pinned by scientific rationalism and the drive for efficiency and pro-ductivity. It became dominant as industrialization took place and after a demise returned in a new form of leadership control through audit and target cultures.

2 *The Therapist leadership discourse*: Therapist leadership focuses on relationships and motivation. It emerged in the post-war period reflecting the endeavor to humanize and democratize the workplace and society. It became dominant after the 1960s boom in

individualism and therapy culture entered the workplace through the human relations movement.

3 *The Messiah leadership discourse*: Messiah leadership focuses on transformational leaders who provide vision and lead by creating strong corporate cultures. The Messiah discourse began to dominate from the early 1980s.

4 *The Eco-leadership discourse*: Eco-leadership is characterized by new understandings of organizations as ecosystems within ecosystems. The focus is on networks, connectivity, and interdependence, where new forms of distributed leadership occur within organizations, and new connections with stakeholders and wider society take place. Ethics is at the heart of Eco-leadership.

(Adapted from Western, 2013, p. 158)

Eco-Leadership as a Meta-Discourse

The four discourses of leadership are all still present in both individual leaders and in organizational life. They do not operate in isolation, but in practice they bump into each other all the time in ad hoc ways. They can contradict or complement each other, integrating or clashing, being in creative tension, or splitting into factions and chaos. However, this ad hoc scenario changes when Eco-leadership is the dominant discourse because then a more conscious and thoughtful process is embedded into the organization. The Eco-leadership discourse acts like *a Meta-Discourse* influencing and shaping how the four discourses work together in organizations. Eco-leaders identify the appropriate leadership approaches within different functions and

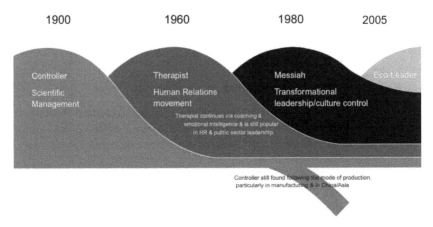

Figure 3.1 The Four Discourses of Leadership
Source: Western, 2013, p. 150.

departments and within the whole organization. A balanced approach is sought to keep the organization in dynamic and creative tension. For example, all organizations need some Controller leadership to run processes and systems efficiently, focus on task, organize work, and control resources and risk (finances and stock for example).

The skills and sensitivities of the Therapist leadership are also necessary to lead the people side of the organization: without a focus on motivation, well-being, and the emotional side of work, any organization will fail. On the one hand, Messiah leadership can be a disruptive force when it's too dominant. Yet all organizations require vision and purpose, and also a "good enough" alignment of a common culture, and employee engagement is required for an organization to function successfully and in a holistic way. The first task of Eco-leadership is to take a meta-position looking inwardly at the organization, to balance the diverse requirements of the parts and the whole, ensuring, for example, enough Controller leadership is in the health and safety and finance functions, while Therapist leadership thrives in team situations. The second task is to look externally at the disruptions in the social, technological, and natural worlds, to be able to adapt quickly to disruptions, either to take advantages of opportunities, or to guard against dangers.

Figure 3.2 (below) shows how Eco-leadership acts as a meta-discourse balancing the other discourse needs within the organizational eco-system, whilst also paying attention to the external eco-systems.

The dotted lines indicate how the boundaries between an organization and the wider eco-systems are more open, fluid, and blurred than our "normative" constructs of organizations allow for. This "structural coupling" (Maturana & Varela, 1987; see also Satterwhite, 2010) between organizations and the wider environment is often marginalized in organizational and management literature that studies organizations as if they were closed systems. The Harvard Business School's famous case study methodology that gets MBAs to study organizations as if they are decision makers in the organization highlights this point, as it leaves very little room for thinking about the fast-changing environment and opportunities and challenges that exist on the outside of the organization.

Overcoming the Ideology[2] of "Individualism-More"

When a leadership team or individual CEO realizes that their organization requires renewal in line with the Eco-leadership four principles, this is nothing short of engaging with a new ideology. I call this an ideology because it is not just another leadership approach, rather it undoes the existing rationale and deeply-set, unconsciously embedded ideology that underpins how organizations and leadership currently functions. The three discourses of Controller, Therapist, and Messiah all reflect the existing ideology, which is underpinned by the pairing of the two Master Signifiers, *Individualism-More*:

Figure 3.2 Eco-Leadership as Meta-Discourse
Source: Western, 2013, p. 289.

a   *Individualism*: individual agency, atomization, fixed roles, position
    power, personality, charisma, talent.
b   *More*: growth, faster, bigger, improved, new, better.

Master Signifiers unleash a chain of signifiers. When people talk about
leadership success, the discussions are limited and contained within the
ideological parameters *Individual* and *More*. For example, people refer to
individual CEOs such as Steve Jobs and speak of "visionary leadership." We
measure their success by *more*, e.g., economic growth, share price increase,
or productivity and output increases.[3] All three leadership discourses –
Controller, Therapist, Messiah – rely on the idea of an individual leader
with agency to deliver *more*. This individual will take up aspects of all three
discourses depending on their personality, social background and the work
context. *There is no outside to the Individualism-More ideology* – it doesn't
exist. There is no space for other possibilities other than individual leaders
and growth.

The radicalism of Eco-leadership is to disrupt this underlying ideology of *Individualism-More* and replace it with a new ideology underpinned by the Master-Signifier pairing of *Network-Ethics*, connoting *interdependency, connectivity, distributed leadership, meaning, purpose, value, social and environmental responsibility, lateral power, and networked-leadership.* Taking up Eco-leadership is therefore a radical change, rather than an incremental one, that requires an ideological shift. When leaders try to take up Eco-leadership they face the ideological challenges this exposes, often without being aware of it.

The Paradox

On the journey to achieve Eco-leadership, there is often a holding onto, or a return to, the ideology of *Individualism-More*, which creates a paradoxical situation. This happens as people backslide to what is known when they meet resistances, or they simply return to what is familiar as they attempt to change. Returning to the ideology of *Individualism-More* can also be a ploy to engage key stakeholders to support the desired transition to Eco-leadership. For if stakeholders have confidence in a charismatic individual, a visionary Messiah leader, and if they are promised increased profit or more success as an outcome, they are more likely to support the radical changes required. There are two clear forms of this paradox that I encounter frequently when working on these challenging transitions within organizations.

Paradox One: Messiah Leadership a PreRequisite for Eco-Leadership?

The common wisdom is that to transform an organization requires an individual leader with the vision to see beyond what is known and familiar, and to create a culture of loyalty and commitment that will deliver this change; i.e., what is needed is Messiah leadership. I meet many leaders in diverse organizational settings who are interested in Eco-leadership and how organizations can be run differently in the networked age. Yet, while there is a conscious understanding of Eco-leadership, a gap exists between the conscious desire for the ideology of *Network-Ethics*, and the unconscious attachments to *Individual-More*. For example, many leaders reference Laloux's popular book, *Reinventing Organizations* (2014). What struck me when reading this book is how it is completely immersed in the Messiah leadership ideology (*Individualism-More*) while at the same time championing the new Eco-leadership ideology (*Network-Ethics*). The paradox and the tensions this produces are glossed over in this book, which offers a romanticized view of the delights of deconstructing hierarchies and replacing them with new forms of self-managing "Teal" organizations.

Herein lies the paradox: Eco-leadership and Messiah Leadership are at odds with each other, at two ends of a spectrum, underpinned by contrasting ideologies. An Eco-leadership-led organization is more akin to a radical social movement with Autonomist leadership everywhere (Western, 2014) than to a traditional organization whose Messiah CEO strives to "engineer culture" (Kunda, 2006) so that employees are loyal and committed to their personal vision.

Paradox Two: Eco-Leadership Driven by Controller Leader

When an organization moves toward embracing Eco-leadership, a second paradox emerges. The Eco-leaders who are most engaged and driving change are often drawn unconsciously into becoming Controller leaders to deliver their longer-term strategic aims. They passionately believe in the new ideology of *Network-Ethics*, but lose sight of this as they attempt to push through change. Controller leaders utilize scientific rationalism, utilitarianism, and functionalism to deliver on specific targets and goals. The Eco-leader can be drawn into taking up a Controller leadership stance when they face resistance or short-term pressures to deliver results (e.g., from the board of directors, shareholders, etc.).

Controller leadership easily becomes a default position when the Eco-leader is under pressure. The Controller discourse is very familiar and deeply embedded in our psyches. If we feel out of control, we reach out for a leader to take control (Controller), or a leader to save us (Messiah). To give away control and power to others, to distribute authority, to democratize strategy, is counterintuitive to the dominant narratives we grow up with and that dominate organizations. The *Individual* Leader pushes for *More* change by applying Controller leadership approaches and techniques.

Eco-leaders who aspire to new ways of distributing leadership can quickly revert back to old ways of leadership. What you then get is a split occurring whereby a leader says one thing and acts in another way, creating confusion and anger and undermining the trust needed to go through a difficult transition. Eco-leadership and sustainable and ethical futures are then put in jeopardy and undermined.

What Is to Be Done?

1. *Changing mindsets*. First, by changing mindsets and transcending the Westernized idea that paradoxes need to be solved, changes the way we approach these challenges. Drawing on Eastern cultures that embrace paradox as ways-of-being that do not need resolution or solution, we move from problem–solution binaries to working-with-differences complexities. For example, the Chinese have "the ability … to hold different propositions simultaneously without distress" (Cotterell, 2002, p. 30; cited in Klein et al., 2018). This latter way is precisely how Eco-leaders view the challenges they face. They don't go for quick solutions but look at the holistic picture; they realize that a quick solution in one part creates new problems in other parts and new dynamics in the whole. Allowing Eco-leadership and Messiah or

Controller leadership to coexist, as does capitalism and communism in China for example, the task is then how to leverage the best outcome within this paradox, rather than trying to attain the purist goal of eliminating one or the other sides that creates the paradox. This Eco-leadership approach therefore works by beginning with the insight that paradoxes are always part of organizational dynamics, and need to be embraced and worked with, rather than "solved." Eco-leadership is about looking outside of the situation for something new in the wider eco-systems. Learning from Asian leadership cultures how to work with paradox is an Eco-leadership approach.

2. *The Eco-leadership formation process.* The first option helps manage the paradox; this second option offers a way to develop Eco-leadership itself that supports the first position. As set out above, the Eco-leadership response to the paradox of having Messiah and Controller leadership is to think integratively at one level, and to be able to hold contradictory positions simultaneously when integration is not possible. It is utopian to focus always on integrative solutions, as this sometimes is not possible or desirable. Developing Eco-leaders over time means that a critical mass within an organization can emerge that is able to reduce a knee-jerk reaction to take up Messiah or Controller leadership at times of pressure.

Eco-leadership formation gives individuals, teams and organizations a shared understanding of the journey to embrace the ideology of *Network-Ethics*. It begins deep within each individual, works through relationships, through to how Eco-leaders influence wider networks, and how they form strategies to deliver change. If we are to address environmental issues and take up an ethical leadership in organizations in radical new ways, we have to develop networks of change agents to foster this change.

Leadership by and large reflects the production methods, functionality, and culture of the organization, alongside the wider societal culture. Some would argue that the leader creates the organization, but I think that by and large the leader internalizes the culture, function, and practices of the organization, and leads from a position of embodying and articulating these. Thus, the industrial factory with its production lines controlled workers without autonomy, set within a "society of prohibition" (McGowan, 2003), produced the Controller leadership discourse. Global corporations, virtual teams, flattened hierarchies set in hyper-consumerist societies and neo-liberal free-market capitalism that increased the wealth of powerful elites, produced Messiah leadership discourse. And now mobile technologies, cloud organizing, technological disruption, and adaptation set in the growing network society, alongside global concerns for social breakdown, digital unemployment and environmental crisis, produce its mirror image, Eco-leadership.

3. *No personal development without organizational development.* There are two key foci in the development of Eco-leadership. The first is to develop individual Eco-leaders who can see that leadership extends beyond the individual. In spite of some critical theorists denying the agency of the individual actor, I am firmly of the belief that the individual leader and

follower are essential to understanding leadership. Working with individuals to enhance their personal capacity to take up Eco-leadership is a key part of any strategy to overcome the potential negative impacts of the paradox, and to influence change in their networks. The second focus is to take an organizational development approach and create formal and informal spaces for Eco-leadership and active followership to flourish everywhere. The task is to work in parallel with both individual leaders and organizational development.

Eco-leadership formation takes place in formal and informal settings. Informal approaches cannot be taught from top-down positions of hierarchy, but senior leaders can support, encourage, and influence informal leadership development, such as *learning from peers*, *learning from practice*, *informal mentoring coaching*, and *informal communities of practice forming*. As for a more formal approach, I will now set out a formal leadership development process that takes an individual through a coaching system that holistically connects different parts of what it takes for an individual to embrace Eco-leadership, termed Analytic-Network Coaching (see Figure 3.3 below).

The Analytic-Coaching System^{TM} provides a framework for developing Eco-leadership. It is a simple yet profound approach that I have used internationally, and we train coaches how to work with leaders using this approach. We now have a network of international coaches who are working with this system. It has five frames (Box 3.2 below), and we take each leader through them, so that as they learn about Eco-leadership through this process, they also internalize the system and use it as a framework to deliver Eco-leadership to others, without reverting back to the ideology of *Individualism-More*.

Box 3.2 The Analytic-Network Five Frame Leadership approach

Frame 1. Depth Analysis (DA) Inner-self
Values, Meaning, Ethics, Authenticity, and Purpose
Frame 2. Relational Analysis (RA) Outer-self
Teamwork, Group Dynamics, Communication
Frame 3. Leadership Analysis (LA) Leader-within
Unique leadership style, Active Followership, Power, and Influence
Frame 4. Network Analysis (NA) Networked self
Internal and External Network Influences, Technology, and People
Frame 5. Strategic Analysis (SA) Strategic mindset
Review four frames above to develop Emergent Strategies for their personal development and leadership focus and for the wider team and workplace they can influence.

(Adapted from Western, 2013, pp. 277–278)

The Analytic-Network Coaching System takes individuals through a process and on a journey from deep within to engaging with the widest

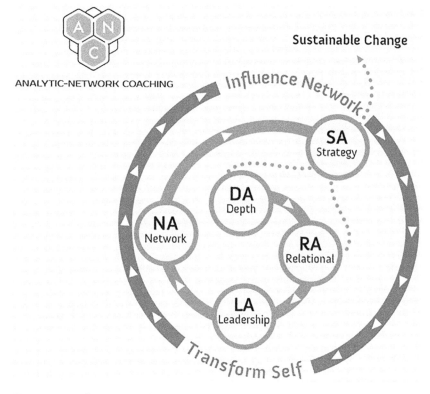

Figure 3.3 Analytic-Network Coaching System
Source: Western, 2013, p. 277.

networks that need to be addressed if Eco-leadership is to be embraced. Drawing on psychoanalytic approaches, we pay attention to the unconscious, the patterns that inhibit us, and the dormant creativity that lies within us. Psychoanalysis provides a method to work between the coach and coachee, where the latter can learn to interpret their own processes and patterns in relation to the coach. This approach recognizes that the unconscious is not only a dynamic deep within our own minds, it is also a dynamic between pairs, groups, organizations, and societies. Analytic-Network Coaching is thus a psycho-social approach to coaching, not simply focused on the internal life of the individual. It gets beyond the coach "fixing" the coachee with expert tools by offering the coachee a way of interpreting themselves, others, and the social, in order to become dynamic change agents. (For more, see Western, 2012).

Conclusion

Eco-Leadership embraces a new ideology departing from the 20th century ideology of *Individualism-More* that entraps leadership thinking in an individual's personal attributes, enacted through the three dominant leader-ship discourses Controller, Therapist, and Messiah leadership. Eco-leadership embraces the Master-Signifiers *Network-Ethics* that change the way organi-zations and leadership are conceptualized. No longer is leadership just the property of the individual and no longer is the outcome only about "more." Individual leaders are one part of an array of actors that comprise a dis-tributed leadership approach within the networks of activity made up of human and non-humans, i.e., technology, society, and nature together.

This eco-system requires a completely new approach to leadership, chal-lenging the top-down hegemony and moving from vertical to lateral axes of power. Conceptualizing organizations as *"eco-systems within eco-systems"* opens up the potential for organizations to be part of the networks of life, and not imagined as closed systems that are separate. These false walls we have built have done untold damage to the environment and social well-being and this is where the new ideology of *Network-Ethics* comes into play. Twentieth-century organizational leadership must embrace a holistic, networked, and ethical approach if we are to retreat from environmental catastrophes and social imbalances that will cause untold suffering and wars.

The challenges to delivering this approach are discussed in the Paradox section above. There is no utopian way forward whereby leadership and organizations suddenly become egalitarian networks filled with distributed leadership. Distributed leadership demands distributed power, authority, resources, and ethics; this is truly challenging and is the cause of paradoxes whereby leaders can call for Eco-leadership and truly believe in it, while enacting Messiah and Controller leadership at both conscious and uncon-scious levels. The answer is not a puritanical drive to dismiss these other forms of leadership, but to find ways of embracing their usefulness under an umbrella of the meta-leadership approach of Eco-leadership. This approach also calls on leaders to embrace other cultural approaches whereby para-doxes are not problems to be solved, but part of the solution because they will always exist and have to be worked with.

This chapter goes beyond the call for new leadership ethics and offers a theoretical approach and the beginning of a methodology to develop new forms of Eco-leadership fit for purpose in the networked society. Furthermore, this approach is getting traction in practice. It has been used in hospices, hos-pitals, and family construction businesses and is currently being used as a concept in a leading global technology company. There is a thirst and a reali-zation by leaders, both from a pragmatic and an ethical perspective, that Eco-leadership is needed, as the old ways are not delivering success anymore.

Notes

1 "A discourse is a linguistic and cultural set of normative assumptions, an institu-tional way of thinking ... A discourse defines what we take for granted and how

we think about something. ... Critical theory attempts to identify normative discourses, so that once revealed they can be critiqued" (Western, 2010, p. 37).

2 Critical theorists/Marxists use the term ideology to describe "false consciousness." By this they mean false ideas that are purposefully spread by political institutions and power elites to dupe the masses, in order to reproduce social, cultural, and material power imbalances that keep these elites in power. However, this no longer works because our diminished trust in authority and institutions means that we don't believe any ideology that is overtly used. Some claim this takes us into a post-ideological era. Žižek (2009) and others claim that a new form of ideology is with us that operates in subtler ways. Ideology today presents itself in non-political yet pervasive everyday ways. Master Signifiers are produced that entrap us in certain ways-of-being, and even though we have a conscious awareness of this ideology, it still entraps us. For example, the onslaught of advertising we constantly experience unleashes the Master Signifiers of "consume" and "be happy" on us. These signifiers repetitively push the social injunctions to buy products and services that will make us happier. While we are aware of being manipulated to consume more, we cannot easily escape our fate to buy, or to feel the "happiness imperative" weigh heavily upon us. This is an example of a non-political ideology, where we experience ourselves as being autonomous individuals, free from ideology and social coercion, and following our own desire to consume. Žižek claims that this new form of ideology is even more powerful as it does not come from an external "big Other" (such as the Communist Party, or establishment elite) but from a "small other" within ourselves. Ideology functions today through our unconscious attachments and investments in our chosen Master Signifiers, which entrap and reproduce the power matrices of late capitalism.

3 This is a particularly westernized view that I explore in a forthcoming book, tentatively titled *Global Leadership Perspectives, Insights and Analysis* (Klein et al., 2018), where new forms of leadership are being unearthed.

References

Cotterell, A. (2002). *East Asia: From Chinese predominance to the rise of the Pacific Rim*. London: Pimlico.

Klein, J., Nai-keung, L., Jian, L., & Chao, C. (2018). Leadership in the Chinese Cultural Space. In S. Western & E.-J. Garcia (Eds), *Global Leadership Perspectives, Insights and Analysis*. London & Thousand Oaks, CA: SAGE Publications, Inc.

Kunda, G. (2006). *Engineering Culture: Control and commitment in a high-tech corporation* (revised ed.). Philadelphia, PA: Temple University Press.

Laloux, F. (2014). *Reinventing Organizations: A guide to creating organizations inspired by the next stage of human consciousness*. Brussels: Nelson Parker.

Latour, B. (2005). *Reassembling the Social: An introduction to actor-network-theory*. Oxford: Oxford University Press.

Maturana, R., & Varela, F. (1987). *The Tree of Knowledge: The biological roots of human understanding*. Boston, MA: Shambhala Publications, Inc.

McGowan, T. (2003). *The End of Dissatisfaction: Jacques Lacan and the emerging society of enjoyment*. Albany, NY: SUNY Press.

Satterwhite, R. (2010). Deep Systems Leadership: A model for the 21st century. In B. W. Redekop (Ed.), *Leadership for Environmental Sustainability* (pp. 230–243). New York & London: Routledge.

Sullivan, L. (1896). The Tall Office Building Artistically Considered. *Lippincott's Monthly Magazine* (March).

Western, S. (2005). *A Critical Analysis of Leadership: Overcoming fundamentalist tendencies*. Doctoral Dissertation, Lancaster University Management School.

Western, S. (2008/2013). *Leadership: A critical text* (1st & 2nd ed.). Los Angeles, CA & London: SAGE Publications, Inc.

Western, S. (2010). Eco-leadership: Toward the development of a new paradigm. In B. W. Redekop (Ed.), *Leadership for Environmental Sustainability* (pp. 36–54). New York & London: Routledge.

Western, S. (2012). *Coaching and Mentoring: A critical text*. London & Thousand Oaks, CA: SAGE Publications, Inc.

Western, S. (2013). *Leadership: A critical text*. Thousand Oaks, CA: SAGE Publications, Inc.

Western, S. (2014). Autonomist Leadership in Leaderless Movements: Anarchists leading the way. *Ephemera: Theory & Politics in Organization*, 14(4), 673–698.

Žižek, S. (2009). *The Sublime Object of Ideology* (2nd ed.). Brooklyn, NY: Verso Books.

4 Sustainable Leadership

Toward Restoring the Human and Natural Worlds

Tina Lynn Evans

Introduction

This chapter develops a theory of sustainable leadership that hinges upon the purposes toward which leadership is applied. Through synthesizing insights from the literatures of a wide range of fields, it argues that sustainable leadership must foster the long-term health, integrity, and resiliency of human communities and nature. Sustainable leadership, comprised of fitting responses to converging socio-ecological crises, is counter-hegemonic, inclusive, place-centered, and learned. Sustainable leadership serves integrative and normative roles in creating/restoring the health of the human/natural world. It is, therefore, highly relevant to the health and survival of both nature and society.[1]

The Crisis of Leadership in the Modern World

Modern Western consciousness abstracts humans from nature, denying that humans can exist only within nature (Spretnak, 1997). This conceptual human/nature divide is not only a division into two, it is a tiered dualism: humans on top, nature acting in all supporting roles (as tool, as resource, as setting) (Shepard, 1995). The subjugated "other," first conceptualized as nature itself, is born with this divide. And there have been many "others" as systems of hierarchy have proliferated to encompass gender, races, non-Western cultures, and more. Cultural systems of hierarchy in Western societies and the projection of a hierarchical worldview upon nature itself surely are among the keystone concepts upholding the house of cards that is the unsustainable, globalized, industrial world (Evans, 2012, p. 55).

   Given the formative role of hierarchy in shaping unsustainable and destructive modern patterns of "development," the concept of leadership itself is often confounded with hierarchy. Given this history, the idea of leadership for sustainability raises suspicion: can modern societies employ leadership in service to sustainability? Or are Western concepts and practices of leadership themselves so infused with notions of hierarchy that they remain irreconcilable with (re)creating[2] sustainable societies? These are crucial questions for sustainability educators and practitioners today, since central to the effort of (re)constructing sustainable societies is the need to dismantle many of the organizing concepts and values of the modern world, concepts and values that feed and are fed by the widespread domination and exploitation of people and of nature by the powerful few – the "leaders" of the globalized capitalist world.

Can we develop leadership today that is not inherently corrupt and manipulative? Can we organize people effectively within systems of leadership and participation in order to (re)cast societies into forms that nurture and justly serve people and nature simultaneously? What might such systems of leadership and participation look like? And on what values and practices would they be based? These are the questions underlying this exploration in search of a leadership for sustainability. At the heart of this exploration is the idea that sustainability cannot be achieved in the absence of social justice because social injustice derives from the same mindset – the same narrowly instrumental orientation to the world and others – that fuels environmental destruction. To pursue sustainability through manipulative and exploitive means would mean creating new systems of domination that would feed the creation of new, unsustainable systems. Can we (re)create leadership that is itself sustainable?

This essay explores this question through developing several claims:

1 Sustainable leadership is centrally defined by the purposes it serves.
2 Sustainable leadership embodies a fitting response to the socio-ecological challenges implicated in the decisions and actions taken.
3 Sustainable leadership is integrative and ultimately place-centered.
4 Everyone must have access to serve as a leader.
5 Leadership must be actively developed in everyone in a sustainable society.
6 Sustainable leadership engages imperfectly in processes of long-term cultural change.

Through developing these claims, this chapter highlights the purposes sustainable leadership must serve and, thereby, constructs a concept of sustainable leadership. This concept is further clarified by illuminating formative characteristics of leadership for sustainability that distinguish it from command and control leadership.[3]

In short, this essay conceptualizes sustainable leadership as a form of community praxis in which one coalesces and directs the energies of a group toward ends that enhance the long-term health, integrity, and resilience of the community and natural systems of which it is a part. Sustainable leadership is also a form of *power with, not power over,* others. Through its praxis, sustainable leadership nurtures the leadership potential of collaborators in the recognition that the leadership of any one individual or group is, and should be, a temporary service to others. Sustainable leadership welcomes new leaders and creates space for their leadership potential to grow. In a world-system replete with entrenched systems of hierarchy and characterized by competition, sustainable leadership is a contradiction. To realize sustainable leadership would entail deep social change that can only happen through a long-term process of cultural change.

Through developing a concept of leadership for sustainability, this essay can inform the character, purposes, and practices of activists, educators, and others whose work continually redefines and teaches leadership in our changing world.

Sustainable Leadership Is Centrally Defined by the Purposes It Serves

Leadership discourse and training that focus on techniques alone portray leadership as a tool that can be used to further *any* human endeavor – whether or not the given activity is just or sustainable. This essay demonstrates that leadership within systems of modern capitalist hierarchy is unequally rewarding to some while oppressive and exploitative to others and nature. Leadership in this context is not leadership at all, but opportunism that creates extreme imbalances among societies and between humans and nature.

In order to understand command and control leadership as the dominant mode of social organization today, it is important to understand the context within which that form of leadership has emerged and thrived.[4] The purposes leadership has served in the world-system have defined its character. Reinventing leadership would mean repurposing it and, consequently, changing societies in deep and important ways.

A Brief History of Opportunistic Leadership in Globalized Political Economy

Systems of inequity in globalized political economy derive from an enforced program through which the winners of old remain the winners indefinitely and continue to manufacture the rules of the game in order to ensure their economic and political advantage (Achbar & Simpson, 2005; Barlow & Clarke, 2002; Black, 2001; Evans, 2012, Chs 3–4; International Consortium of Investigative Journalists, 2003; Manley, 1987; Marcuse, 1964; Norberg-Hodge et al., 2002; Scheer, 2002). The world-system is not sustainable, but predatory and opportunistic.

Examples of opportunistic leadership abound in modern capitalist societies. Centuries of European colonization laid the foundations for modern capitalist opportunism to spread globally, creating persistent economic and political inequities between former imperialist colonizer nations and former colonies whose lands and peoples were the objects of conquest. Inequity was built into the colonial system by the leaders of empire: the colonial system created an intentional hierarchy in which colonies served their rulers in multiple ways. Colonies were never intended by their conquerors to be allowed to develop diverse, healthy economies in which wealth was distributed widely. Such a formula would, after all, create colonies that could eventually challenge their rulers. Instead, colonies served as the extraction grounds for empire, producing or otherwise delivering up raw materials for empires while employing conquered peoples in the processes of extraction through systems of slavery and low-wage labor (Miller, 1999).

This colonial system was perhaps the most significant factor in creating the uneven "development" of the modern capitalist world today that Wallerstein (1974, 1976, 2003, 2005, 2006, 2007, 2008) explicates in his world-system theory of core, semi-periphery, and periphery nations and regions within globalized political economy. Once the former colonies were free to compete on their own in a rapidly globalizing marketplace, they found themselves hopelessly behind their former rulers who had become the modern industrialized nations of the world. Because they served for so long as resource extraction grounds and sources of cheap labor for empire, former colonies had not developed strong modern infrastructures, accessible and modern education systems, diversified manufacturing sectors capable of producing a wide variety of finished goods, or resilient traditions of democracy. The value of at least some aspects of these developments within a context of sustainability is questionable, but their importance to effective participation in a globalized, industrial economy is clear (Evans, 2012, Chs 3–4; Miller, 1999; Wallerstein, 1974, 1976, 2003, 2005, 2006, 2007, 2008).

Although colonialism as a command and control system of direct territorial rule by dominant national powers is waning, the unequal power relationships between the industrialized and the developing worlds persist through imperialism. Imperialism manifests itself as a form of economic, cultural, and political domination similar in its effects to colonialism but without direct administration of foreign territories by nation states (Evans, 2012, Chs 3–4; Miller, 1999). Under this more recent hegemonic order, the industrialized powers of the world, acting through a system of international free trade agreements, continue to extract raw materials from afar and take advantage of cheap labor (Evans, 2012, Ch. 4). Free trade within such a system benefits the wealthy at the expense of the poor because it drives down the prices of commodities to match the lowest prices globally. For those individuals, companies, and nations who sell raw materials and agricultural products and who tend to operate on a very thin margin of profit, opening local markets to global competition can be devastating. While many products can be produced in many places, there are some environments that are better than others for doing so, and it is generally in these locations that production can be accomplished most cheaply. When other producers in less advantageous locales must compete with advantaged producers, they often cannot make ends meet. In this circumstance, diversity (and, therefore, resilience) is lost in the local economy. Small producers lose their economic security while the big players in the global economy – who can produce virtually anywhere they like at low cost by locating where environmental, labor, and other costs are low – use their advantage to dominate global markets (Douthwaite, 2004; Norberg-Hodge et al., 2002).

International finance and debt serve as additional tools for opportunistic leaders to create dependency (Evans, 2012, Ch. 4; Miller, 1999, pp. 85–86; Stiglitz, 2002). Developing nations, in their attempts to create the infrastructure that would allow them to compete in the global economy, have assumed extremely heavy debt loads, borrowing from sources such as the World Bank and regional development banks. And, due to their historically generated, lopsided development, they have not been able to compete effectively with the industrialized world. For these nations, the playing field is impossibly tilted in favor of industrialized powers. Meanwhile, the United States, the world's foremost debtor nation, continues as the world economic leader due to its historical position of dominance and the economic and political systems that were constructed to reinforce that dominance (Evans, 2012, pp. 132–135).[5]

In the interest of justice and sustainability, it matters a great deal where we are being led and for what purposes. The global economic system described here functions as if there are no limits (physical or ethical) to exploiting both people and nature to fuel the engines of economic growth and secure profits for economic leaders. Wealth has also become concentrated in fewer and fewer hands (Piketty, 2014). Leadership for "success" in such a system is not sustainable leadership; it is simply domination.

An exploration of the history of global inequity, capitalist concentration of market control, and profits reaped by imperial interests reveals that the purposes served by leadership 1) inform all meaningful discussion of the character of leadership and 2) create a foundation for developing a concept of sustainable leadership. Our discussion here breaks sharply with leadership literature and training that seeks to be apolitical. Seemingly apolitical leadership training and literature is, in fact, *very* political precisely because it does not overtly question the purposes of leadership and, thereby, tends to reinforce the notion that beneficial models of leadership can be practiced in any context. Such a conception of leadership tends not to question hierarchy in that the boss and the leader are conflated, as though it does not matter whether one follows a leader by choice or must submit to follow a "leader" solely in order to keep earning a living. In the context of such overt hierarchies, any technique or practice of leadership, however profound or worthy, can be used for manipulation and control of the followers as well as for ecologically destructive ends. Effective leadership techniques practiced in ultimate service to destructive systems may even mask social contradictions and harsh divisions and thereby delay radical action for social justice.

To reveal the ideological basis of much leadership training and literature, though, is not to say that work in areas such as industrial democracy has no merit. Because most people now live and survive through an unjust and unsustainable capitalist system, we are walking contradictions, supporting ourselves and our families in the short term while participating in the long-term undoing of the natural world as well as the continued breakdown of social justice and coherent, collaborative communities. But we cannot simply extract ourselves from historical realities, and our choices in how we live are in fact limited. This is the struggle of leadership: how can one, several, or many lead toward a just and sustainable future in these times of converging socio-ecological crises created and upheld by pervasive exploitive leadership?

Sustainable Leadership as a Continuum

Three important constituents of the purpose of leadership can help us define a continuum of leadership character: degree of centralization of authority, level of abstraction, and scale of operation. The continuum of leadership ranges from exploitive to sustainable leadership. Within this continuum, those forms of leadership that are less abstract tend to be more sustainable (Evans, 2012, Ch. 5; Kemmis, 1990), while the distancing afforded to practitioners of highly abstract forms of leadership tends to encourage exploitation in the form of collective violence. Collective violence can be defined as large-scale damage inflicted on people and the environment by large numbers of people (Summers & Markusen, 2003, p. 215). People are less likely to inflict harm in service to personal gain on those people and places with whom/which they share meaningful and intimate relationships – especially when they intend to stay put in place and community (Abrams, 2008; Shuman, 1998/2000). Similarly, scale of activity also matters: the larger the scale of operations, the greater the opportunities for abstraction. Scale, in turn, relates to an additional important factor in characterizing the purposes and practices of leadership along a continuum ranging from exploitive to sustainable: degree of centralization of control. Potential for hierarchical domination and exploitation increases with centralization of control, and this same centralization of decision making and concentration of profits are perhaps the most useful tools to those who would use leadership to exploit.

The leadership continuum, as a whole, holds at one extreme the leadership of exploitation that uses everything and everyone necessary to perpetuate the leader's privileged status. This form of leadership is essentially manipulative and instrumental. At the other end of the continuum is sustainable leadership. Pittman (2007) defines "living sustainability" as "the long-term equilibrium of health and integrity maintained dynamically within any individual system (organism, organization, ecosystem, community, etc.) through a diversity of relationships with other systems" (n.p.). This concept of sustainability is flexible in that what is sustainable in any instance is deeply influenced by the socio-ecological context within which action or change takes place (Evans, 2012, p. 17). What may be sustainable in one context may not be in another.

In sustainable leadership, choices and actions foster the *long-term health and integrity* of the system. Because the integrity of oppressive or socioecologically damaging or deleterious systems is not a goal of sustainability,

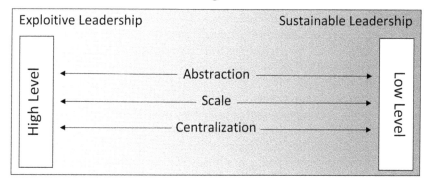

Figure 4.1 The Leadership Continuum. Abstraction, scale, and centralization tend to be inversely related to level of sustainability in leadership.
Source: Evans, 2011.

health must be the primary defining quality of sustainable leadership, with integrity as an essential supporting factor. In pursuing health and integrity, leaders must also focus on resiliency with regard to the socio-ecological system in question. Resiliency is the ability of a system to bounce back from damage or disturbance while maintaining is essential functions. I offer the rationale for these claims in the following section.

The distinction I draw between exploitive leadership and sustainable leadership is one that hinges on the *purposes* to which leadership is applied. If we are to lead toward sustainability, we must ultimately concern ourselves with the effects of our leadership on the health and integrity of other people and nature. When acting within a model of exploitive leadership, one's central aim is to remain in a position of (perceived) advantage over other people and nature.

Sustainable Leadership Embodies a Fitting Response to the Socio-Ecological Challenges Implicated in the Decisions and Actions Taken

A response is fitting because it supports the health, integrity, and resiliency of human communities and natural world. In exploring sustainable leadership as a *fitting* response to one's socio-ecological context, it is helpful to begin with an exploration of nature and societies as complex adaptive systems.

Nature as Context

In nature, ecosystems utilize the potential of their given contexts (incoming sunlight, water, nutrients, and more) as they move from simple states characterized by little differentiation among organisms and functions to complex states characterized by many types of organisms carving out specific niches and sharing tightly knit interdependencies. The Earth as a natural system is comprised of nested subsystems of varying scales, both living and nonliving (for example, individual organisms and animal communities as well as rivers, oceans, and the entire hydrological cycle). Natural systems move through cycles of rising complexity followed by varying levels of disturbance/disintegration. The disturbance/disintegration phase unleashes potential for new configurations of complexity to arise. In natural systems, resiliency is also inversely related to complexity. Very simple systems bounce back from disturbance more easily than do complex systems with tightly coupled interrelationships of organisms inhabiting specific niches (Homer-Dixon, 2006, Ch. 9).

The rising and falling complexity of the nested systems that comprise the Earth's planetary system has typically not been synchronized, meaning that, as some systems have all or partially unraveled, others at different scales have provided relative stability. Human actions have, however, synchronized the disintegration phase of multiple systems such as ocean fisheries, topsoil, and coastal aquatic systems – perhaps the largest scale and most important of these being the Earth's climate itself (Homer-Dixon, 2006, Ch. 9).

A Dangerous Synchronicity

We live in a time of converging sustainability crises that include climate change, resource depletion, pervasive pollution, a rapid rate of species extinction, global concentration of wealth and power, massive poverty, and more. The synchronicity of the disintegration phase of so many natural systems that has been brought about by human actions threatens the survival of our species and that of many others. Its creation has coincided with the rise of the Western cultural notion that humans are not embedded in and dependent upon nature, but instead are conquerors and users of nature. This broad cultural construct has swept the globe through colonialism, imperialism, and economic/cultural globalization. Within this cultural and economic context, forms of leadership have emerged that are highly abstract, large scale, and centralized.

This dangerous synchronicity of converging sustainability crises is also driven in many ways by leaders and their influence. The elements of human choice and will as well as social power that form the center of gravity for the convergence of the sustainability crises we face differentiates this convergence markedly from the movement of complex adaptive systems in nonhuman nature. The crisis itself is, therefore, a subject for leadership work – and perhaps the most important subject of all. The sustainability crisis is the crucible for defining leadership within a normative framework: forms of leadership that contribute to the health, integrity, and resiliency of human and natural systems and, by extension, to the potential for human survival and thriving, are the only forms of leadership that can be called sustainable.

Counter-hegemony as Fitting Response

Fitting responses to the converging crises of sustainability must be based in political clarity and counter-hegemony. Developing politically clear insights involves reading the world in deeply critical ways. As the central vehicle for understanding and addressing oppression, Freire (1970/2000) argued the critical importance of political clarity. In his *Pedagogy of the Oppressed* (1970/2000), he advocated educational praxis aimed at helping people develop deep understandings of social power and how that power informs the ideas and actions of people across social strata. I have argued similarly elsewhere (Evans, 2012) the importance of counter-hegemony in the field of sustainability education.

Engaging in counter-hegemony means critiquing and attempting to dismantle hegemonic economic and political powers. The actions of these powers tend to fall at the exploitive end of the leadership continuum, at best ignoring and at worst destroying the long-term health, integrity, and resiliency of socio-ecological systems. Counter-hegemonically informed leadership seeks to dismantle historically created inequities and exploitation while fostering the health, integrity, and resiliency of communities and nature. Doing so involves cultivating people's critical thinking (Brookfield, 1987, 2000) and related transformative capacities (Mezirow, 2000). Counter-hegemony is a fitting response to globalized political economy and, therefore, an essential aspect of sustainable leadership (Evans, 2012).

Sustainable leadership serves as a vehicle for the expression of counter-hegemonic social values. Sustainable leadership can adapt appropriately to serve sustainable ends for the long term if it remains flexible and inclusive of diverse insights about hegemony and counter-hegemony within the changing contexts of socio-ecological systems. Sustainable leadership maintains an outward focus on the world. It exists as a dynamic, yet normative, interaction with the world rather than as a rigidly fixed set of beliefs. Sustainable leadership is open, flexible, and responsive to the influx of new ideas (and the bearers of these ideas). It represents the potential for realizing a normative leadership that explicitly rejects totalitarian embodiments.

Reciprocity and Mutualism as Fitting Responses

Examples of sustainable indigenous inhabitation of place (Armstrong, 1995; Berkes, 1999; LaDuke, 1999; Martinez, 1997; Nelson, 1983; Salmon, 2000; Sveiby & Skuthorpe, 2006) indicate that for humans to live sustainably, their actions must be guided by an ethic of reciprocity in relationships with other people and nature. An ethic of reciprocity in action translates to healthy interdependence and care for nature and society. This care promotes the human potential for thriving. Sustainable leaders strive to create reciprocal, mutually nurturing, sustaining relationships among people and between humans and nature.

Despite the myth, broadly accepted as common sense in Western culture, that competition brings out the best in people and society, the human tendency for collaboration is more personally fulfilling and appropriate to a wider range of social situations than is the drive for competition (Kohn, 1986). Indeed, the failure of leaders to maintain a focus on helping others and a turn toward egoism and self-aggrandizement typically causes leaders to fall (Keltner, 2016). Social capital in the forms of nurturing reciprocity and collaboration that create strong relational bonds can also contribute significantly to community resiliency to disturbance and breakdown (Adger, 2003; Petzold & Ratter, 2015, p. 40). Nature, despite years of grade school science education focusing on survival of the fittest as the principle vehicle for biological evolution, is now becoming recognized as a network (Borrett et al., 2014) comprised of interacting components that mutually generate a holism that is much more than the sum of its parts (Patten, 2016). Nature, it seems, is more collaborative than competitive in its formative capacities. The recognition of human societies as part of and dependent upon nature is also rapidly emerging within the field of sustainability science (Folke et al., 2016). This recognition points to the need for human collaborative co-evolution with nature rather than domination over and destruction of it.

These insights make a great deal of sense when one considers human indigenous heritage. Although competing tribes and cultures have fought each other for millennia, the day-to-day workings of indigenous societies have been based in collaboration and care manifested in both direct and diffuse forms of social reciprocity and in reciprocal duties associated with nature care. The cutthroat culture of globalized industrial capitalism is a very recent departure within that human tradition (Hall & Klitgaard, 2012, Ch. 2). Being slow and not so physically fierce creatures whose young are highly vulnerable and do not fully mature for many years, humans would not have survived as a species without mutuality. Many indigenous societies have developed various forms of gift cultures wherein sharing the necessities of life within the tribe or community has played a defining role in the survival of the group (Jensen, 2000, p. 212; Polanyi, 1944/1957, p. 46). Indigenous societies have also developed ethical frameworks of reciprocity with nature rather than domination over it. Both reciprocity with nature and the sharing of food and other necessities with others promote the health, integrity, and resiliency of socio-ecological systems – the very purposes served by sustainable leadership. These actions also create deep and lasting relationships among people and between people and nature. Jeannette Armstrong (1995), a member of the Okanagan tribe, notes that, in her culture, it is the ability to form such relationships (the strength of the heart self) that defines the ability to lead: "the strength with which we bond in the widest of circles gives us our criterion for leadership" (p. 321).

Leadership as a fitting response to the converging crises of sustainability is characterized by counter-hegemonic social engagement and the forging of collaborative and mutually beneficial relationships among people and with nature. Sustainable leaders seek mutually beneficial and liberating ends in communities that include both people and nature as members.

Sustainable Leadership Is Integrative and Ultimately Place-Centered

To lead sustainably, we must act from an ecological worldview, in full recognition that everything is connected to every other thing and that what goes around does indeed come around. If we want to live meaningful lives and enjoy the respect of others, we must recognize the meaning inherent in other people and in nature, and we must honor the integrity and the life-ways of others, both human and nonhuman. I believe this living reciprocity is what Armstrong (1995) refers to when she describes the Okanagan experience of bonding with ancestral homelands:

> As Okanagans, our most essential responsibility is to learn to bond our whole individual selves and our communal selves to the land. Many of our ceremonies have been constructed for this. We join with the larger self, outward to the land, and rejoice in all that we are. We are this one part of Earth. Without this self we are not human: we yearn; we are incomplete; we are wild, needing to learn our place as land pieces. We cannot find joy because we need place in this sense to nurture and protect our family/community/self. The thing Okanagans fear worst of all is to be removed from the land that is their life and their spirit.
>
> (pp. 323–324)

As suggested by Armstrong, social bonds and bonds between people and nature are most effectively understood and enacted within the context of real places that offer a shared context of community and nature extending over long periods of time. In such communities, actions and ideas – and their benefits and consequences – are most immediately known and visible (Armstrong, 1995; Shuman, 1998/2000, p. 8).

Centering sustainable leadership in place does not, however, mean that we should wall ourselves off from the world or disregard distant or global environmental and social problems. To extract ourselves in such a way from the world as a whole would be unspeakably irresponsible given our current context. Global capitalism has created an unhealthy inter-dependence – a *codependence* – from which it will be difficult to extract ourselves and our communities unscathed. In order to name this world and transform it, even by (re)localizing, we must know *this* world. We must know what we are up against and, to the best of our ability, think through the ramifications of our local actions in a world where everything has indeed been made to affect every other thing within perhaps the most unhealthy system of interdependence possible. Sustainable leadership must address globalization while simultaneously creating place-centered communities. Terry (1993) recognizes this need for a comprehensive approach to leadership. He notes that we must seek to be inclusive of a broad and deep understanding of and intimacy with the world: "Comprehensiveness is the most inclusive quality of meaning. It seeks to add depth of insight, celebrate wisdom, and in its creation of meaning, affirm the joy and tragedy of existence" (p. 227). To move this world toward sustainability, we must engage with it, not recoil from it. This engagement should, in large measure, take the form of place-centered praxis that consciously and simultaneously contributes to socio-ecological sustainability on a global scale (Evans, 2012, Chs 3–5).

Everyone Must Have Access to Serve as a Leader

Totalitarian leadership systems limit access to positions and roles of leadership throughout society. Totalitarian systems attempt to centralize and control ideas generated within a society about the state of the world, both as it is and as it should be. Totalitarian systems are inherently unjust and unsustainable in that they ignore or forego responses that are fitting to the health, integrity, and resiliency of people and nature and, in service to a few, seek to dictate a given reality into existence. The modern capitalist economy as described above is totalitarian. Totalitarian systems both refuse to actively promote the potential for leadership throughout society and also refuse to respond fittingly and justly. In taking these actions, totalitarian systems may sow the seeds of their own destruction: forms of oppression that negate the value of people invariably generate social resistance, and often violent action.

In contrast to totalitarian leadership, sustainable leadership must offer paths to differential authority that are open to everyone in a given society (Barbour, 1993, p. 37). This notion opposes totalitarian tendencies to attach political offices and powers to hereditary lines and to social ranks and categories from which many are totally and indefinitely excluded. Totalitarian leadership embodies and solidifies hierarchies consisting of paths to power that are unassailable and hopelessly remote to the vast majority of people. Kingdoms and dictatorships come to mind, but even nominal democracies and "free" markets can be totalitarian in these respects.

In order to maintain open paths to leadership and to encourage broad political participation and the development of leadership potential throughout society, differential authority should change hands periodically. Although monarchies and dictatorships that are more benevolent than some democracies today may exist and certainly have existed, perpetual concentration of power can be dangerous, particularly within the context of modern capitalism where power most naturally manifests in manipulation and exploitation (Marcuse, 1964). In order for any society to be benevolent in comparison to modern capitalist societies, the people need to exercise meaningful control over key aspects of their own lives. In any comparatively just society, sustainable leadership must be active throughout society on multiple levels.

Such was the case within the kingdom of Ladakh before it was subsumed under Indian government rule, and it remains the case to some extent today although Ladakh has become increasingly entangled with the globalized capitalist world (International Society for Ecology and Culture, 1993; Norberg-Hodge, 1991/1992). In traditional Ladakhi society, leadership that meaningfully shaped the lives of people was developmental, small scale, and local. It also was decidedly *not* abstract in that the Ladakhi people, in order to prosper in their isolated and demanding environment, exercised an ecological leadership of place that emphasized reciprocal practices of working directly with nature and each other.

Many indigenous traditions of recognizing the leadership of elders offer examples of leadership that are open to all who attain the proper level of experience as evidenced by age. Sustainable leadership of elders would also remain open and responsive to the voices and concerns of youth.

Leadership Must Be Actively Developed in Everyone in a Sustainable Society

In keeping with the idea that sustainable leadership offers fitting responses to environmental and social crises, and building upon the notion that paths to leadership must be open to all, it follows that leadership should be actively developed in everyone in ultimate service to sustainability. Greenleaf's concept of servant leadership offers a clearly defined ethical and relational foundation for leadership that aids in formulating responses to the world that are both fitting to socio-ecological context and inclusive. According to Greenleaf (1970/1991), a servant leader works to build the leadership capacities of others rather than simply to maintain his/her own position of power. The servant as leader sows the seeds of long term change because s/he shares ownership of the changes s/he leads with others who participate in the change. Greenleaf (1970/1991) contrasts the servant leader with the dominator leader who is "leader first, perhaps because of the need to assuage an unusual power drive or to acquire material possessions" (p. 7):

> The difference manifests itself in the care taken by the servant-first to make sure that other people's highest priority needs are being served. The best test, and difficult to administer, is: do those served grow as persons; do they, while being served, become healthier, wiser, freer, more autonomous, more likely themselves to become servants? And, what is the effect on the least privileged in society; will he benefit, or, at least, will he not be further deprived?
>
> (Greenleaf, 1970/1991, p. 7)

Greenleaf's emphasis on the public sharing of the fruits of leadership also coincides well with the notion that sustainable social systems do not concentrate power in the hands of the few while causing the vast majority to live in misery.

Terry (1993) offers additional theories on leadership that extend and further clarify Greenleaf's (1970/1991) concept of the servant leader. According to Terry, leaders must be concerned not only with what decisions are made, but also with how they are made. Decisions must be made in transparent and open ways while they fittingly "acknowledge the significant features of the human condition" (Terry, 1993, p. 108). In taking this approach, leaders treat people with respect and acknowledge that they have a right to engage in decisions that affect their lives and communities. For Greenleaf (1970/ 1991) and Terry (1993), leaders should engage justly in service to justice.

The faith of sustainable leaders in the power of average people to create meaningful and beneficial change in the world articulates well with Paul Rogat Loeb's (1999) argument that leadership is *learned*, step by developmental step, when properly nurtured and supported in community (Ch. 3). For Loeb, leadership is not *inborn*, but a possibility for all. Fostering the potential for learning sustainable leadership ought, therefore, to be a central focus for sustainable leaders acting within multiple contexts. Philosophies and practices enacted through shared leadership are also more likely to survive and evolve over the long term than are the philosophies and practices of single, dominant leaders. They are therefore more likely to foster the long-term integrity and resiliency aspects of sustainability.

Sustainable Leadership Engages Imperfectly in Processes of Long-Term Cultural Change.

In the current world-system, damage and destruction visited upon people and nature are both integral and pervasive. Large-scale, centralized businesses and organizations practice abstract leadership from afar, and the potential for realizing sustainable leadership may appear to be nearly entirely precluded. Sustainable leaders deciding and acting within unsustainable contexts face the intense challenges of acting within institutional, community, and cultural settings where choices open to them are likely to have mixed results in terms of fostering sustainability. Terry (1993) describes the dilemmas faced by leaders:

> Leadership ... confronts an abyss of unknown consequences and obligations in any action it does take. The ripple effects of action are so vast and complex that no computer or cost-benefit analysis can totally analyze them. Duties often conflict; ethical choices are usually not made between right and wrong or good and bad but between conflicting rights and goods.
>
> (p. 260)

Given the contexts within which many leaders operate today, those who strive to be sustainable must recognize that they are engaged in a long-term project of cultural change and that their contributions to that change will be imperfect and embody contradictions. Loeb (1999) warns us against attempting to adhere to the "perfect standard," the notion that, if our ideas and actions are not entirely consistent, we should see ourselves as hypocrites and refrain from acting (pp. 38–39). According to the perfect standard, for example, one should not oppose the building of oil pipelines or fight air pollution if one drives a car. The notion that, in order to move toward sustainability, one must be completely sustainable in one's own life could leave all or most of us in paralysis or in a state of simply not attending to the implications of our actions. If leaders are to be part of and effective within the current social context, they must be able to live and work in gray areas while continually moving toward sustainability. Their work is unlikely to reach the defining point of sustainability on the leadership continuum. Still, leaders must work inclusively to identify widely set guideposts for decisions and actions. They must also acknowledge their own limited knowledge and trust others with whom they collaborate to bring to the table differing and useful ideas (Abrams, 2008).

The commitment of sustainable leaders to fittingly responsive socio-ecological change must also be deep-rooted and lifelong. The sustainability challenges we face collectively did not emerge within a single human life-time, and they will not be resolved within the lifetimes of any of us alive today. Sustainable leadership is a lifelong commitment to ideas and pro-cesses that fittingly address the socio-ecological crises we face. Sustainable leaders are cultural change-makers, and cultural change takes time and patience. Sustainable leaders have hope that their work will contribute to renewed health, integrity, and resiliency of human societies and nature, and they also have the humility to recognize that there are no guarantees of this desired outcome.

Conclusions

The self-destructiveness of exploitive leadership is currently evidenced by the widespread social inequity and environmental destruction that characterize our world today and foretell disaster for all if modern societies do not radically change course. As a fitting response to converging socio-ecological crises, sustainable leadership is a means of coalescing and directing group action in ways that promote living sustainability (Pittman, 2007). Such lea-dership represents a normative commitment to health, integrity, and resi-liency for individuals, communities, and nature. Power for its own sake is antithetical to sustainable leadership.

Sustainable leadership offers a normative, but inclusive, dynamic, and open (imperfect) framework for long-term cultural transformation in service to a more just and resilient world. It serves the needs of people for material sufficiency, dignity, and meaningful and consequential participation in deci-sions that affect their lives. It takes people seriously as subjects in the world rather than seeing them as tools to be manipulated and controlled in order to serve the ends of a powerful global elite.

Sustainable leadership is a historically and culturally embedded concept and practice. Rather than being inwardly focused on the values of the leader (that may be informed by the "common sense" of powerful but unsustainable systems) or being focused on personal characteristics or individual leadership style, sustainable leadership focuses outwardly in order to create fitting responses to the twin crises of social justice and environmental destruction. These responses are counter-hegemonic and aimed at creating and nurturing reciprocal and sustaining relationships among people and between humans and nature. Sustainable leadership is also an exercise in cultural change. As such, it requires humility, listening, empathy, and taking others and nature seriously as subjects and community members in their own right. Sustainable leadership can embody the best of human agency. If widely practiced, it can contribute to realizing the best possible outcomes in these dangerous times.

Notes

1 This chapter is an extensive and substantive revision of an article by the same author published in the *Journal of Sustainability Education* (Evans, 2011; copyright held by the author). Material drawn directly from the earlier article does not appear with quotations in this chapter.

2 I place "re" in parentheses here and in other places throughout this essay in recognition that relatively nonhierarchical, place-based cultures and remnants of these cultures remain in diverse places globally. For members of these cultures, the "re" in phrases such as "re-create sustainable leadership" may not apply. The parenthetical "re" also recognizes that, for some peoples and places, examples never have existed or no longer exist to draw upon for sustainable leadership and living, meaning that sustainable social systems must be created for the first time from scratch.

3 See Wheatley (2007) for a discussion of the failings of command and control leadership. This essay is also inspired, in part, by Wheatley's call for forms of leadership that are up to the task of reinventing the culture and practices of leadership in order to make it inherently life-enhancing, life-giving, and life-supporting rather than life-destroying.

4 Forms of command and control leadership (slavery, for example) have long existed in human history, but the way most of us experience that form of leadership today is through our interactions with many dominant systems of social organization such as the globalized economy. Because the globalized economy organizes the leadership/followership experience of so many people worldwide in such important ways, understanding command and control systems within that system is particularly important to understanding current conceptions of leadership.

5 An important difference between this current economic imperial system and that of colonialism is that capital is now less anchored in and dependent upon nation states as platforms for capital accumulation and political sources of legitimacy. Presently, capital has become mobile and abstract, and its legitimacy in acting independently of nation state controls is supported and enforced through international free trade agreements such as the North American Free Trade Agreement (NAFTA) and the General Agreement on Tariffs and Trade (GATT) as well as through the World Trade Organization (WTO). The NAFTA treaty even gives multinational corporations chartered in its three signatory nations (the United

States, Mexico, and Canada) the right to sue a signatory nation directly for regulatory and other actions deemed "tantamount to expropriation" (which has been at times interpreted to include government regulatory interference with potential profits) (Moyers, 2002).

References

Abrams, J. (2008). *Companies We Keep: Employee ownership and the business of community and place*. White River Junction, VT: Chelsea Green.

Achbar, M., & Simpson, B. (Producers), Bakan, J., Crooks, H., & Achbar, M. (Writers), Achbar, M., & Abbott, J. (Directors). (2005). *The Corporation* [Motion picture]. United States: Zeitgeist Films.

Adger, W.N. (2003). Social Capital, Collective Action, and Adaptation to Climate Change. *Economic Geography*, 79(4), 387–404.

Armstrong, J. (1995). Keepers of the Earth. In T. Rozak, M.E. Gomez, & A.D. Kanner (Eds), *Ecopsychology: Restoring the earth, healing the mind* (pp. 316–324). San Francisco, CA: Sierra Club Books.

Barbour, I. G. (1993). *Ethics in an Age of Technology: The Gifford lectures, 1989–1991, Vol. 2*. San Francisco, CA: Harper.

Barlow, M., & Clarke, T. (2002). *Blue Gold: The fight to stop the corporate theft of the world's water*. New York: The New Press.

Berkes, F. (1999). *Sacred Ecology: Traditional ecological knowledge and resource management*. Philadelphia, PA: Taylor & Francis.

Black, S. (Producer/Director). (2001). *Life and Debt* [Motion Picture]. New York: New Yorker Films.

Borrett, S.R., Moody, J., & Edelmann, A. (2014). The Rise of Network Ecology: Maps of the topic diversity and scientific collaboration. *Ecological Modelling, 293*, 111–127.

Brookfield, S.D. (1987). *Developing Critical Thinkers: Challenging adults to explore alternative ways of thinking and acting*. San Francisco, CA: Jossey-Bass Publishers.

Brookfield, S.D. (2000). Transformative Learning as Ideology Critique. In J. Mezirow & Associates (Eds), *Learning as Transformation: Critical perspectives on a theory in progress* (pp. 125–148). San Francisco, CA: Jossey-Bass Publishers.

Douthwaite, R. (2004). Why Localization is Essential for Sustainability. *Growth the Celtic Cancer. FEASTA Review*, 2, 114–124.

Evans, T. (2011). Leadership without Domination? Toward Restoring the Human and Natural World. *Journal of Sustainability Education*, 2(1), 1–16. Available at: www.jsedimensions.org/wordpress/wp-content/uploads/2011/03/Evans2011.pdf.

Evans, T.L. (2012). *Occupy Education: Living and learning sustainability*. New York: Peter Lang.

Folke, C.et al. (2016). Social-ecological Resilience and Biosphere-based Sustainability Science. *Ecology and Society*, 21(3), 431–446.

Freire, P. (1970/2000). *Pedagogy of the Oppressed* (30th Anniversary ed.). New York: Continuum International Publishing Group.

Greenleaf, R.K. (1970/1991). *The Servant as Leader*. Indianapolis, IN: The Robert K. Greenleaf Center.

Hall, C.A.S., & Klitgaard, K.A. (Eds). (2012). *Energy and the Wealth of Nations: Understanding the biophysical economy*. New York: Springer.

Homer-Dixon, T. (2006). *The Upside of Down: Catastrophe, creativity, and the renewal of civilization.* Washington, DC: Island Press.

International Consortium of Investigative Journalists. (2003). *Water Barons: How a few powerful companies are privatizing your water.* Washington, DC: Public Integrity Books.

International Society for Ecology and Culture (Producer). (1993). *Ancient Futures: Learning from Ladakh.* Bristol: International Society for Ecology and Culture.

Jensen, D. (2000). *A Language Older than Words.* New York: Context Books.

Keltner, D. (2016). *The Power Paradox: How we gain and lose influence.* New York: Penguin.

Kemmis, D. (1990). *Community and the Politics of Place.* Norman: University of Oklahoma Press.

Kohn, A. (1986). *No Contest: The case against competition.* Boston, MA: Houghton Mifflin.

LaDuke, W. (1999). *All Our Relations: Native struggles for land and life.* Cambridge: South End Press.

Loeb, P.R. (1999). *Soul of a Citizen: Living with conviction in a cynical time.* New York: St. Martin's Griffin.

Manley, M. (1987). *Up the Down Escalator: Development and the international economy – A Jamaican case study.* Washington, DC: Howard University Press.

Marcuse, H. (1964). *One-dimensional Man: Studies in the ideology of advanced industrial society.* Boston, MA: Beacon Press.

Martinez, D. (1997). American Indian Cultural Models for Sustaining Biodiversity. In Proceedings of the Sustainable Forestry Seminar Series, Oregon State University, 1995. Special Forest Products: Biodiversity Meets the Marketplace. https://www.fs.fed.us/pnw/pubs/gtr63/gtrwo63g.pdf.

Mezirow, J., & Associates. (2000). *Learning as Transformation: Critical perspectives on a theory in progress.* San Francisco, CA: Jossey-Bass Publishers.

Miller, A. (1999). Economics and the Environment. In C. Merchant, (Ed.) *Ecology: Key concepts in critical theory* (pp. 78–87). Amherst, NY: Humanity Books.

Moyers, B. (Host). (2002). *Bill Moyers Reports: Trading democracy* [Motion picture]. Princeton, NJ: Films for the Humanities & Sciences.

Nelson, R.K. (1983). *Make Prayers to the Raven: A Koyukon view of the northern forest.* Chicago, IL: University of Chicago Press.

Norberg-Hodge, H. (1991/1992). *Ancient Futures: Learning from Ladakh.* San Francisco: Sierra Club.

Norberg-Hodge, H., Merrifield, T., & Gorelick, S. (2002). *Bringing the Food Economy Home: Local alternatives to global agribusiness.* London: Zed Books.

Patten, B.C. (2016). The Cardinal Hypotheses of Holoecology: Facets for a general systems theory of the organism–environment relationship. *Ecological Modeling, 319,* 63–111.

Petzold, J., & Ratter, M.W. (2015). Climate Change Adaptation under a Social Capital Approach: An analytical framework for small islands. *Ocean and Coastal Management, 112,* 36–43.

Piketty, T. (2014). *Capital in the Twenty-First Century.* Cambridge, MA: Belknap Press of Harvard University Press.

Pittman, J. (2007, August). Whole Systems Design and Living Sustainability. Presentation given at the orientation to the Prescott College Ph.D. Program in Sustainability Education, Prescott, AZ.

Polanyi, K. (1944/1957). *The Great Transformation: The political and economic origins of our time.* Boston, MA: Beacon Press.

Salmon, E. (2000). Kincentric Ecology: Indigenous perceptions of the human-nature relationship. *Ecological Applications*, 10, 1327–1332.

Scheer, H. (2002). *The Solar Economy: Renewable energy for a sustainable future.* London: Earthscan.

Shepard, P. (1995). Nature and Madness. In R. Rozak, M.E. Gomes, & A.D. Kanner (Eds), *Ecopsychology: Restoring the earth, healing the mind* (pp. 21–40). San Francisco, CA: Sierra Club.

Shuman, M.H. (1998/2000). *Going Local: Creating self-reliant communities in a global age.* New York: Free Press.

Spretnak, C. (1997). *The Resurgence of the Real: Body, nature, and place in a hypermodern world.* Reading, MA: Addison-Wesley.

Stiglitz, J.E. (2002). *Globalization and its Discontents.* New York: W. W. Norton.

Summers, C., & Markusen, E. (2003). The Case of Collective Violence. In M. D. Ermann & M. S. Shauf (Eds), *Computers, Ethics, and Society* (3rd ed.) (pp. 214–231). New York: Oxford University Press.

Sveiby, K., & Skuthorpe, T. (2006). *Treading Lightly: The hidden wisdom of the world's oldest people.* Crow's Nest, New South Wales, Australia: Allen & Unwin.

Terry, R.W. (1993). *Authentic Leadership: Courage in action.* San Francisco, CA: Jossey-Bass Publishers.

Wallerstein, I. (1974). *The Modern World-system: Capitalist agriculture and the origins of the European world-economy in the sixteenth century.* Studies in Social Discontinuity. New York: Academic.

Wallerstein, I. (1976). A World-system Perspective on the Social Sciences. *British Journal of Sociology*, 27, 343–352.

Wallerstein, I. (2003, July–August). U.S. Weakness and the Struggle of Hegemony [Electronic Version]. *Monthly Review*.

Wallerstein, I. (2005). After Developmentalism and Globalization, What? *Social Forces*, 83, 1263–1278.

Wallerstein, I. (2006). The Curve of American Power. *New Left Review*, 40, 77–94.

Wallerstein, I. (2007). Precipitate Decline: The advent of multipolarity. *Harvard International Review*, 50–55.

Wallerstein, I. (2008, August 4). Theory talk #13 – Immanual Wallerstein on World-systems, the Imminent End of Capitalism and Unifying Social Science. *Theory Talks.* www.theory-talks.org/2008/08/theory-talk-13.html.

Wheatley, M. (2007). *Finding Our Way: Leadership for an uncertain time.* San Francisco, CA: Berrett-Koehler Publishers.

5 Eco-Leadership, Complexity Science, and 21st-Century Organizations

A Theoretical and Empirical Analysis

D. Adam Cletzer and Eric K. Kaufman

Introduction

Throughout the 20th century, the traditional approach to leadership was based on "machine metaphors and machine-like assumptions" (Allen et al, 1999, p. 67; Rost, 1997). Leadership was seen as derived from position, vested in an individual, top-down in nature, and "driven by power for the purpose of control" (Allen et al., 1999, p. 67). The leader and his or her actions were viewed as "more critical than those of any other member of the group" (Wielkiewicz, 2000, p. 335). Those individuals within an organization who were "most competent and loyal" were appointed to leadership positions and assumed responsibility for the organization's overall success; they provided vision for the organization and direction to followers (Chemers, 1997, p. 11). The focus of leadership studies, then, became to make these individuals better leaders, and, indeed, "much of empirical research on leadership focuses on predicting outcomes that reside at the individual level of analysis" (DeChurch et al., 2010, p. 1069).

However, in today's rapidly changing, increasingly complex, and interdependent world, our models of leadership simply have not yet fully caught up with the leadership dynamics of a 21st century, knowledge-driven society (Avolio et al., 2009). Scholars increasingly argue that the traditional notion of leadership as "having a vision and aligning people with that vision is bankrupt" (Heifetz & Laurie, 1997, p. 126). Relying on a few, elite positional leaders is "inadequate for dealing with the complexities of the modern world" (Wielkiewicz, 2000, p. 335). The romantic notion of a heroic individual leader may simply no longer be tenable (Avolio et al., 2009). Such approaches leave us ill-equipped to meet today's complex challenges because their reliance on singular individuals to provide "the leadership" fails to leverage the collective intelligence, energy, and creativity of all actors in a system. The complexity of new, adaptive challenges – along with the sheer speed of scientific, technological, and societal change – is simply too much to depend entirely on a small, upper-echelon of positional leaders to provide "the leadership" for an organization (Allen et al., 1999; Western, 2013). It will take all of us. Wielkiewicz (2000) warns of an "urgent need" to radically rethink leadership in a way that "matches the complexity of the systems to which organizations must respond" (p. 335).

Western (2010, 2013) critically examined this shift in society's understanding of leadership through a meta-analysis of historical, socio-political, and economic perspectives, and identified four distinct discourses of leadership occurring in Europe and North America during the past century: (a) Controller, (b) Therapist, (c) Messiah, and (d) the emerging Eco-leader discourse. The latter discourse emerged in the early 2000s and is characterized by collective decision making, collaboration, shared leadership, and grassroots organization. This discourse reflects a 21st-century society's attempt to adapt in the face of increasingly complex and interconnected challenges that require the resources of whole organizations – to heed the warning that our mechanisms for enacting leadership are becoming outdated (Wielkiewicz & Stelzner, 2005).

As the eco-leader discourse evolves in society, scholars, too, are beginning to understand and study leadership as a complex social phenomenon – "an emergent property of a social system, in which 'leader' and 'follower' share in the process of enacting leadership" – rather than a simple set of traits, skills, or behaviors (Jackson & Parry, 2012, p. 105). The 20th century's long-running, mechanistic view of leadership seems inadequate for explaining leadership as the emergent phenomenon it is increasingly understood to be in today's more interconnected and interdependent world (Western, 2013). Therefore, just as scholars turned from mechanical to ecological metaphors for explaining the phenomenon of leadership, they have also utilized – and been influenced by – new scientific paradigms in which to ground their theories. One such "new science" influencing worldviews is complexity science (Lichtenstein et al., 2006; Marion & Uhl-Bien, 2001; Regine & Lewin, 2000). Though a nascent science, Regine & Lewin (2000) write that complexity science represents a "Kuhnian shift" in the physical sciences, and is expected to have a similar impact in the social sciences. Scholars who have studied business, politics, trends in the stock market, the emergence of life on Earth, the fall of the Soviet Union, the rise of the Arab Spring, or even the movements of flocking birds have all drawn upon complexity science when attempting to explain the complex interactions inside complex adaptive systems (Davis, 2004). The connectivity among actors within a system is one of the hallmarks of both the ecological approaches to leadership and complexity science; it also directly applies to leadership studies (Allen et al., 1999; Western, 2013).

This chapter provides one example of how an ecological approach to leadership might be studied in an effort to empirically support conceptual claims that ecological forms of leadership are good for organizations. Heretofore, there have been few, if any, empirical studies linking an ecological approach to leadership with organizational success (Lowhorn, 2011; Wielkiewicz, 2000, 2002). We address this gap by offering findings to support the claim that an ecological approach will lead to more adaptive organizations that have greater success over time. In what follows, we first discuss the promise of complexity science in leadership studies, and the 21st century organization as an ecological system, before turning to our empirical findings and discussion of what an eco-leader might do to help his or her organization to become truly ecological in form and function.

The Promise of Complexity Science in Leadership Studies

At its core, complexity science is a repudiation of the reductionist approach to scientific inquiry. Richardson, Cilliers, & Lissack (2001) write: "Where we once focused on the parts of a system and how they functioned, we must now focus on the interactions between these parts, and how these relationships determine the identity, not only of the parts, but of the whole system" (p. 6). Complexity science is, therefore, typically applied to complex – social movements, flocking birds, the emergence of life on Earth – whose internal structure cannot easily be reduced to a mechanistic system where cause and effect are more linear in nature (Allen, 2001). This is in contrast to the traditional approach to science (and the traditional study of leadership), which involves trading the complexity of the real world for a simpler, reduced representation (Allen, 2001). This reduction is based on the assumption that it is possible to: (a) establish a system's boundaries, excluding factors that are less relevant; (b) reduce the "full heterogeneity to a typology of elements"; (c) study individuals of average type; and (d) study processes that run at an average rate (Allen, 2001, p. 24). This process of reduction takes much of the "messiness" out of studying a complex phenomenon like leadership. However, as Finkelstein (2002) writes, "I understand that as researchers we need to simplify very complex processes to study them carefully, but what are we left with when we remove the messiness, the back-and-forth, the reality?" (p. 77).

There is a belief that the use of reductionist approaches has led leadership scholars to fixate on the individual leader's "symbolic, motivational, or charismatic" actions for too long – trading the messy reality of leadership for the clean deficiency of individual variables (Lichtenstein et al., 2006, p. 2). However, through the lens of complexity science – just as through an ecological approach to leadership – leadership is no longer viewed as a simple, rational exchange between leader and followers. That view "won't fly in terms of explaining the full dynamics of leadership" (Avolio et al., 2009, p. 430). Instead, leadership is viewed as an "interactive system of dynamic, unpredictable agents that interact with each other in complex feedback networks" (Ibid., p. 430). These interactions foster learning, innovation, and the dissemination of knowledge (Uhl-Bien et al., 2007).

Moreover, leadership is seen not necessarily as the *intentional* actions or effects of leaders. Instead, leadership "can be enacted through *any interaction* in an organization ... leadership is an emergent phenomenon within complex systems" (Hazy et al., 2007, p. 2). Moreover, through the lens of complexity science, leadership is understood not only as the product of these interactions, but also as the interactions of the unpredictable agents in a system themselves. When levels of leader–follower interaction "reach a critical mass, patterns begin to emerge and the group self-organizes," giving rise to social movements, organizational initiatives, even governments (Guastello, 2007, p. 606). This is a sea change in leadership studies.

As scholars begin to view leadership as "an emergent property of a social system," the next step then is to explain *how* leadership emerges (Jackson & Parry, 2012, p. 105). Emergence is a central component of complexity science. Indeed, complexity science's purpose is largely to explain emergence. The study of emergence is not a new one. One of the first written explanations of this concept was by English philosopher G.H. Lewes, who made the distinction between "resultant" and a term he coined, "emergent," when writing on chemical reactions:

> Although each effect is the resultant of its components, we cannot always trace the steps of the process, so as to see in the product the mode of operation of each factor. In the latter case, I propose to call the effect an emergent. It arises out of the combined agencies, but in a form which does not display the agents in action.
>
> (Lewes, 1875, as cited in De Wolf & Holvoet, 2005, p. 2)

Emergence takes place in a complex adaptive system with a high degree of interactivity among agents; the interactivity is nonlinear in nature and contains numerous feedback loops (Richardson et al., 2001). This makes it nearly impossible to establish a simple cause and effect, and some would argue the cause is irrelevant, which led Lewes to use the term emergent. Emergence, therefore, is best described as "a phenomenon where global behavior arises from the interactions between local parts of the system" (De Wolf & Holvoet, 2005, p. 2). To understand how these micro level interactions (e.g., the continued interactions between disenchanted workers) yield macro level structures (e.g., a strike or larger social movement) gives us insight into how leadership works and what roles so-called leaders may play in the process.

The basic processes that explain emergence within complex adaptive systems include three factors: microdynamics, macrodynamics, and complex natural teleology. Microdynamics represents the bottom-up behavior that is created when individuals interact; these behaviors can be either coordinated or random. Small groups, dubbed "aggregates," or ensembles (groups of aggregates) begin to form through interaction. In the social sciences, the term aggregates typically describes "small groups of directly interacting actors who have a sense of common identity" (Marion & Uhl-Bien, 2001, p. 400). The effect of this interaction "imparts both a measure of stable order within and among ensembles and a collateral measure of unpredictability" (Ibid., p. 394).

Macrodynamics, on the other hand, is concerned with the resulting "structures and behaviors that emerge unbidden out of an interactive network of ensembles – behaviors that are self-generative, the products of interactive dynamics rather than external force" (Marion & Uhl-Bien, 2001, p. 396). In other words, macrodynamics is concerned with what emerges from the micro-level interactions of individual agents. In the realm of leadership, "persistently interacting social networks create order, innovation, and fitness" (Ibid., p. 396). However, because macro-level structures and behaviors arise in non-intuitive ways, "they ultimately elude control and prediction" (Ibid., p. 396). Yet, uncertainty, unpredictability, and non-linearity – while they may confound and conceal – are actually what afford complex systems the ability to be dynamic and adaptable. Order and stability in a complex system are necessary and good, but they do not allow for the variation that is crucial to the ongoing survival of the system. When you consider that macro-level structures arise from the various interactions of multitudes of individual actors over time, that there is variety is not what is surprising; it is the emergence of order that is interesting and difficult to explain. Marion & Uhl-Bien (2001) have dubbed the collection of forces that enable this macro-level order "complex natural teleology."

Complex natural teleology is the mechanism that translates micro-level interactions into an order that is recognizable to us as macro-level structures and behaviors, such as leadership in its many forms: social movements, businesses, and governments. Complex natural teleology is comprised of: (a) autocatalysis, the automatic catalysts that foster interaction among actors, particularly "tags," which is any person or structure that speeds interaction; (b) need, the innate desires that drive the autocatalysis process, such as status, power, or resources; (c) physics, the demands or limitations either internal or external that shape the interaction; and (d) natural selection, "the selection of forms from among sets of possible forms (as restricted by physics)," (Marion & Uhl-Bien, 2001, p. 400). Together, these forces are the requisite conditions for micro-level interactions to emerge into an ordered macro-level behavior or structure.

How Complexity Science Impacts Leadership Studies

At its most basic level, and from a complexity lens, leadership as we know it arises in the following way: micro-level interactions among individual actors (i.e., so-called leaders and followers), called autocatalytic interactions, occur. These micro-level interactions are driven by need, enabled by human and technological catalysts (or tags), limited by physics, and culled by natural selection. These autocatalytic interactions cause the emergence of macro-level structures and behaviors that yield order, innovation, and dissemination of information – things we would recognize as leadership and the products of leadership (i.e., organizations, movements, flocking birds, etc.) (Marion & Uhl-Bien, 2001). All of this occurs within the complex adaptive system.

The complex adaptive system (CAS), for its part, is the environment – nurturing or otherwise – in which the emergence of leadership occurs. In recent years, scholars searching for a model to "more accurately reflect the complex nature of leadership as it occurs in practice" have employed the CAS as the fundamental unit of analysis for leadership – a shift away from the individual leader (Uhl-Bien & Marion, 2009, p. 631). Complex Adaptive System theory is one of four major schools of thought in complexity science (De Wolf & Holvoet, 2005). Levy (1992, as cited in Uhl-Bien & Marion, 2009) describes complex adaptive systems this way:

> A complex (adaptive) system is one whose component parts interact with sufficient intricacy that they cannot be predicted by standard linear equations; so many variables are at work in the system that its overall behavior can only be understood as an emergent consequence of the holistic sum of the myriad behaviors embedded within. Reductionism does not work with complex systems, and it is now clear that a purely reductionist approach cannot be applied; ... in living systems the whole is more than the sum of its parts. This is the result of ... complexity which allows certain behaviors and characteristics to emerge unbidden.
>
> (p. 631)

Complex adaptive systems can be found nearly everywhere: "ecosystems, the brain, ant colonies, stock markets, just to name a few" (Regine & Lewin, 2000, p. 7). CAS also provides a new paradigm for studying leadership in a way that "more easily explores issues that confound us from a traditional view – issues of shared, distributed, collective, relational, dynamic, emergent and adaptive leadership processes" – all approaches that fall within the emergent eco-leader discourse and ecological forms of leadership (Uhl-Bien & Marion, 2009, p. 631; Western, 2013). Regine & Lewin (2000) conclude, "the avenue most relevant to understanding organizational dynamics within companies ... is the study of complex adaptive systems" (p. 6).

Organizations as Ecological Systems

It is easy to see how complexity science supports eco-leadership's explanation of leadership as an emergent process co-created by both leaders and followers operating in fluid roles. Many organizations, which exist as macro-level manifestations of these interactions, could be described as complex adaptive systems, which are characterized by redundancy, diversity, interaction, and decentralization (Davis, 2004). However, the conventional understanding of leadership as emanating from individual positional leaders undermines these four requisite factors of complex systems. By relying on few positional leaders to provide leadership for an organization, redundancy is reduced, diversity is limited, interaction is lessened, and power is centralized, all of which reduce the capacity for the organization to learn and adapt as an organism in the changing environment.

Not every organization is an appropriate venue to apply an ecological approach to leadership, however. Organizations like banking or manufacturing, which require specific tasks to be performed in an efficient manner, are predisposed to a more mechanistic approach (Western, 2013). Schools and hospitals, despite the highly personal nature of the work that is performed, are also associated with a more mechanistic approach to leadership because of the rigid hierarchies within them. An ecological approach, on the other hand, is well-suited to organizations that feature flattened hierarchies, a more educated workforce, and collaborative decision-making processes (Gockel & Worth, 2010). The ecological approach to leadership is also particularly suited to a knowledge-driven economy that requires rapid generation of new knowledge and innovation in order to be competitive; the flattened hierarchies and collaborative decision-making processes allow the eco-leader to harness the creativity, energy, and intelligence of the entire system to provide leadership for the organization rather than relying on a few positional leaders (Western, 2013). The ecological approach is also particularly well suited for organizations that purposefully seek out connections with other organizations and communities. Where the mechanistic paradigm conceives of an organization as a bounded system, ecological approaches view organizations as interconnected and interdependent ecosystems (Western, 2013).

One quintessential example of an organization functioning as a complex adaptive system – and the focus of this study – is the Florida Cooperative Extension Service. As a federal, state, and local partnership, Extension brings educational programming to diverse communities (Bonnen, 1998). Extension represents the interconnected, nested systems described by Western (2013). Among its programs is the 4-H Youth Development Program, which, in addition to existing at the federal, state, and local levels, also consists of innumerable connections with local communities, organizations, nonprofits, businesses, schools, and families. The Florida 4-H program is led in each county by an Extension agent (i.e., a positional leader), with the support from a cross-section of the program's stakeholders, organized in the form of the county 4-H association (Diem & Cletzer, 2011). These 4-H associations maintain a roster of members with deep ties to the community in which they live. These associations exist to provide input and resources to the county 4-H program. They represent a collective leadership body. However, in Extension and 4-H, the focus is often heavily on the Extension agent as the leader of the county 4-H program.

This view of Extension agents as traditional positional leaders, however, is problematic for aspects of the program – most noticeably turnover. The National Association of State Universities and Land-Grant Colleges identified retention of Extension agents as a "challenge area" (Extension Committee on Organization and Policy's Leadership Advisory Council, 2005). Turnover among county Extension faculty results in "disrupted educational programs, unmet citizen needs, low morale among remaining Extension professionals, and wasted financial and material resources dedicated to

Extension agent on-boarding and in-service training" (Safrit & Owen, 2010, para 4). Efforts to reduce the effects of turnover on Extension programs have primarily focused on addressing issues related to the positional leader – burnout, salary and benefits, work-life balance, skills and competencies, or job satisfaction – rather than a more systemic approach. Unfortunately, each of these approaches to addressing turnover fails to acknowledge an emerging generational shift occurring in the workforce and its long-term effects on the retention of new agents and program resiliency: Millennials. As Baby Boomers exit the workforce, organizations often replace them with Millennials. Where Baby Boomers sought employment stability, 74 percent of Millennials report expecting to have as many as five or more employers in their lifetime, and 38 percent of those currently employed are actively searching for a new position now (Price Waterhouse Coopers, 2011). Indeed, more than 60 percent of Millennials leave their positions in fewer than three years (Schawbel, 2013). Turnover is both costly and damaging to program momentum, leaving employers facing an expensive revolving door (Schawbel, 2013).

Still, efforts to mitigate these effects focus on preparing heroic positional leaders through skill and competency development, despite evidence that generational trends point to continued turnover among this generation that accounts for a growing percentage of Extension 4-H agents. The effect is a leadership development approach focusing almost entirely on the positional leader when, in fact, the problem is systemic in nature. By taking a more ecological approach and distributing leadership, turnover among agents may be less disruptive and detrimental to the organization because responsibility for the program is not vested in a single person. Extension is failing to adapt to an external shift.

Adaptability Becomes the Chief Aim of 21st Century Organizations

Assuming an organization can carry out its mission successfully, it will usually turn its attention to longevity. It is the primary role of the leaders of an organization to structure and position the organization for continued relevance and success (Selznick, 1997). This necessitates the organizational capacity to continually interpret and react to external environmental factors. Barnard (1948) writes that the external environment is comprised of "physical, biological, and social materials, elements, and forces," and, further, is "at root the cause of instability and limited durability of organizations" (p. 6).

Though Barnard's (1948) description of an organization's need to contend with the external environment was appropriate for his time, how organizations seek to adapt has changed. During the time that Barnard wrote, organizations sought to find "equilibrium" with the external environment by enacting controlling internal policies governing employees' behavior. This model situated power and control in the hands of positional leaders and relegated employees to worker status (Western, 2013). This model may have been effective when the purpose of an organization was efficient physical production, but in today's knowledge-driven economy, "knowledge is a core commodity and the rapid production of knowledge and innovation is critical to ... survival" (Uhl-Bien et al., 2007, p. 299). The challenges today's organizations face demand a new, more flexible, adaptive, and creativity-inducing model.

An ecological perspective is concerned with the way in which an organization interrelates to other parts of its ecosystem (i.e., society, economy, the environment), as well as inflows of information and resources, all in an attempt to be adaptive and generative (Western, 2013). To structure and position an organization for survival in a modern, knowledge-driven society, Wielkiewicz & Stelzner (2005, 2010) propose an ecological perspective that is characterized by four factors: (a) interdependence, (b) open systems and feedback loops, (c) cycling of resources, and (d) adaptation. This ecological model stresses the individual responsibility of actors in an ecosystem, developing the capacities of individuals within organizations, and a long-term perspective (Allen et al., 1999). Rather than chasing equilibrium, the goal becomes maximizing the *adaptability* of the organization to better contend with changing external factors. This ecological perspective posits that the long-term adaptability of an organization will be determined by the management of the tension between situating power and control in the hands of positional leaders, and having a "diverse sample of organization members influence the leadership process" (Wielkiewicz & Stelzner, 2005, p. 331). This is also described as the tension between the mechanistic, or industrial, paradigm, and the ecological paradigm. Western (2010) sums it up, writing that the environment "change[s] so quickly these days that the adaptive companies with capability for change are the winners" (p. 49).

In the case of county 4-H programs, their ability to adapt in the face of external threats to continue to meet community needs by providing youth programs will largely determine their programmatic success. When properly employed, we argue that the county 4-H associations, with their close ties to the community and collective leadership model, represent an ecological approach to leadership that has the capacity for ensuring success.

Results and Discussion of Findings

To empirically link an ecological approach to leadership with programmatic success, though, you must first define programmatic success. In this study, a researcher-developed index was used to score and rank county 4-H programs. The index drew on mandatory federal enrollment reporting data, along with United States Census Bureau data, to track per capita enrollment and five-year enrollment trends in all of Florida's county 4-H programs. We then ranked county 4-H programs using z-scores. Based on these results, we invited association members and Extension agents from three of the highest scoring counties and three of the lowest scoring counties to participate in qualitative focus groups. These focus groups encouraged participants to share in their own words their experience with leadership in their county 4-H programs. The focus groups centered on three primary questions: (a) What factors do you feel have contributed to the success of this group? (b) How does this group approach decision making?; and (c) How does this group ensure continued improvement?

As the high performing and low performing groups were compared and contrasted, we discovered that they diverged markedly on two of Wielkiewicz & Stelzner's (2005) four factors of eco-leadership: Open Systems & Feedback Loops, and Interdependence.

Low Scoring County 4-H Associations Are More Inwardly Focused and Connected

Low scoring county 4-H programs' associations differentiated themselves, in part, by exhibiting a greater tendency to be inwardly focused and connected. In an organization meant to connect the 4-H program to the community in order to gather input and resources, the composition of low scoring county 4-H associations' members was almost entirely from within the program. For example, a 4-H club leader may represent her individual club's interests on the county association. Moreover, when association members were asked what they considered their primary role in 4-H, more than half of association members cited some other role, most often club leader.

Low scoring counties also tended to dwell exclusively on inwardly focused procedural matters – scholarship deadlines, banquet plaques, camp fees, etc. – rather than focusing outward on meeting community needs and identifying new challenges. One association member, who had just recently assumed the role of association secretary said, "I just went through a year's worth of meeting minutes and there's really not a whole lot in there other than what we've discussed as far as policies and procedures."

In contrast, high scoring county programs, while also tackling procedural matters, were the only associations to discuss vetting program-related issues, such as deciding which programs to offer, how they may meet community needs, and how to recruit new volunteers to carry them out. In a perfect example, one 4-H agent described a scene where she balked at the local association's guidance on how best to build her new program in a rural county. When members suggested she begin with school programs, rather than the community clubs favored by the state leaders, she said: "'Blasphemy! We can't do that.' I was almost defiant to them. We cannot go to the schools, we have to do community clubs, and they said, 'Listen, if you're going to be successful in *this county* with 4-H you have got to start in the schools, libraries, and churches.'"

She went on to say that after six months of failure she acquiesced. She began to heed their advice and "Two years later, we have, I mean, *quadrupled* our numbers, and I have way more volunteers and community support. They were right."

In this same vein, high scoring county 4-H associations were also more likely to cite their external connections in terms of actual communities – "the west side of town," "past the river," minority communities, or businesses groups – rather than formalized, entity-to-entity connections, such as having a Farm Bureau or Cattlemen's Association representative. Formalized connections were more common among low scoring counties.

These findings are consistent with Wielkiewicz & Stelzner's (2005) ecological leadership principle of open systems and feedback loops, which states that an organization is dependent on inflows of information and other resources. Each organization is itself part of a larger, more complex open system (e.g., communities, economies, societies). Organizations that squelch feedback loops place the organization at risk by lessening its ability to adapt to the environment as it changes (Wielkiewicz & Stelzner, 2010). Low scoring associations that select members from within the 4-H program for the purpose of representing and connecting internal constituencies (e.g., sub-advisory groups or individual 4-H clubs), therefore, have a more inwardly focused, closed system with fewer feedback loops. This leaves the 4-H program with little inflows of new information, less feedback on programming, and fewer resources from the larger community. Having the organization structured in this way may contribute to increasingly ineffective county 4-H programming over time as the organization fails to adapt to external changes.

High Scoring County 4-H Programs Attribute Success to a Greater Number of Factors

County 4-H associations diverged on the question "To which factors do you attribute the success of the county 4-H program?" Low scoring county association members attributed success to only one factor: positional leaders. This usually meant the county 4-H agent. One participant remarked, "We've had other agents who didn't take the program to the level that Rhonda has." However, it just as often meant the 4-H club leaders, who are adult volunteers who manage a 4-H club. Another participant commented, "I think it has to do with the leaders that we have in our clubs. We really have strong leaders, and that's where you're going to get your strong clubs."

High scoring counties, in contrast, attributed success to a range of factors that did include positional leaders, such as the 4-H agent, but also other factors. A commonly cited factor was strong involvement from parents: "Parent involvement, I think, is number one. You have to have parent involvement for it to be successful." Another was a tight-knit community: "I guess it's the tight knit community. They're gonna make sure the kids get what they need." The same associations often cited vested county commissioners, both in terms of budgetary support and a general understanding of the purpose of the 4-H program.

This is consistent with Wielkiewicz & Stelzner's (2005) ecological leadership principle of interdependence, which posits that any attempt to understand or direct an organization by focusing on its positional leaders is incomplete and bound to fail. Leadership must be understood in the complex context of the organization and its environment, and success can be attributed, in part, to a group's ability to see the connectedness of social systems and the way they influence one another. Therefore, the specific factors to which high scoring counties attribute success are not important in and of themselves. Rather, it is the number and variety of factors contributing to success identified by high scoring counties that makes it illustrative of this concept. High scoring counties' association members are more apt to see the myriad factors affecting their county 4-H program, rather than fixating on individual positional leaders.

The Eco-Leader in the 21st Century Organization

If ecological approaches to leadership are, indeed, better for helping organizations be more adaptive in the knowledge economy, the next important question is: So, what does an eco-leader do? With so-called leaders and followers serving in more fluid roles, and the potential for all actors to provide leadership at different points, the answer might not be immediately clear. However, there is surprising agreement in the literature. Positional leaders continue to play an essential role by: (a) influencing the structure of the ecological system and (b) managing tension to create adaptive change.

First, rather than creating change through directives or selling their vision to followers, positional leaders act as organizational architects, creating the right conditions for leadership to flourish (Western, 2013). This is similar to the concept of physics with regard to complex natural teleology; physics refers to "external and internal demands and restrictions that limit or enable system behavior" (Marion & Uhl-Bien, 2001, p. 399). Positional leaders can nurture the organizational ecosystem by acting as an organizational architect in several ways, with the most obvious being designing the physical structure in which people live and work. Following the destruction of the British Parliament's House of Commons chamber during World War II, Winston Churchill was faced with the question of keeping the traditional adversarial rectangle design, wherein the governing and opposition parties faced each other, or opt for the more common semi-circle layout. Churchill remarked that the adversarial rectangle design was responsible for the two-party system of government Britain had come to know, saying, "We shape our buildings and afterwards our buildings shape us" (United Kingdom Parliament, 2017, para 1).

Similarly, how organizations are structured socially also matters. Western (2013) contrasts the Quakers – whose humility and austere lifestyle is reflected in their flattened hierarchy, eschewal of churches, and locally elected ministers – with the Catholic faith's traditional focus on hierarchy and projection of power: "The size of the church mimics the power of the leader ... the Pope has his own city" (p. 253). This is of particular importance in the realm of 4-H and other nonprofit organizations. Should power and decision-making processes be concentrated in the hands of the positional leader, or should there be substantial delegation of authority to volunteers when carrying out a program? Satterwhite (2010) writes, "The organization has to respond to external stimuli, which it can only do in ways that are consistent with its structure" (p. 232). In this way, function follows form. Those positional leaders responsible for structuring the organization should "constantly work on form and structure to make them consistent with organizational purpose" and best equipped to respond to the relevant external stimuli (Western, 2013, p. 254).

Additionally, if the nature of an ecological approach to leadership is redistributing leadership and power from a centralized, hierarchical structure throughout the organization, then inherent in the leader's role as organizational architect is the need to critically examine organizational hegemony and uncover structural inequities where they exist. By emphasizing a leadership-centric philosophy, rather than leader-centric, positional leaders can "go beyond simply serving the disadvantaged to the harnessing of their power" (Ospina et al., 2012, p. 255). If an organization is to harness the energy and creativity of the entire system to be successful, then all actors in the system should be included and valued.

Second, positional leaders play a critical role in what Wielkiewicz & Stelzner (2010) call "optimiz[ing] the tension between the 'Old School'/industrial perspective and the 'New School'/ecological perspective" (p. 23). The tension is between structure and process, efficiency and adaptability, order and chaos. This need for balance has long been understood on some level in leadership studies; examples of the yin and yang of this industrial/ecological tension abound: transactional versus transformational leadership (Pearce & Sims, 2002); organic versus mechanistic (Courtright et al., 1989); democratic versus autocratic leadership (Gastil, 1994), the individual versus relationship orientation (Rost, 1997); etc.

The difficulty for the positional leader is in achieving a balance over time. Recall that Barnard (1948), writing from a mechanistic perspective, believed the purpose of leadership in an organization was to help achieve an equilibrium with the external environment through creating complementary internal structures. Structure can create order, efficiency, and high productivity, but too much structure can also leave an organization unable to adapt quickly to a changing environment. Conversely, an ecological model, with its focus on process, can lead to disintegration if carried too far; should all structure and hierarchy be eschewed, the ecosystem becomes too chaotic (Wielkiewicz & Stelzner, 2010). To demonstrate the successful navigation of the tension between these two paradigms, Regine & Lewin (2000) provide the example of Andy Grove, then CEO of Intel. Facing adaptive challenges, he chose not to deliberately restructure the hierarchy of the organization in a top-down, mechanistic manner. Instead, he "pushed [the organization] into a degree of chaos by creating uncertainty and ambiguity" in order to free all the actors within the Intel ecosystem to generate their own order in response to the external adaptive challenge (Regine & Lewin, 2000, p. 11).

The benefits of nurturing an ecosystem and balancing the tension between structure and process is clear. Complexity science and the ecological approach it supports "dramatically expands the potential for creativity, influence, and positive change in an organization" (Lichtenstein et al., 2006, p. 8). Further, it provides a clear set of procedures for distributing leadership, fostering self-organization, and overall making an organization more adaptive.

Conclusions and Future Research

By continuing the work of empirically connecting an ecological approach to leadership with long-term organizational success, it should be possible to provide further evidence and insight into eco-leadership. The basic premises of this study could be replicated in a wide variety of contexts: business, rural communities, agricultural organizations, civic groups, etc. Empirical studies of leadership approaches' effects on organizations, communities, or programs are rare. By using the structure provided – complexity science as a theoretical framework and mechanistic-to-ecological continuum indicators as a measure – replication would only then require the creation of an index of success in the complex adaptive systems under study.

There is more work to be done, though, to better study this phenomenon. A measure of ecological leadership practices occurring in an organization should be developed. While there are instruments like the Leadership Attitudes and Beliefs Scale III (LABS-III) that provide a useful proxy for measuring individuals' attitudes and beliefs on the mechanistic–ecological continuum, they often do not assess the reality of leadership within the organization, as long-running institutional practices and structures may trump even the association members' individual attitudes and beliefs about leadership (Wielkiewicz, 2000, 2002). This would be accomplished by reviewing the literature on leadership in mechanistic and ecological organizations, and then identifying indicators of where an organization may fall on a continuum between mechanistic and ecological. This would likely be further broken down into sub-scales based on Wielkiewicz & Stelzner's (2005) four factors of ecological leadership: interdependence, open systems and feedback loops, cycling of resources, and adaption.

After identifying superlative ecological organizations through quantitative means, more qualitative work also needs to be done to describe best practices for the eco-leader. How does the eco-leader best structure his or her organization to encourage leadership to flourish in unexpected places? What are the exemplary cases of optimizing the tension between mechanistic and ecological processes over time?

By studying the ecological approach to leadership in action, we expand our understanding of leadership from "the isolated, role-based actions of individuals to the innovative, contextual interactions that occur across an entire social system" (Lichtenstein et al., 2006, p. 2). We also "increase the relevance and accuracy of leadership theory by exploring how leadership outcomes are based on complex interactions, rather than 'independent' variables" (Ibid.). Complexity science, for its part, provides a framework for exploring the phenomenon of leadership more deeply and could be utilized more often as a theoretical framework for leadership studies. The notion that leadership is a linear process affecting few variables in isolation is at odds with what we know both scientifically and intuitively about leadership. Focusing only on roles and actions of specific leaders is just the tip of the iceberg.

References

Allen, P. (2001). What is complexity science? Knowledge of the limits to knowledge. *Emergence: Complexity and Organization*, (3)1, 24–42.

Allen, K. E., Stelzner, S. P., & Wielkiewicz, R. M. (1999). The Ecology of Leadership: Adapting to the challenges of a changing world. *Journal of Leadership & Organizational Studies*, 5(2), 62–82.

Avolio, B. J., Walumbwa, F. O., & Weber, T. J. (2009). Leadership: Current theories, research, and future directions. *Annual Review of Psychology*, 60(1), 421–449.

Barnard, C. I. (1948). *Organizations and Management*. Cambridge, MA: Harvard University Press.

Bonnen, J. T. (1998). The Land Grant Idea and the Evolving Outreach University. In R. M. Lerner & L. K. Simon (Eds), *University-Community Collaborations for the Twenty-First Century* (pp. 25–70). New York: Routledge.

Chemers, M. M. (1997). *An Integrative Theory of Leadership*. Mahwah, NJ: Lawrence Erlbaum.

Courtright, J., Fairhurst, G., & Rogers, L. (1989). Interaction Patterns in Organic and Mechanistic Systems. *Academy of Management Journal*, 32(4), 773–802.

Davis, B. (2004). *Inventions of Teaching: A genealogy*. Mahwah, NJ: Lawrence Erlbaum.

DeChurch, L. A., Hiller, N. J., Murase, T., Doty, D., & Salas, E. (2010). Leadership Across Levels: Levels of leaders and their levels of impact. *The Leadership Quarterly*, 6(21), 1069–1085.

Diem, K.G., & Cletzer, D.A. (2011). *Florida 4-H Implementation Guide to Maintain Tax Exempt Status for your County 4-H Program*. Retrieved from: http://florida4h.org/staff/taxexempt/.

De Wolf, T. & Holvoet, T. (2005). Emergence Versus Self-Organization: Different concepts but promising when combined. In G. Di Marzo Serugendo (Ed.) *Engineering Self-Organising Systems: Nature-inspired approaches to software engineering* (pp. 1–15). New York: Springer.

Extension Committee on Organization and Policy's Leadership Advisory Council. (2005). *2005 Report*. Washington, DC: National Association of State Universities and Land-Grant Colleges.

Finkelstein, S. (2002). Planning in Organizations: One vote for complexity. In F. Yammarino and F. Dansereua (Eds), *The Many Faces of Multi-Level Issues* (Research in Multi-Level Issues, Volume 1) (pp. 73–80). Oxford: Elsevier.

Gastil, J. (1994). A Meta-Analytic Review of the Productivity and Satisfaction of Democratic and Autocratic Leadership. *Small Group Research*, 25(3), 384–410.

Gockel, C., & Werth, L. (2010). Measuring and Modeling Shared Leadership: Traditional approaches and new ideas. *Journal of Personnel Psychology*, 9(4), 172–180.

Guastello, S. J. (2007). How leaders really emerge. *American Psychologist*, 62(6), 606–607.

Hazy, J.K., Goldstein, J.A., & Lichtenstein, B.B. (2007). Complex Systems Leadership Theory: An introduction. In J. K. Hazy, J.A. Goldstein, and B. B. Lichtenstein (Eds), *Complex Systems Leadership Theory: New perspectives from complexity science on social and organizational effectiveness* (pp. 1–13). Mansfield, MA: ISCE.

Heifetz, R. A., & Laurie, D. L. (1997). The Work of Leadership. *Harvard Business Review*, 75, 124–134.

Jackson, B., & Parry, K. (2012). *A Very Short, Fairly Interesting and Reasonably Cheap Book about Studying Leadership*. Thousand Oaks, CA: SAGE Publications, Inc.

Lichtenstein, B. B., Uhl-Bien, M., Marion, R., Seers, A., Orton, J. D., & Schreiber, C. (2006). Complexity Leadership Theory: An interactive perspective on leading in complex adaptive systems. *Emergence: Complexity and Organization*, 8(4), 2–12.

Lowhorn, G. L. (2011). A Confirmatory Factor Analysis of the Leadership Attitudes and Beliefs Scale-III. *International Journal of Arts and Sciences*, 4(6), 284–296.

Marion, R., & Uhl-Bien, M. (2001). Leadership in complex organizations. *The Leadership Quarterly*, 12(4), 389–418.

Ospina, S., Foldy, E. G., El Hadidy, W., Dodge, J., Hofmann-Pinilla, A., & Su, C. (2012). Social Change Leadership as Relational Leadership. In M. Uhl-Bien & S. Ospina (Eds), *Advancing Relational Leadership Research: A dialogue among perspectives* (pp. 255–302). Charlotte, NC: Information Age Publishers.

Pearce, C., & Sims, H. (2002). Vertical Versus Shared Leadership as Predictors of the Effectiveness of Change Management Teams: An examination of aversive, directive, transactional, transformational, and empowering leader behaviors. *Group Dynamics: Theory, Research, and Practice*, 6(2), 172–197.

Price Waterhouse Coopers. (2011). Millennials at Work: Reshaping the workplace. Retrieved from: www.pwc.com/m1/en/services/consulting/documents/millennials-at-work.pdf.

Regine, B., & Lewin, R. (2000). Leading at the Edge: How leaders influence complex systems. *Emergence: Complexity and Organization*, 2(2), 5–23.

Richardson, K. A., Cilliers, P., & Lissack, M. (2001). Complexity Science. *Emergence*, 3(2), 6–18.

Rost, J. C. (1997). Moving from Individual to Relationship: A postindustrial paradigm of leadership. *Journal of Leadership & Organizational Studies*, 4(4), 3–16.

Safrit, R. D., & Owen, M. B. (2010). A Conceptual Model for Retaining County Extension Program Professionals. *Journal of Extension*, 48(10), Article 2FEA2. Retrieved from: www.joe.org/joe/2010april/pdf/JOE_v48_2a2.pdf.

Satterwhite, R. (2010). Deep Systems Leadership: A model for the 21st century. In B. W. Redekop (Ed.), *Leadership for Environmental Sustainability* (pp. 230–243). New York & London: Routledge.

Schawbel, D. (2013, December 16). 10 Ways Millennials Are Creating the Future of Work. *Forbes*. Retrieved from: www.forbes.com/sites/danschawbel/2013/12/16/10-ways-millennials-are-creating-the-future-of-work/.

Selznick, P. (1997). *Leadership in Administration: A sociological interpretation*. Oxford: Oxford University Press.

Uhl-Bien, M., Marion, R., & McKelvey, B. (2007). Complexity Leadership Theory: Shifting leadership from the industrial age to the knowledge era. *The Leadership Quarterly*, 18(4), 298–318.

Uhl-Bien, M., & Marion, R. (2009). Complexity Leadership in Bureaucratic Forms of Organizing: A meso model. *The Leadership Quarterly*, 20(4), 631–650.

United Kingdom Parliament. (2017). Churchill and the Commons Chamber. Retrieved from: www.parliament.uk/about/livingheritage/building/palace/architecture/palacestructure/churchill/.

Western, S. (2010). Eco-leadership: Toward the development of a new paradigm. In B. W. Redekop (Ed.), *Leadership for Environmental Sustainability* (pp. 36–54). New York: Routledge.

Western, S. (2013). *Leadership: A Critical Text*. Thousand Oaks, CA: SAGE Publications, Inc.

Wielkiewicz, R. M. (2000). The Leadership Attitudes and Beliefs Scale: An instrument for evaluating college students' thinking about leadership and organizations. *Journal of College Student Development*, 41(3), 335–347.

Wielkiewicz, R. M. (2002). Validity of the Leadership Attitudes and Beliefs Scale: Relationships with personality, communal orientation, and social desirability. *Journal of College Student Development*, 43(1), 108–118.

Wielkiewicz, R. M., & Stelzner, S. P. (2005). An Ecological Perspective on Leadership Theory, Research, and Practice. *Review of General Psychology*, 9(4), 326–341. doi:10.1037/1089-2680.9.4.326.

Wielkiewicz, R. M., & Stelzner, S. P. (2010). An Ecological Perspective on Leadership Theory, Research, and Practice. In B. W. Redekop (Ed.), *Leadership for Environmental Sustainability* (pp. 36–54). New York & London: Routledge.

6 Toward an Understanding of the Relationship Between the Study of Leadership and the Natural World

Robert M. McManus

Introduction

Several years ago, I had the opportunity to hike Peru's Salkantay trail that ends at the famed ruins of Machu Picchu. The five-day pilgrimage led my fellow travelers and me past snow-capped mountains, through lush rain forests, and across the raging Urubamba River. The path summits at 15,500 feet above sea level (4,724.4 meters). At the time, I was in my early 40s, so I was one of the oldest people in our group of mostly 20-something college students. Where they seemed to effortlessly skip like young mountain goats across the rocks and gorges on our path, I staggered and plodded along, gasping for breath. Our guide, Carlos, who truly was impervious to the effects of the altitude, would run ahead with the students and then circle back to provide me with company and encouragement until we made it to camp, sometimes hours after our fellow travelers. In those hours alone together on the trail, Carlos and I developed a rapport.

On the fourth day, we stumbled into a little cantina near the end of the trail that served hikers winding up their journey. I bought everyone in our group a cold beer to celebrate nearing the end of our excursion. I made a brief toast and thanked my guide and fellow hikers for their patience during our time together. We all quickly raised our bottles and began to enjoy our well-earned libation. Our guide, however, did something unexpected. Before he took a sip of his beer, he poured a bit of it on the ground. I was stunned. Why would my new friend waste something as "precious" as a cold beer at the end of such a difficult journey? Carlos explained that it was his way of thanking the Incan goddess Pachamama, the goddess of the earth, for her kindness and generosity on our journey. Indigenous people from the Andes believe Pachamama is angered and problems develop when humans take too much from the earth or take nature for granted. Our guide taught me a valuable lesson that day – one that I believe we must all learn if we are to better understand the relationship between leadership and the natural world. This is something that my Peruvian guide had learned as a child, but it is something that we in the field of leadership need to learn today.

I propose that leadership scholars must more fully incorporate the natural world in their understanding of leadership if we are to better understand the leadership process. In our book, *Understanding Leadership: An Arts and Humanities Perspective* (2015), my co-author Gama Perruci and I provide our readers with a definition of leadership. We argue that leadership is a *process* that incorporates several components that function together to produce the phenomenon we call "leadership." These components include the leader, the followers, the goal, the context in which the leaders and followers pursue their goal, and the unique cultural values and norms that influence the entire leadership process. Thus, we argue: "Leadership is the process by which leaders and followers develop a relationship and work together towards a goal (or goals) within … . context shaped by cultural values and norms" (McManus & Perruci, 2015, p. 15; Perruci, 2011, p. 83). We call this The Five Components of Leadership Model. What we propose with this model is an architectural plan to better understand and map the field of leadership studies. Rather than proposing to add another "brick" to the leadership literature – that is, another particular theory – we suggest that the many theories of leadership can fit into the Five Components of Leadership Model to make better sense of the field and add to our overall understanding of the leadership process.

Review of Relevant Literature

Most leadership scholars are familiar with these five components of leadership, but they are usually studied in isolation. For example, many theorists have spent considerable time studying the particular traits or behaviors of leaders forming a "leader-centric" approach to the study of leadership, such as trait, behavior, and charismatic leadership theories (e.g., Blake & Mouton, 1964; House, 1976; Stogdill, 1948). Likewise, the study of followership has grown a great deal in recent years as scholars have recognized the importance of followers to the leadership process (e.g., Chaleff, 2009; Kellerman, 2008; Kelley, 1988; Riggio, Chaleff, & Lipman-Blumen, 2008). The relationship between the leader and the follower has also been analyzed with theories such as Leader–Member Exchange Theory, Transformational Leadership, and Servant Leadership (e.g., Bass & Avolio, 1994; Graen & Uhl-Bien, 1995; Greenleaf, 1970). Many scholars have focused upon leaders and followers achieving the goal, which is the heart of the leadership process, such as Path-Goal Theory and Contingency Theory (e.g., Fiedler, 1967; House & Mitchell, 1974). Organizational scholars have long examined the contextual factors influencing leadership, such as the way an organizational or political culture may affect leadership in a particular situation (e.g., Bolman & Deal, 2013; Kellerman, 2015; Schein 2016). Likewise, cultural theorists have recently paid increasing attention to the effect culture has upon the leadership process (e.g., Hofstede, 2001; House et al., 2004; Trompenaars & Hampden-Turner, 2012). All of these components of

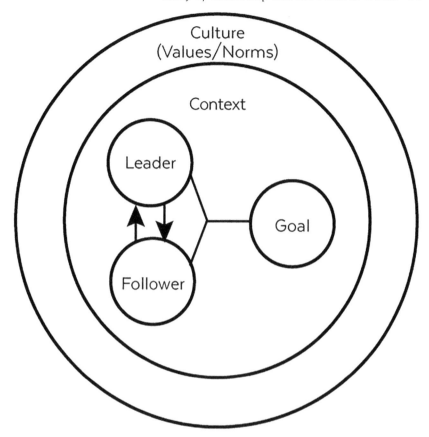

Figure 6.1 The Five Components of Leadership Model
Source: Reprinted with permission of the publisher. From *Understanding Leadership: An Arts and Humanities Perspective*, copyright © by Robert M. McManus and Gama Perruci, Routledge, Abingdon. All rights reserved.

leadership are readily acknowledged in the journals and textbooks in the field of leadership studies (e.g., Northouse, 2016; Yukl, 2013). *What has not been generally acknowledged is the role the natural environment plays in the leadership process.* However, there are some exceptions to this observation.

There are scholars in the field of leadership studies who have previously identified a relationship between leadership and the natural environment, at least tangentially or as an emerging area of interest. Benjamin Redekop provides an extensive literature review of this scholarship in his edited volume *Leadership for Environmental Sustainability* (2010, pp. 1–8). Other scholars have more directly linked the study of leadership and the natural world. For example, Peter Senge specifically identifies the natural world as a vital aspect of systems thinking (Senge, 2006; Senge et al., 2010), and Mark Van Vugt (2012) links leadership to evolutionary biology.

More recently, Deborah Gallagher (2012) assembled a two-volume text, *Environmental Leadership: A Reference Handbook,* that brings together a variety of scholars from multiple disciplines who present a wide range of perspectives to study the connection between leadership and the natural world. Gallagher defines environmental leadership as "a process by which Earth's inhabitants apply interpersonal influence and engage in collective action to protect the planet's natural resources and its inhabitants from further harm" (2012, p. 5). Gallagher's text presents a wealth of literature on environmental leadership, and has become a definitive text for those who study environmental leadership. *What I am proposing here, however, is that the natural world not be seen as a component of only environmental leadership, but as a vital component of the general phenomenon of leadership.*

There are two chapters in Redekop's anthology mentioned earlier that are of particular importance to our discussion here. The first is Simon Western's (2010) chapter "Eco-Leadership: Towards the Development of a New Paradigm." In his chapter, Western summarizes and builds upon the concept of "eco-leadership" that he originally presented in his *Leadership: A Critical Text* (2008/2013). Although Western is quick to point out that his focus on the natural world is not the exclusive emphasis of his theory, he does acknowledge the natural world as playing a part in the process of leadership and the "reciprocal relationship between leadership and its environment" (p. 36). The other chapter found in Redekop's anthology that is of particular relevance to our discussion of the connection between the process of leadership and the natural world is Rian Satterwhite's (2010) "Deep Systems Leadership: A Model for the 21st Century". Satterwhite's Deep Systems Leadership emphasizes the couplings between systems and their environments, people and systems, and the environment and people. These couplings form intersections between systems theory, deep ecologies, and systemic leadership, which Satterwhite places within the broadest context of cultural biology. Satterwhite's model directly ties the *broad* practice of leadership to the natural world and serves as an impetus for the argument presented in this chapter. However, what I propose to do in this chapter is to somewhat simplify Satterwhite's basic thesis and place the process of leadership directly in the context and constraints of the natural world.

The Connection Between Leadership and the Natural World

Let me begin my argument with a syllogism – a basic argument with a major premise, a minor premise, and a conclusion:

Major Premise: Human beings are a part of nature, and, thus, operate within and are constrained by the natural world.
Minor Premise: Leadership is a universal human process.
Conclusion: Consequently, the process of leadership operates within and is constrained by the natural world.

Let us first begin with our major premise: "Human beings are a part of nature, and, thus, operate within and are constrained by the natural world." Darwin's seminal text *On the Origin of the Species* (1859/2008) proposed biological evolution as a grand biological system directly tying humanity to the natural world. Twelve years later in his book *The Descent of Man* (1871/2004), Darwin focused on the processes that led to the development of human beings. Here Darwin made it clear that he thought that human thinking and actions, as well as our physical characteristics, have an evolutionary origin. Rather than conceiving human beings as *above* nature – or "a little lower than the angels" – as did those who held a religious view of the cosmos before him, Darwin made the argument that human beings were *a part of nature* and subject to all of its physical processes. Scientists now widely accept this principle. Biologist and Pulitzer Prize winner E.O. Wilson encapsulates this point when he states:

> Nature is the birthright of everyone on Earth. The millions of species we have allowed to survive are our phylogenetic kin. Their long-term history is our long-term history. Despite all our fantasies and pretensions, we always have been and will remain a biological species tied to this particular biological world.
>
> (Wilson, 2014, p. 132)

More recently, leadership scholars have echoed Darwin's and Wilson's claim as they have explored the embodiment of leadership in contexts ranging from a leader's physical environment to neuroscience (e.g., Ropo & Parviainen, 2001; Waldman et al., 2011). These authors and studies support my major premise that human beings are subject to the constraints of the natural world just as is the rest of the universe. To think otherwise is to remove human beings from their natural embodied context, thus ignoring the interdependency between human beings and their environment and disregarding the relationship between leadership and the natural world. At first blush, this statement may seem self-evident – indeed, I believe it is – however, *leadership practitioners and scholars have overlooked this fundamental fact for too long, adding to our present climate crisis.* We will return to this idea later in this chapter, but for now, we must establish our minor premise, which is "Leadership is a universal human process."

Our minor premise is more directly related to leadership. Perruci and I also propose "For leadership studies ... the central intellectual focus revolves around human beings' purposeful interaction" (McManus & Perruci, 2015, p. 17). It is worth taking some time to unpack this statement. The first concept that needs some explanation is what is meant by "purposeful interaction." Refer back to the definition of leadership provided earlier in this chapter: "Leadership is the process by which leaders and followers develop a relationship and work together towards a goal (or goals) within a context shaped by cultural values and norms." This is an often-overlooked ubiquitous process. Some illustrations immediately come to mind. For example, a coach (leader) working with a team (followers) to win game three (goal) of the national championship (context) of the Brazilian Football Confederation (cultural values and norms) is leadership. Similarly, a CEO (leader) motivating her employees (followers) to develop a new product and bring it to market (goal) in the technology industry (context) that faces competition from domestic and foreign markets (cultural values and norms) is also leadership. What we often fail to recognize is the more quotidian forms of leadership, such as that of a parent (leader) helping a child (follower) to complete the child's project (goal) for the local middle school science fair (context) in a highly competitive school district in Japan (cultural values and norms); *this is also leadership.* One thus does not have to venture into the confines of a national football stadium or a Fortune 500 company to find leadership. The phenomenon is a part of our daily lives. This is not to say that non-human animals do not practice leadership (see Van Vugt, 2012), but leadership studies most often conceive of leadership as a *human* process, and this is the focus of our discussion here. Now that we have explored our minor premise, let us turn our attention to our conclusion: The process of leadership operates within and is constrained by the natural world.

One way to conceptualize the ubiquitous nature of leadership and its relationship to the natural world is found in the duality between action and motion. Action is marked by intentionality and free choice as an expression of one's values. This places the leadership process squarely in the realm of action. Motion, contrarily, is marked by the natural world and a *lack of intentionality.* Events may *happen* in the natural world that can be seen, for example, bodily functions performed by the respiratory and circulatory system or rain falling, but there is *no intent* to such events. *However, this difference is not to disregard the fact that motion is still a fundamental requirement for action. This fact also does not preclude leader and follower agency – self-awareness and free will – that separates leaders and followers from the context and allows for purposeful interaction.*

As we have established, the central focus of leadership can be conceptualized as human beings' *purposeful interaction.* If we were to once again refer to the examples listed above – the football team, technology company, and the parent and child – these actions imply an explicit or implicit purpose to the interaction between leaders and followers. Once again referring to our examples above, the football team must have the physical ability to play the game (motion) if they are to win the championship (action). The CEO and employees experience hunger (motion); they may find a variety of ways to feed themselves, but they choose to do so by producing a particular good to sell to consumers (action). The parent and child must have the required cognition (motion) if they are to present a successful experiment at the science fair (action). This inter-linkage between action and motion can be summarized thus:

(A) There is no action without motion.
(B) There is motion without action.
(C) Action is not reducible to motion.

(Burke, 1978, 1989)

Said another way:

(A) There is no leadership without the natural world.
(B) The natural world exists without leadership.
(C) Leadership is not reducible to the natural world.

The key to the relationship between leadership and the natural world is found in the first point: *There is no action without motion, and there is no leadership without the natural world.*

The Five Components of Leadership and their Relationship to the Natural World

Now that we have established our syllogism, let us turn our attention to the way the natural world manifests itself in each of the other five components of leadership.

Leader

As we discussed above, the literature surrounding the embodiment of leadership has grown a great deal in recent years. This literature draws our attention to the fact that leaders are living, breathing human beings, and that their corporeal bodies have an effect upon the leadership process. The International Leadership Association recently recognized this trend in the field of leadership studies in their annual Building Leadership Bridges' volume *The Embodiment of Leadership* (2013), in which the contributors explore the embodiment of leadership in a number of contexts. The volume's editor observes:

> In life, leaders have bodies that think, move, act, have emotions and desires, age, hurt, and sense. The corporality [*sic*] is raced, gendered, cultured, sexual, instinctual, and emotional. Too often, however, in both academic literature and mainstream media, leaders are treated as disembodied, their leadership qualities referred to in ways that not only suggest leadership involves only cerebral functions but fail to recognize that cerebral functions originate and are actualized in the body.
>
> (Melina, 2013, p. xiii)

This idea is echoed in the literature surrounding trait leadership and attribution theory and its relationship to leadership; e.g., does a person "look" like a leader? (Re et al., 2013). This may take on an explicitly physical dimension, such as in the studies that have illustrated the role that one's physical height may play in an election (Lawson et al., 2010). Likewise, the more subtle forms of physicality, such as body language, facial expression, and vocalics may play a role in the way leaders are perceived and their ability to relate to and motivate followers (Riggio & Feldman, 2005). The literature cited here illustrates just a few of the ways the leadership process is tied to the natural world. Leaders are intimately tied to their corporeal bodies. Critics may say that this is self-evident. However, most scholars in the field of leadership studies have for too long failed to recognize the material limits in which the process of leadership operates. This failure has consequences that we will examine later in this chapter. For now, we turn to the way the natural world encompasses followers.

Followers

Just as leaders are tied to the natural world through their physical bodies, so are followers. However, there are other facets of followership that further illustrate this point. To further understand the constraints the natural world places on followers, we turn to two early theories of human motivation developed by Abraham Maslow and Frederick Hertzberg.

Those familiar with the field of leadership studies know that there is a rich river of thought that runs from the field of psychology. Maslow developed one of the germinal theories laying the foundation for the psychological study of leadership and followership in his 1943 article "A Theory of Human Motivation." In his article, Maslow proposed his Hierarchy of Needs Pyramid. Many are familiar with this theory; the basic thesis is that people must have their most basic level needs met before they can hope to pursue their higher-level needs. Leaders and followers must meet their basic physiological needs at the bottom of the pyramid (food, water, warmth, rest), along with their need for safety and security, before they can hope to meet their psychological needs, such as love and belonging or their need for self-esteem. These needs must be met before either leaders or followers can hope to meet their need for self-actualization and experience their full potential located at the top of Maslow's pyramid. Although there is room for moving up and down the pyramid as the context changes, the basic premise is that people's natural needs must be met before they can hope to achieve their higher-level needs (Maslow, 1943).

Another theory that reinforces this point can be found in Frederick Hertzberg's *Work and the Nature of Man* (1966) in which the author identifies two forms of human motivation: hygiene factors and motivation factors. Hygiene factors include company policy, supervision, interpersonal relations, working conditions, and salary as basic needs for personal satisfaction. In some ways, this list mirrors Maslow's basic and mid-level needs. If a person does not make enough of a salary to put food on the table, is fearful for their safety on the job, or does not enjoy the people with whom they interact on a day-to-day basis, they are not having their physiological, safety, and love and belonging needs met. If these needs are not met, followers will be dissatisfied. However, Hertzberg argues that these factors alone are not enough to motivate followers. Followers also have motivators to make them *want* to follow the leader and pursue a goal – factors such as achievement, recognition, the work itself, responsibility, and advancement. These needs correspond to Maslow's higher-level needs of self-esteem and self-actualization. Hertzberg summarizes this duality:

> The human animal has two categories of needs. One set stems from his animal disposition, that side of him previously referred to as the Adam view of man [based upon the Biblical myth of the Garden of Eden]; it is centered on the avoidance of loss of life, hunger, pain, sexual deprivation, and on other primary drives, in addition to the infinite varieties of learned fears that become attached to these basic drives. The other segment of man's nature, according to the Abraham concept of the human being [based upon the Biblical founder of the monotheistic religions of Judaism, Christianity and Islam], is man's compelling urge to realize his own potentiality by continuous psychological growth … If man is to be understood properly, these two characteristics must be constantly viewed as having separate biological, psychological and existential origins.
>
> (Herzberg, 1966, p. 56)

These are two basic theories of follower motivation that illustrate the point that followers must first have their needs met in the natural world before they can hope to engage in the leadership process to achieve a goal. This is not unlike the difference between motion and action that we discussed earlier in which motion was tied to the natural world, and action was tied to purposeful interaction. In short, motion animates; action motivates, but you cannot have action without motion. I reference these two well-known theories of human motivation simply to illustrate a point: just like leaders, followers are tied to the natural world and cannot engage in the leadership process effectively without considering the constraints imposed upon them by the natural world. We now turn our attention to the next component in our model, the goal.

Goal

The goal is that portion of the Five Components model that unites leaders and followers in a common purpose. It is also the linchpin in the argument that claims the central focus of leadership revolves around human beings' purposeful interaction. There are some obvious ways in which goals are tied to the natural world. Once again, we refer to our examples of a Brazilian soccer team winning a championship, a technology company producing a product for market, and a parent and a child working to produce a project for a science fair. In the case of the technology company, the link to the natural world is explicit. Leaders and followers work together to create a physical object to sell to consumers. This process is constrained by the availability of the natural resources needed to produce the object. Likewise, in the example of a parent and child working to produce a project for a science fair, the resources available place a constraint upon the project. The example of the Brazilian football team is a bit different. True, there is a great deal of physicality needed to achieve the goal of winning the championship. There is also likely a financial reward tied to the accomplishment; thus, there is a reasonable tie to the natural world, but the championship itself is not so much about a physical object, such as a trophy or a financial reward, as much as it is about the pride that comes from winning the title. Likewise, in the examples of the technology company, both leaders and followers may be motivated by the importance of their work and the contribution they can make to science and technology as much as, or even more than, the physical product they are creating. The parent working with a child to complete the science fair project probably does not care so much for the project itself as much as the parent cherishes the time he or she can spend with the child, or the knowledge that the child gains from doing the project. Where does the natural world fit into these less tangible and more altruistic and emotional/personal goals?

These more altruistic and emotional factors often seem more important to leaders and followers than do the physical goals they may be attempting to achieve. Can human goals be reduced to exclusively meeting physiological purposes? Perhaps not, but that does not mean that altruistic and emotional factors are not rooted in the natural world. Many scholars have asked why humans seem to possess pro-social qualities, such as altruism, that do not seem to comport immediately with the broad concept of natural selection. Although there is a plurality of reasons for this kind of phenomenon, many of them come from the field of biological science. For example, Darwin argued that such pro-social traits gave tribes a natural advantage over other tribes (Darwin, 1871/2004). Likewise, various authors since Darwin's time have argued that such pro-social traits help enable group selection and adaptation, although their ultimate explanations for such traits may differ (Wilson, 1975; Dawkins, 2004). Likewise, even emotions as complex as love may have a biological basis in an evolutionary social contract between persons within groups and protection of oneself and one's progeny, in addition to cultural and environmental influences that may influence such emotions (Dawkins, 2004; Pinker, 1997, 2003.) One scholar argues:

> Darwin's theory of evolution through natural selection (1871) makes clear that human psychology is ultimately a product of biological evolution – in the same way that our bodies are evolutionary products – consisting of many different traits that evolved because they enable our

ancestors to cope better with the demands of the environments in which they were living.

(Van Vugt, 2012, p. 142)

This is not to imply that all goals are based exclusively in the realm of motion. The way one chooses to reach a goal and one's responses to the emotion attached to obtaining or not obtaining a goal is certainly within the realm of action. Nevertheless, altruistic and emotional action is *grounded* in the realm of motion, as we have described earlier. Leaders and followers developing a relationship and working toward a goal is a part of the process of leadership, but that is only a portion of our model; we must also consider the next component of the Five Components of Leadership Model.

Context

Leadership does not occur in a vacuum. We must also consider the context in which this process takes place. When considering context and its relationship to the natural world, we will consider the immediate framework in which the leaders and followers pursue their goal and work our way out to the larger systems that encompass this process. Let us once again consider our recurring examples. The Brazilian soccer team may practice for their games on a green field set within a grand stadium in downtown Rio de Janeiro. The technology company may be a startup in a small office somewhere in the heart of Silicon Valley, whereas the parent and child may be working on their science project at a kitchen table in their home located in a suburb of Tokyo. Each of these contexts possesses its own unique organizational culture that is a part of any team, working group, or family, as organizational leadership scholar Edgar Schein observes (Schein, 2016).

Certainly, these micro-cultures affect the way these leaders and followers go about reaching their goal, as well as the general climate and working norms within these organizations. On a larger scale, however, each of these organizations are members of much larger systems with a wide variety of stakeholders. The Brazilian football team is just one team among many in the Brazilian Football League, complete with the coaches, players, employees, fans, and bars and restaurants that make their living through their connection to the team. The technology company may produce a product that might potentially affect the lives millions of consumers, not to mention its connection to global manufacturers and supply chains. Even the little family working away the evening at their kitchen table somewhere in the suburbs of Tokyo is connected to a web of organizations throughout the world that may be exhibited in the physical objects in the home – from the materials for their project, to the chairs on which they sit, to the music on the radio. These scenarios are to simply illustrate the complexity of the open systems of which we are all a part (Senge, 2006; Wheatley, 2006). What we often fail to realize, however, is the way the natural world relates to these systems.

However, a growing number of individuals and organizations are beginning to understand the importance of the natural world. As more organizations now acknowledge their corporate social responsibility, the natural
world is increasingly being acknowledged as a major stakeholder for these
organizations (Enkvist et al., 2008; World Commission on Environment and
Development, 1987). For example, consider the thousands of paper cups
used at an average football game and their impact on landfills, the petroleum products used to power global manufacturing and supply chains, and
even the amount of resources used and energy consumed by a single family.
These organizations all take much more than they give to the natural world.
As organizations become more aware of their impact upon the environment,
they are increasingly starting to acknowledge the inputs and outputs that are
a part of the grand systems of which they are a part. Satterwhite, Miller,
and Sheridan echo this when they say: "Natural systems surround and define
our lives. We are active participants in them. Indeed, any sense of separation
from them is false; we *are* them and they *are* us" (Satterwhite, Miller, &
Sheridan, 2015, p. 61). (Emphasis in the original.)

One line of research that illustrates this well is found in Evolutionary
Leadership Theory (ELT). This line of research calls on fields such as evolutionary theory, biology, social neuroscience, and neurosciences to examine
the biological implications of leadership. Scholars in this field argue that
leadership and followership are products of biological processes, adaptation,
and natural selection that help ensure the survival of the species (Van Vugt,
2012; Van Vugt & Ahuja, 2011; Van Vugt et al., 2008).

Hence, leadership and followership are natural extensions of the evolutionary
process and part of the natural world. Although we may comprehend this,
most leaders and followers do not appreciate the larger ecological systems of
which we are a part, which points to the need for an ecologically-informed
leadership theory and practice.

Cultural Values and Norms

Thus far we have examined four components of our model and their connection to the natural world. We now turn to examine the fifth component in
our model, cultural values and norms. As briefly mentioned above, leadership scholars such as Edward Hall, Geert Hofstede, Fonz Trompenaars, and
Robert House have explored the way culture affects the leadership process
(Hall, 1973; Hofstede, 2001; House et al., 2004; Trompenaars & Hampden-
Turner, 2012). These theorists have examined elements of culture such as
individualism and collectivism, power distance, and performance orientation, among others. Perhaps the cultural theorists who have had the most to
say about the connection between a culture's view of leadership and its
connection to the environment are Trompenaars and Hampden-Turner.
These scholars propose that cultures have two basic ways they relate to
nature: those cultures that hold an internal locus of control and those

cultures that hold an external locus of control. Those cultures that have more of an internal locus of control believe they can control their environment to reach their goals, whereas those cultures that have an external locus of control believe that their environment controls them and that they must work with the environment to reach their goals (Trompenaars & Hampden-Turner, 2012.)

Although there are many ways this theory can be interpreted, we can use this division as a starting point to examine the different ways cultures may view the natural world in the leadership process. We started our conversation with a classic example of this dichotomy. My guide, Carlos, possessed an external locus of control. He believed we were to *work with nature* and be careful to respect it and treat it well if we were to have a safe journey and complete our hike. As a Westerner, I possessed more of an internal locus of control. If we completed our hike, it was because we had the fortitude to soldier on and subdue nature. Remember, I toasted myself and my fellow pilgrims and our strength in completing our journey; Carlos toasted Pachamama for her benevolence.

There are some cultures that are more inclined to acknowledge the role of the environment in the leadership process than are others. The example above illustrates this point. However, all cultures have an ethic of environmental responsibility that can be called upon to compel leaders and followers to more fully consider the natural world in the leadership process. Many times, this ethic can be found in the realm of religion. The monotheistic religions of Judaism, Christianity, and Islam have rich histories and current philosophies that call for the thoughtful stewardship of nature (Blanchard & O'Brian, 2014; Foltz et al., 2003; Francis, 2016; Yaffe, 2001). Likewise, Eastern wisdom traditions such as Hinduism, Buddhism, Taoism, and Confucianism also have traditions that honor the natural world (Jenkins et al., 2017); as do Native American and other indigenous cultures (Holthaus, 2013; Marchand & Vogt, 2016). Religion is just one way scholars and practitioners can better understand the link between the environment and cultural values and norms, but it does help to further illustrate the natural world's connection to the leadership process. It is important to remember Lao Tzu's admonition in the *Tao te Ching*: "Man is ruled by the earth" (Stenudd, 2015, p. 123).

For too long leadership scholars have failed to fully acknowledge the natural world as a fundamental part of the broad context in which leadership takes place. As mentioned above, most leadership scholars have only briefly touched upon this topic or identified it as an emerging trend or of tangential interest to the field of leadership studies. This is a blind spot in the discipline (Redekop, 2010, p. 2). We now turn to a potential remedy to this problem. There are a variety of ways scholars can visualize the role of the natural world in the leadership process. I am proposing here a model to further develop our understanding of this connection, and to encourage other scholars to critically analyze this model and its heuristic potential.

The Natural World as a Sixth Component of Leadership

Building upon the Five Components of Leadership Model presented throughout this chapter, I propose the natural world be conceived as having *an equal role as the other five components of the model, thus revising the model to a Six Components of Leadership Model.* Here once again is our proposed revised definition of leadership: "Leadership is the process by which leaders and followers develop a relationship and work together towards a goal (or goals) within a context shaped by cultural values and norms, *and functions within and is constrained by the natural world.*" We can picture this with a circle labeled "natural world" encompassing the other components of the model as was presented earlier in this chapter.

The implication of Figure 6.2 above is that the natural world is just as much a part of the process of leadership as is the leader, the follower, the

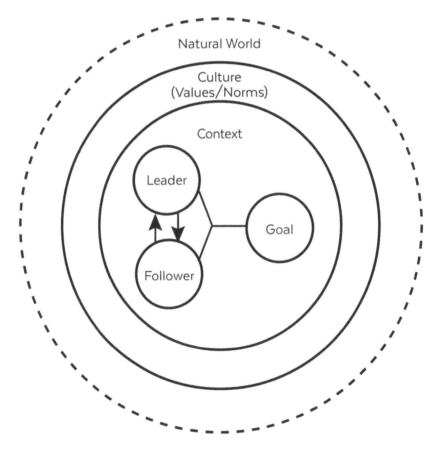

Figure 6.2 The Five Components of Leadership Model Set Within the Natural World
Source: Reprinted with permission of the publisher. From *Understanding Leadership: An Arts and Humanities Perspective*, copyright © by Robert M. McManus and Gama Perruci, Routledge, Abingdon. All rights reserved. Alteration made with permission from the authors.

goal, the context, and the cultural values and norms that we have discussed in this chapter. Certainly, such a definition and representation of leadership highlights the important role the natural world plays in the leadership process. As we have seen in this chapter, the natural world touches upon every other aspect of the model. Such a definition of leadership would also encourage leadership practitioners to more fully consider the natural world when making all sorts of leadership decisions.

Another aspect of this definition is that it identifies the natural world as a constraint imposed upon the leadership process. Leaders and followers can only reach their goals inasmuch as the natural world allows. We are all a part of nature; ultimately, nature can exist without human beings, but human beings cannot exist without nature. Depicting the natural world as a part of the leadership process in this way emphasizes this fact.

Critics of this approach may argue that the natural world does not exert as much influence as do other aspects of the model, such as the leader. Leadership is essentially situational. If a goal does not directly affect the natural world, should the natural world be considered as a component of leadership writ large? There is a difference between a football team deciding to use recycled cups at their concession stands, a technology company deciding to use carbon neutral power, and a family spending an evening working away at their kitchen table on a child's science project. Critics may also argue that humankind has, indeed, harnessed nature on many occasions, such as by building dams, creating means of refrigeration and heating, and even through geothermal and solar power. Can scholars really claim that nature constrains the leadership process with the myriad of examples that may suggest otherwise? Those responding to this criticism might argue that these critics miss the point: all of the other components of leadership are a part of the natural world, and to think otherwise is to dismiss the limitations the natural world imposes as well as the opportunities it provides.

Critics of the model might also ask why it is so important to consider the natural world as a part of the leadership process? One might reply that anthropogenic climate change, air and water pollution, overpopulation, loss of biodiversity, deforestation, and ocean acidification are just a few of the "wicked" problems that leaders and followers have created by not considering the natural world when attempting to achieve their goals. Thoughtless leadership created these problems; thoughtful leadership must seek to correct them. If leaders continue to fail to address the natural world as a vital part of the leadership process, the problems humans have created will ultimately place the human species itself in jeopardy as we enter the period of the earth's six great extinction. Some may say that it is already too late to reverse many of the problems that humans have created. Regardless, leadership scholars and practitioners have a responsibility to fully consider the natural world as an integral part of the leadership process if our species and others will have any hope of long-term survival.

Conclusion

In this chapter, we examined the role the natural world plays in the leadership process. We also explored the way leadership is a pervasive human process that is distinguished by purposeful action, but is animated by natural motion. In so doing, we used McManus and Perruci's Five Components of Leadership Model to consider the way leaders, followers, goals, contexts, and cultural values and norms relate to the natural world. Finally, we considered adding the natural world as a vital component of leadership and suggested that it be acknowledged as a vital sixth component to the leadership process. As we conclude, I encourage other leadership scholars and practitioners to consider what I have proposed here as they research, test, and practice leadership. What I have proposed is what I hope to be a part of continuing conversation regarding the way scholars and practitioners can better understand the role of the natural world in the leadership process and address the multitude of problems our failure to acknowledge this fundamental fact has created. I close with the words of the biologist E.O. Wilson: "Perhaps the time has come to cease calling it the 'environmentalist' view, as though it were a lobbying effort outside the mainstream of human activity, and to start calling it the real-world view" (2003, p. 28). Perhaps the time has also come to cease calling the incorporation of the natural world into the process of leadership simply "environmental leadership" and start calling it real-world leadership.

References

Bass, B.M., & Avolio, B.J. (1994). *Improving Organizational Effectiveness through Transformational Leadership*. Thousand Oaks, CA: SAGE Publications, Inc.

Blake, R.R., & Mouton, J.S. (1964). *The Managerial Grid*. Houston, TX: Gulf Publishing Company.

Blanchard, K.D., & O'Brian, K.J. (2014). *An Introduction to Christian Environmentalism: Ecology, virtue, and ethics*. Waco, TX: Baylor University Press.

Bolman, L.G., & Deal, T.E. (2013). *Reframing Organizations* (5th ed.). San Francisco, CA: Jossey-Bass.

Burke, K. (1978). (Nonsymbolic) Motion/(Symbolic) Action. *Critical Inquiry*, 4(4), 809–838.

Burke, K. (1989). The Nature of Human Action. In J. R. Gusfield (Ed.), *Kenneth Burke: On symbols and society* (pp. 53–55). Chicago, IL: University of Chicago Press.

Chaleff, I. (2009). *The Courageous Follower: Standing up to and for our leaders* (3rd ed.). San Francisco, CA: Berrett-Koehler Publishers.

Darwin, C. (1859/2008). *The Origin of Species*. New York: Bantam Dell.

Darwin, C. (1871/2004). *The Descent of Man*. London: Penguin Books.

Dawkins, R. (1976/2004). *The Selfish Gene* (4th ed.). Oxford: Oxford University Press.

Enkvist, P., Nauclér, T., & Oppenheim, J. M. (2008). Business Strategies for Climate Change. *The McKinsey Quarterly*, 2, 24–33.

Fiedler, F.E. (1967). *A Theory of Leadership Effectiveness.* New York: McGraw-Hill.

Foltz, R.C., Denny, F.M., & Baharuddin, A. (Eds) (2003). *Islam and Ecology: A bestowed trust.* Cambridge, MA: Center for the Study of World Religions.

Francis, Pope. (2016). *Laudato Sí: Praise be to you: On care for our common home.* North Palm Beach, FL and Erlanger, KY: Beacon Publishing/Dynamic Catholic Institute.

Gallagher, D. R. (2012). *Environmental Leadership: A reference handbook* (2 Vols.). Thousand Oaks, CA: SAGE Publications, Inc.

Graen, G. B., & Uhl-Bien, M. (1995). Relationship-Based Approach to Leadership: Development of a leader–member exchange (LMX) theory of leadership over 25 years: Applying a multi-level, multi-domain perspective. *Leadership Quarterly*, 6 (2), 219–247.

Greenleaf, R.K. (1970). *The Servant as Leader.* Westfield, IN: Greenleaf Center for Servant Leadership.

Hall, E.T. (1973). *The Silent Language.* New York: Random House.

Herzberg, F. (1966). *Work and the Nature of Man.* Cleveland, OH: World Publishing Company.

Hofstede, G. (2001). *Culture's Consequences: Comparing values, behaviors, institutions, and organizations across nations* (2nd ed.). Thousand Oaks, CA: SAGE Publications, Inc.

Holthaus, G. (2008/2013). *Learning Native Wisdom: What traditional cultures teach us about subsistence, sustainability, and spiritualty.* Lexington: University Press of Kentucky.

House, R.J. (1976). A 1976 Theory of Charismatic Leadership. In J. G. Hunt & L. L. Larson (Eds), *Leadership: The cutting edge* (pp. 189–207). Carbondale, IL: Southern Illinois University Press.

House, R.J., Hanges, P.J., Javidan, M., Dorfman, P.W., & Gupta, V. (2004). *Culture, Leadership, and Organizations: The globe study of 62 societies.* Thousand Oaks, CA: SAGE Publications, Inc.

House, R.J., & Mitchell, R.R. (1974). Path-Goal Theory of Leadership. *Journal of Contemporary Business*, 3, 81–97.

Jenkins, W., Tucker, M.E., & Grim, J. (2017). *Routledge Handbook of Religion and Ecology.* Abingdon: Routledge.

Kellerman, B. (2008). *Followership: How followers are creating change and changing leaders.* Boston, MA: Harvard Business Press.

Kellerman, B. (2015). *Hard Times: Leadership in America.* Stanford, CA: Stanford Business Books.

Kelley, R. (1988). In Praise of Followers. *Harvard Business Review*, 66(6), 142–148.

Lawson, C., Lenz, G.S., Baker, A., & Myers, M. (2010). Looking like a Winner: Candidate appearance and electoral success in new democracies. *World Politics*, 62(4), 561–593.

Marchand, M.E., & Vogt, K.A. (Eds). (2016). *The River of Life: Sustainable practices of Native Americans and indigenous peoples.* East Lansing, MI: Michigan State University Press.

Maslow, A.H. (1943). A Theory of Human Motivation. *Psychological Review*, 50(4), 370–396.

McManus, R.M., & Perruci, G. (2015). *Understanding Leadership: An arts and humanities perspective.* Abingdon: Routledge.

Melina, L.R., Burgess, G. L., Falkman, L.L., & Marturano, A. (Eds). (2013). *The Embodiment of Leadership*. San Francisco, CA: Jossey-Bass.

Northouse, P.G. (2016). *Leadership: Theory and practice* (7th ed.). Thousand Oaks, CA: SAGE Publications, Inc.

Perruci, G. (2011). Millennials and Globalization: The cross-cultural challenge of intragenerational leadership. *Journal of Leadership Studies*, 5(3), 82–87.

Pinker, S. (1997). *How the Mind Works*. New York: W. W. Norton and Company.

Pinker, S. (2003). *The Blank Slate: The modern denial of human nature*. New York: Penguin Books.

Re, D.E., Hunter, D.W., Coetzee, V., Tiddeman, B.P., Xiao, D., DeBruine, L.M., Jones, B.C., & Perrett, D.I. (2013). Looking Like a Leader: Facial shape predicts perceived height and leadership ability. *Plos One*, 8(12). Retrieved from: http://journals.plos.org/plosone/article?id=10.1371/journal.pone.0080957.

Redekop, B. (Ed.). (2010). *Leadership for Environmental Sustainability*. New York & London: Routledge.

Riggio, R.E., Chaleff, I., & Lipman-Blumen, J. (2008). *The Art of Followership: How great followers create great leaders and organizations*. San Francisco, CA: Jossey-Bass.

Riggio, R.E., & Feldman, R.S. (2005). *Applications of Non-Verbal Communication*. New York: Psychology Press/Routledge.

Ropo, A., & Parviainen, J. (2001). Leadership and Bodily Knowledge in Expert Organizations: Epistemological rethinking. *Scandinavian Journal of Management*, 17(1), 1–18.

Satterwhite, R. (2010). Deep Systems Leadership: A model for the 21st century. In B. Redekop (Ed.), *Leadership for Environmental Sustainability* (pp. 230–242). New York & London: Routledge.

Satterwhite, R., Miller, W.M., & Sheridan, K. (2015). Leadership for Sustainability and Peace: Responding to the wicked challenges of the future. In M. Sowcik, A.C. Andenoro, M. McNutt, & S. Murphy (Eds), *Leadership 2050: Critical challenges, key contexts, and emerging trends* (pp. 59–74). Bingley: Emerald Group Publishing.

Schein, E.H. (2016). *Organizational Culture and Leadership* (5th ed.). Hoboken, NJ: Wiley.

Senge, P.M. (2006). *The Fifth Discipline: The art and practice of the learning organization*. New York: Currency/Doubleday.

Senge, P.M., Smith, B., Kruschwitz, N., Laur, J., & Schley, S. (2012). *The Necessary Revolution: How individuals and organizations are working together to create a sustainable world*. New York: Broadway Books/Crown Publishing.

Stenudd, S. (2015). *Tao Te Ching: The Taoism of Lao Tzu explained*. Charleston, SC: Create Space.

Stogdill, R.M. (1948). Personal Factors Associated with Leadership: A survey of the literature. *Journal of Psychology*, 25, 35–71.

Trompenaars, F., & Hampden-Turner, C. (2010). *Riding the Waves of Culture: Understanding diversity in global business* (3rd ed.). New York: McGraw-Hill.

Van Vugt, M. (2012). The Nature in Leadership: Evolutionary, biological, and social neuroscience perspectives. In D.V. Day & J. Antonakis (Eds), *The Nature of Leadership* (2nd ed.) (pp. 141–175). Thousand Oaks, CA: SAGE Publications, Inc.

Van Vugt, M., & Ahuja, A. (2011). *Naturally Selected: Why some people lead, why others follow, and why it matters* (Kindle ed.). New York: HarperCollins e-books.

Van Vugt, M., Hogan, R., & Kaiser, R. (2008). Leadership, Followership, and Evolution: Some lessons from the past. *American Psychologist*, 63, 182–196.

Waldman, D.A., Balthazard, P.A., Peterson, S.J. (2011). Leadership and Neuroscience: Can we revolutionize the way that inspirational leaders are identified and developed? *Academy of Management Perspectives*, 25(1), 60–74.

Western, S. (2008/2013). *Leadership: A critical text* (2nd ed.). Thousand Oaks, CA: SAGE Publications, Inc.

Western, S. (2010). Eco-leadership: Towards the development of a new paradigm. In B. Redekop (Ed.), *Leadership for Environmental Sustainability* (pp. 36–54). New York & London: Routledge.

Wheatley, M.J. (2006). *Leadership and the New Science: Discovering order in a chaotic world* (3rd ed.). San Francisco, CA: Barrett-Koehler.

Wilson, E. O. (1975). *Sociobiology: The new synthesis*. Cambridge, MA: Belknap Press.

Wilson, E.O. (2003). *The Future of Life*. New York: Vintage Books.

Wilson, E.O. (2014). *A Window on Eternity: A biologist's walk through Gorongosa National Park*. New York: Simon & Schuster.

World Commission on Environment and Development. (1987). *Our Common Future*. Oxford: Oxford University Press.

Yaffe, M.A. (2001). *Judaism and Environmental Ethics: A reader*. Lanham, MD: Lexington Books.

Yukl, G.A. (2013). *Leadership in Organizations* (8th ed.). Upper Saddle River, NJ: Pearson/ Prentice Hall.

7 The Unseen Revolution

Leadership for Sustainability in the Tropical Biosphere

Paul Kosempel, Linda G. Olson and Filiberto Penados

Introduction

The predominant Achilles heel of leadership research in the last century has been researchers' overreliance on data and models from the minority world[1] (Henrich et al., 2010). Such reliance has often been paired with research in leadership that reifies messianic notions of leadership and traditional power structures of domination (Shriberg, 2012; Western, 2013). It is more common than not for scholars to focus on the minority world, and research on leadership for sustainability does not provide an exception to this pattern (Cui, 2017). A few exceptions in the realm of leadership for sustainability in addition to this volume should be noted (Gallagher, 2012). Focusing research efforts in majority world countries has the benefit of both understanding leadership for sustainability efforts more thoroughly, but also better understanding these efforts from a critical, alternative lens. While research privileges minority world efforts, an unseen revolution is taking place at the local level in the majority world. Our aim in this chapter is to explore numerous unseen sustainability leadership efforts that are taking place amidst the tropical biosphere in Belize.

Sustainable development has included a tripartite emphasis on social, economic, and environmental factors since the report of the Brundtland Commission (1987). In exploring the distinction between sustainability leadership and leadership for sustainability, Wilson and Kosempel (2016) reinforce the notion that leadership for sustainability must include economic, environmental, and social dimensions. However, current bodies of research often place greater emphasis on the environmental dimension of sustainability and in fact, specifically narrow the focus to just climate change to the neglect of other environmental problems (Gallagher, 2012). Taken alone, environmental leadership has been defined as "a process by which Earth's inhabitants apply interpersonal influence and engage in collective action to protect the planet's natural resources and its inhabitants from further harm" (Gallagher, 2012, p. 5). Expanding upon Gallagher's argument for the need to think beyond climate change, we contend that those who study leadership for sustainability need to focus outside just the environmental dimension. In the developing world, issues of economic and social development take on an even greater concern, and as such, need to be considered for anyone taking on the topic of leadership for sustainability.

Leadership for sustainability demands attention to the multiple efforts of diverse stakeholders from many perspectives. Edwards (2005) describes the work of multiple small entities simultaneously effecting change with respect to sustainability; what we would call an "unseen revolution." These efforts range from a village in Borneo replacing diesel generators with hydro-generators to a model public transportation system in Curitiba, Brazil. At the heart of these efforts is leadership: leadership at the local community level. Western (2010) laments the preponderance of top-down approaches to leadership for sustainability and espouses the need to progress to a new paradigm called eco-leadership. Rather than limiting leadership to a few individuals in high positions in government, Western (2010) suggests that "Eco-leadership redistributes leadership and power from the center to the edges, recognizing the impossibility of 'going it alone' when we are independent of each other and on planet Earth" (p. 42). Western suggests that eco-leadership relies on a spiritual approach, something akin to solidarity among members of an organization. He describes it as either a religious or spiritual belief or a compassion for justice and belief in the capacity for human good. Gallagher (2012) also emphasizes the point that environmental leadership does and should take place at all levels of organizations, from "conference rooms ... [to] ... small towns in China" (p. 9).

Applying a critical lens to leadership for sustainability similarly emphasizes the need to focus on local approaches. Alvesson and Spicer (2012) argue that a critical approach requires asking whether leadership is always desirable and to consider the notion that leadership efforts may exist simply to create conditions of domination and control. They further describe the need to maintain healthy skepticism that leadership is needed and to expose the blind faith that is often put in the hands of the power of leadership. Additionally, the critical study of leadership yields an understanding that leadership can become an ideology of its own and exclusionary in its practice given the focus on specific leadership roles. As such, leadership needs to be understood and transformed in more democratic and critically grounded ways due to its ideology being rooted in hero worship and positional authority (Bendell & Little, 2015). Exploring leadership at the local level, particularly as enacted in majority countries, is an essential part of this necessary transformation (Alvesson & Spicer, 2012). Additionally, research is needed to determine if the patterns of domination and exclusion are prevalent in other non-Western countries, and to identify alternatives to hegemonic leadership models. In this chapter, we answer the call to examine leadership efforts in the developing world. More specifically, we seek to understand how these leadership efforts reflect the characteristics of the approaches suggested by Western (2010) and Gallagher (2012).

One of the most vital areas to examine and learn from leadership focused on sustainability is in the intersection of the developing world and the tropical biosphere. Countries like Belize, Costa Rica, Guatemala, Ecuador, and Brazil play an essential role in environmental stewardship and leadership given the importance of their ecosystem to the rest of the planet. These areas include tropical rainforests that have been described as the lungs of the planet for their abundant ability to absorb carbon dioxide and produce oxygen. The minority world has much to learn from the majority world related to protecting our environment. In Belize, important examples exist of community, government, and business leadership paying close attention to environmental sustainability. Specifically, this chapter will explore several cases of Belizean leaders and leadership aimed at increasing the resilience of this ecosystem.

Examples of the Unseen Revolution

The country of Belize is a hidden gem of a natural paradise situated on the eastern coast of Central America. Formerly British Honduras, this young nation's land is covered with over 60 percent forest and is bordered by Guatemala to the south and west, Mexico to the north, and the Caribbean Sea on the east. Its great biodiversity includes a 600-mile-long coastline, home to the world's second largest barrier reef, that is sprinkled with 1,000 cays, coastal lagoons, and three atolls: Turneffe, Glover's, and Lighthouse. Known as the Mesoamerican Reef, this area boasts over "500 species of fish ... 60 species of coral ... and diverse marine species including sea turtles, sharks and dolphins" (Ministry of Agriculture and Fisheries, n.d.). The Belize Barrier Reef Reserve System (BBRRS), a UNESCO World Heritage site, includes seven protected areas and attracts accomplished divers from all over the world, particularly at the Great Blue Hole. Unfortunately, human impact in the form of overfishing, human-made land, and air pollution from increased coastal habitation and agriculture, poor tourism practices, and mangrove deforestation is threatening this unique ecosystem.

The models and approaches suggested in current research are being enacted in multiple local sustainability efforts in Belize. Friends for Conservation and Development, Long Caye at Lighthouse Reef Atoll, and The Nature Conservancy-Belize are three such efforts that make significant contributions to sustainable development within the tropical biosphere. Their work is largely unseen by the larger world, but essential to their nation and our world. Understanding how they manage these efforts is important for scholars and practitioners dedicated to leadership for sustainability.

Friends for Conservation and Development

Friends for Conservation and Development (FCD) is a nongovernmental organization that comanages[2] the Chiquibul National Park, one of the most complex and complicated protected areas to manage. To begin with, the national park is one of the utmost isolated and rugged terrains, making it difficult and expensive to monitor. Second, it is part of a larger ecosystem in which multiple state and non-state agencies are involved. It is part of the Chiquibul forest that includes the Chiquibul Forest Reserve managed by the Forestry Department, the Caracol Archaeological Park managed by the Institute of Archaeology (IA), and the Chiquibul National Park managed by FCD, together accounting for 7.7 percent of the total area of Belize. The Chiquibul forest also contains one of the largest cave systems in the western hemisphere, under the jurisdiction of IA, and a hydroelectric dam with its reserve managed by a private company. The protection of the Chiquibul cannot be accomplished without coordination and partnerships with the multiple agencies that have jurisdiction in the larger Chiquibul forests.

Perhaps the factor that makes management of the forest particularly complicated is that the Chiquibul is located along a disputed border with Guatemala and most of the threats come from the Guatemalan side. The Chiquibul has a long history of use by Belizeans, but several buffer zones stand between the park and the communities, making it easier to manage. From the Guatemalan side, individuals enter Belize and the park illegally to log, mine, poach, and farm. Mostly these are landless peasants, some of whom may be connected to bigger interests and at times these peasants are armed. Protection of the Chiquibul therefore involves FCD in questions of sovereignty, national security, and international politics. FCD must work with immigration officers, the Belize Defense Force, the Ministry of Foreign Affairs, and National Security agencies.

The Chiquibul area contains resources, timber and non-timber products, minerals, water, and tourist attractions that many see as unexploited economic opportunities. That Guatemalans are illegally exploiting the Chiquibul makes justifying conservation of the protected area difficult among some Belizean sectors and increases demands for opening it for Belizean economic exploitation. Currently the Ministry of tourism is developing a tourism initiative in and around the attractions in the Chiquibul forests.

FCD acknowledges the inherent complexity and has engaged it by recognizing the need to think creatively, the need to act with urgency and integrity and above all the need to act collectively. FCD has been able to build alliances both within Belize and across Guatemala. In Belize, it has been able to engage with environmental organizations, communities, private agencies, individuals, and state agencies including national security agencies and foreign affairs. The national borders and international politics have not stopped FCD. Recognizing that the protection of the Chiquibul goes beyond the border, it has been able to engage Guatemalan state and non-state environmental agencies to work with their citizens to create alternative livelihood opportunities.

FCD has been able to mobilize state and non-state actors by communicating a sense of urgency about the protection of the Chiquibul. FCD has made Chiquibul a household word and drawn attention to the problem from the relevant state agencies. It has done the latter in a non-antagonistic manner by sharing the beauty of the Chiquibul and communicating in objective but forceful ways the reality on the ground. A major part of its strategy has been to infect people with their passion for the protection of the Chiquibul by what people at FCD call infecting them with the *Chiquibul-FCD bug*. In 2014, for example, it was able to raise over $300,000 through a telethon with donations from individuals and organizations – a staggering amount for a country with a population of just over 350,000.

Part of recognizing and responding to complexity has meant that FCD has adopted a notion of sustainability that goes beyond environmental protection to include the importance of social and economic dimensions. FCD recognizes the economic reality of peasants and the larger political context in which they exist and has sought to address these economic issues. It has recognized the economic opportunities that the Chiquibul has to offer and has engaged with economic actors to examine these opportunities in a way that guarantees the other dimensions of sustainability. Perhaps even more importantly, it has sought to address the institutional dimension of sustainability by acting with integrity in a Belizean landscape where the integrity of politicians, and sometimes NGOs, has been called into question. FCD is recognized as a leader by many Belizeans including the Prime Minister, who, in his 2013 Independence Day address, noted that "Enough cannot be said in praise of FCD. Their awareness-raising as well as operational efforts, have been phenomenal" (Barrow, 2013). FCD has established itself as a communal leader by demonstrating enormous commitment, persistence, and determination. They have demonstrated the highest level of integrity, professionalism, passion, and action largely by mobilizing local and international organizations around the importance and urgency of protecting the Chiquibul.

To understand the leadership of FCD, it is necessary to consider its roots. FCD was started in the mid-1980s as the Youth Environmental Action Group (YEAG), which was a group of young people from a small village with a population of about 2,000. This collection of energetic young people was concerned and wanted to do something about the well-being of their community and its surrounding environment. The group engaged in the exploration of their natural environment through hiking and camping in the Chiquibul, developing a connection to the place and, in the process, creating spaces for dialogue and reflection about the reality of their community and dreams for the future. They engaged in environmental education programs with schoolchildren about the value of the natural environment and the importance of caring for it; they engaged in cleanup and garbage collection campaigns to improve the quality of the environment surrounding the community and educating community members; and they also engaged in riverside cleaning and tree planting to protect the watershed.

The results of YEAG's work were small and the process sometimes frustrating: cleared garbage dumps would be filled back again and planted trees sometimes uprooted; and the young people would at times be taunted that they had too much spare time and additional garbage would pile up during village cleanup campaigns. While the garbage dumps disappeared after many years, the impact of YEAG was much more in the thinking and behavior of the involved young people. Many gave up their slingshots and bird-shooting hobby and made changes in the management of garbage at home. Above all, they persevered with YEAG and developed a form of leadership and understanding of sustainability that today informs FCD.

In speaking to three founding members of FCD, who were once YEAG students who are now staff of FCD, plus a new staff member, they revealed key leadership characteristics that kept this work alive. The most important is a passion and sense of cause for the protection of the Chiquibul. They talk about the magic of the Chiquibul and about how there is an FCD-Chiquibul bug that bites everyone that comes in contact with it. They seek to infect partners, stakeholders, and staff with this bug often by taking them there. But the bug is not only the majesty of the Chiquibul but the passion with which they speak about what they do. Second, they communicate a sense of urgency and determination about its protection. They demonstrate relentlessness in getting their message across to everyone, from community members to the prime minister. This relentlessness has proven effective in making the Chiquibul a national concern.

Third is the question of integrity. For these members, FCD is principled, and one of the reasons they continue to be engaged is because they know that FCD will not sell out on its principles. Fourth is an orientation toward learning and adaptability. The Executive Director of FCD, Rafael Manzanero, explains their adaptive style in acknowledging that when starting FCD there were not many environmental organizations that they could learn from (personal communication, June 15, 2017). They practiced and learned; when they took over the Chiquibul it was similar, and today as they engage present challenges, they come up with ideas, put them into practice, and learn together. For Rafael and for the other members, FCD has been a truly grassroots initiative.

Last is the importance of alliances and partnerships. For three of the staff members, one of the greatest assets of the executive director and FCD is its capacity to convene actors and develop partnerships, in effect recognizing that to achieve the protection of the Chiquibul requires collective action.

Long Caye at Lighthouse Reef

Long Caye at Lighthouse Reef is another model effort of leadership for sustainability in Belize. It is an island community comprised of a for-profit business and a nonprofit conservation institute. It was founded in 1967 and has remained in family ownership since its founding. The business venture on the island is a combination of real estate development and an island resort. The nonprofit conservation institute seeks to maintain the island as a preserve and partner with other nonprofits and academic entities to conduct research. Currently, the island has three principal owners.

Their organization follows their own model called the Lighthouse Model for Resilience and Sustainability, which attempts to balance community, culture, and conservation in all that they do. Their adherence to this model can be enumerated in multiple examples. First, the owners of the island community established comprehensive eco-guidelines initially in 2003 with significant revisions in 2010. The eco-guidelines are intended to balance the community's needs for economic development with environmental conservation and resilience, and have been lauded as exemplary by the Coastal Zone Management Authority and Institute of Belize (n.d.). Some of the more significant guidelines include:

- Restricting landowners to only using 30 percent of land plots for construction with all construction built on stilts at a minimum of 4 feet above the island surface.
- Requiring each building on the island to be self-contained, providing its own power, waste management, and water using rain collection, solar/ wind systems, and composting toilets.
- Restricting the construction of individual docks/piers in order to preserve essential mangrove around the island.

Additionally, the island owners have followed an operating principle of "the land drives the plan" rather than the opposite. An example of this principle in action is the protection of 1/3 of the island as an official preserve with the Government of Belize to ensure that it is never developed. On a smaller, and perhaps no less important a scale, no fences or landscaping are allowed on individual plots of land. Last, to create walkways on the island, the owners built the narrow walkways within a 40-foot-wide corridor, which allowed them to shape them around unique features of the island such as a large, old buttonwood tree or massive ferns. Decisions on development are made specifically with the natural design of the land as the driver in decisions.

The practices of this organization align closely with the approaches and models previously discussed. Western's (2010) model of eco-leadership discusses the presence of a spiritual approach of solidarity toward the environment (pp. 49–51). The founders of Long Caye consider the Earth to be an island community not unlike their own island, and have solidarity around their mission and model. Solidarity was not easily achieved by the owners. In fact, the sustainability of the island was threatened when this solidarity was not shared by a co-owner who prioritized economic development over the environmental conservation of the island. One owner wanted to develop the lagoon portion of the island, whereas the current owners knew that it would be nearly catastrophic from an environmental perspective. An ownership change was necessitated and led to the current solidarity.

Being comprised of only three members, the leadership/ownership group of the island is small. As such, the leadership structure seems fairly traditional given that all decisions are made by those with positional authority. However, the ownership team's decision making is entirely by consensus, which represents a more distributed form of leadership. One owner described how every decision is made through consensus with a focus on sustainability, from a decision to not allow plastic water bottles on the island to decisions about potential investors. Both the small size of the leadership team and the consensus decision-making style are potential exemplars for other sustainable development efforts.

The Nature Conservancy

The Nature Conservancy (TNC) is an international environmental nonprofit agency operating in over 65 countries and committed to the mission of "conserving lands and water on which all life depends" (The Nature Conservancy, n.d.). In 1989, when the Conservancy began working in Belize, it was natural for them to take up a dual focus on marine and terrestrial habitats given the rich ecosystem. Largely, the focus of this leadership example will concentrate on the critical marine habitats, since they are of such great importance to the local and Caribbean region. As fishing and tourism are the backbone of Belize's coastal communities' economic health and food security, both need to be considered in approaches to sustainability efforts.

The coastal communities of Belize share a strong dependence on fishing for food and livelihood. Marked by low-tech and subsistence fishing, many fisheries experienced a significant decline in fish size and quantity from 1970–1990s, exacerbating coastal poverty (The Nature Conservancy, n.d.). The introduction of bottom trawling and other destructive fishing methods competes unfairly with traditional cast net fishing and increases discarded fish, threatens larger sea animals and reefs, and decreases the pristine appeal for tourism (Stiles et al., 2010). In addition, TNC scientists have discovered "more than 13 spawning aggregation sites of endangered reef fish" along the barrier reef (The Nature Conservancy, n.d.). The Conservancy realized early on that governmental regulations without fishers' involvement did not create shared and sustained stewardship of the coastal waters. Moreover, the government ministries had limited resources to maintain and enforce regulations that would limit exploitation of the coastal natural resources. Ms. Julie Robinson, a Belizean and Conservancy marine researcher and conservationist, has spent nearly 20 years working with fishing communities to help them organize for diversification of their fisheries, develop stronger fishing practices, and organize for self-monitoring and innovation. Co-management of the waters using fishing cooperatives and associations alongside non-governmental and government entities has facilitated fishers becoming what she calls "great ocean stewards" (The Nature Conservancy, n.d.). Fishers have played a prominent role in designing their own monitoring system, and with co-laborers from the cooperatives as well as the Conservancy, Belize has a self-management standard unique in the region (Cruz et al., 2015).

Innovating and developing diverse economies that relieve reliance on a fragile marine fishing environment has also been a focused goal of the Conservancy. One such successful project is the Belize Placencia Fisherman's Cooperative and their development of an aquaculture seaweed industry. Robinson notes that this new industry provides promising alternatives to fishing reliance by offering a sea product that offers a new food source from the ocean with local and global acclaim, while providing balancing chemical stabilization properties to the reef system. In addition, this particular project has incorporated women, bringing greater gender equity to co-management and innovations for solutions (Julie Robinson, personal communication, December 4, 2016).

Management of Belize's marine areas has demanded a style of leadership that best reflects eco-leadership, in that success has not been possible without generative and co-leadership efforts. The power to make changes has been vested in the members most impacted and who live in the area where firsthand feedback and knowledge of consequences are intertwined. Coastal Belizeans have developed agency and overcome the lack of government resources through more local, generative problem-solving.

Belize Natural Energy

A final example worth exploring that demonstrates unique leadership approaches within the majority world is Belize Natural Energy (BNE). We have previously written about it, so will not spend as much time in the space here (Kosempel & Olson, 2016). BNE is the single largest taxpayer in the country of Belize, and it is the only company to have discovered oil in Belize. BNE has been a model corporate citizen throughout its relatively short history. It was started in 2005, and in addition to its economic success, it has also developed numerous social and environmental initiatives and received national and global recognition for its efforts. It is especially unique in that it is a fossil fuel generating company that has been bestowed the Green Business Award from the University of Belize and national industry associations. Specifically, it was recognized for its environmental safety processes and its investment in a Liquefied Petroleum Gas Processing Plant. The driving force behind this plant was to reduce natural gas emissions that are created in the production of oil. It has since developed into a lower-cost source for butane and propane for Belizean citizens. BNE has also been recognized for its social and economic programs, such as its award-winning adult education program and development of the BNE Charitable Trust. Probably the most significant attribute of the company is its employment of over 95 percent Belizean citizens, a unique practice among foreign-owned oil companies in majority countries (Orr & McVerry, 2007) including the hiring of their Belizean CEO in 2006. BNE has surprisingly achieved significant results in terms of the tripartite emphasis on economic, environmental, and social aspects of sustainability.

Implications

Examples of leadership for sustainability in the majority world abound, providing ample evidence in support of Edwards' (2005) contention that an unseen revolution is afoot. In the country of Belize, we provided three examples of unique approaches to sustainability that reflect leadership practices essential for our world moving forward, leadership practices that are consistent with critical leadership perspectives. FCD provides an example of an organization that successfully negotiates relationships with multiple, highly diverse stakeholders in order to preserve a pristine environmental area of our planet. Their organization is reflective of Western's (2013) notion that "leadership is not boundaried, it accompanies, complements, and merges with other relational interactions of followership, teamwork, collaboration and participation" (p. xiv). At Long Caye at Lighthouse Reef, "the land drives the plan" for development. Rather than situating humans at the center of this endeavor, the owners of Long Caye place the island ecosystem at the center of all of their decisions, demonstrating a better understanding of our inter-dependencies with nature (Western, 2013). Alvesson and Spicer (2012) suggest that a critical performative approach to leadership would include alternatives to leadership such as cooperation and collaborative communities. The long-term relationships between The Nature Conservancy, the Belizean government, and local fishing communities are evidence that such alternatives exist and are critical in moving forward sustainable initiatives.

Finally, BNE provides a unique example of a business in a majority country that makes strides toward sustainable development. Although their overall structure is fairly traditional with positional authority throughout, their practice of hiring mostly Belizeans and developing its workers in significant ways through all levels for personal fulfillment provides close alignment with Western's quality of organizational belonging (2013, pp. 263–266). A key factor in BNE's sustainable development is their strong national identity (Kosempel & Olson, 2016). This national identity is exemplary of Western's (2013) contention that businesses and corporations belong to the social fabric of the community and cannot operate separately. These four organizations provide new and diverse examples from the majority world that illustrate the power of critical perspectives in leadership.

Notes

1 We are intentionally using the term "majority world" to describe what is normally thought of as the "developing world." The term "developing world" is relatively problematic. Inherent in the term is an expectation that some parts of the world are still in progress. Perpetuating the use of this term has the potential to frame a

country such as Belize as underdeveloped or inferior to the "developed world." An alternative we considered was the classification system used by The World Bank based on gross national income (GNI) per capita. Given that it's solely based on a statistical ranking, it has less potential for bias. The limitation to using this categorization is basically that it is too simplistic. Belize is classified as an "upper middle income" category country, which distinguishes it from high-income countries like the United Kingdom, Germany, and Japan, but aligns it with qualitatively different countries like China, Russia, and Turkey. Belize is a country with over 40 percent of the population living below the poverty line, so a category such as "upper middle income" seems to lack validity on its face. We use the term "majority world" as a reminder that countries that are typically considered "developing" make up the vast majority of the world's population. Correspondingly, the "developed world" is referred to as the "minority world" in this chapter.

2   Co-management in Belize is a system in which the Forestry Department that has the responsibility for and authority over national parks delegates the management responsibility to a nongovernment or community organization. The Forestry Department retains overall authority including the possibility of de-reserving. The nongovernmental or community organization on the other hand has the responsibility for developing and implementing management plans, including raising the necessary funds.

References

Alvesson, M., & Spicer, A. (2012). Critical Leadership Studies: The case for critical performativity. *Human Relations*, 65(3), 367–390.

Barrow, D. (2013). 2013 Independence Day Address. Retrieved from: www.belize hub.com/pm-dean-barrows-independence-day-address/.

Bendell, J., & Little, R. (2015). Seeking Sustainability Leadership. *The Journal of Corporate Citizenship*, 60(December), 13–26.

Brundtland, G.H. (1987). Our Common Future: Report of the World Commission on Environment and Development. Oxford University. Retrieved from: www.un-do cuments.net/our-common-future.pdf.

Coastal Zone Management Authority and Institute. (n.d.). Retrieved from: www.coa stalzonebelize.org/archives/31.

Cruz, S., RobinsonJ.S., & Tingey, R. (2015). Integrating Participatory Planning in the Design of Belize's Marine Replenishment Zones. In T. Nishida & A. Caton (Eds), *GIS/Spatial Analyses in Fishery and Aquatic Sciences, Vol. 6* (pp. 135–152). Saitama, Japan: International Fishery GIS Society.

Cui, L. (2017). Fuzzy Approach to Eco-Innovation for Enhancing Business Functions: A case study in China. *Industrial Management and Data Systems*, 117(5), 967–987.

Edwards, A.R. (2005). *The Sustainability Revolution: Portrait of a paradigm shift.* Gabriola Island, BC: New Society Publishers.

Gallagher, D.R. (2012). Why Environmental Leadership? In D.R. Gallagher (Ed.), *Environmental Leadership: A reference handbook, Vol. 1* (pp. 3–10). Los Angeles, CA: SAGE Publications, Inc.

Henrich, J., Heine, S.J., & Norenzayan, A. (2010). The Weirdest People in the World? *Behavioral and Brain Sciences*, 33, 61–135.

Kosempel, P., & Olson, L. (2016). Enactment of a Sustainable Vision in the Dual Context of the Tropical Biosphere and the Developing World: A case study of Belize Natural Energy. *Journal of Leadership Studies*, 9(4), 65–69.

Orr, B., & McVerry, B. (2007). Talent Management Challenge in the Oil and Gas Industry. *Natural Gas and Electricity*, 24(5), 18–23.

Ministry of Agriculture and Fisheries: Belize. (n.d.) Retrieved from: www.agri culture.gov.bz/Statutory_Bodies.html.

Shriberg, M. (2012). Sustainability Leadership as 21st-Century Leadership. In D.R. Gallagher (Ed.), *Environmental Leadership: A reference handbook, Vol.2* (pp. 469–478). Los Angeles, CA: SAGE Publications, Inc.

Stiles, M.L., Stockbridge, J.S., Lande, M., & Hirshfield, M.F. (2010). Impacts of Bottom Trawling on Fisheries, Tourism, and the Marine Environment. Oceana Central America. Available at: http://oceana.org/sites/default/files/reports/Tra wling_BZ_10may10_toAudrey.pdf.

The Nature Conservancy: Central America-Belize. (n.d.). Retrieved from: www.na ture.org/ourinitiatives/regions/centralamerica/belize/index.htm.

Western, S. (2010). Eco-Leadership: Towards the development of a new paradigm. In B. Redekop (Ed.), *Leadership for Environmental Sustainability* (pp. 36–54). New York & Abingdon: Routledge.

Western, S. (2013). *Leadership: A critical text*. Thousand Oaks, CA: SAGE Publications, Inc.

Wilson, S.G., & Kosempel, P. (2016). Introduction to the Symposium on Sustainability Leadership. *Journal of Leadership Studies*, 9(4), 43–46.

8 Heroes No More: Businesses Practice Collaborative Leadership to Confront Climate Change

Deborah Rigling Gallagher

The time is ripe for enlightened business leaders to scale up corporate sustainability by engaging responsibly on climate policy.

Georg Kell, Executive Director, United Nations Global Compact

Introduction

In June 2012, more than 2,000 corporate leaders and investors, government officials, representatives of non-governmental organizations, and academic observers gathered in Rio de Janeiro, Brazil, the site of the United Nations Rio +20 Conference on Sustainable Development. They were there to attend a side event, "Rio+20 Corporate Sustainability Forum: Innovation & Collaboration for the Future We Want." Attendees dined on local delicacies, gathered in anterooms to network, and shared stories in conference halls as they celebrated past successes and made plans for future efforts. The event was the latest in a 10+ year history in which the United Nations, having long been unsuccessful in convincing its stakeholders to formally engage with the private sector (Tesner & Kell, 2000), has harnessed the economic and political power of transnational corporations to address critical global challenges such as poverty, inequality, and climate change through the agency of its trisector partnership, the United Nations Global Compact (UNGC).

The Rio + 20 summit attracted 30,000 participants, many more than the UNGC side event, and included heads of state, whose representatives spent long hours negotiating a declaration on sustainable development, "The Future We Want." The overarching message of both events was that the private sector should play an increasingly prominent role in making progress on the United Nations Millennium Development Goals[1] (Kettunen & ten Brink, 2012), and in addressing the impacts of climate change.

But many UNGC members present in Rio, corporate environmental leaders all, recognized that a global, government-supported climate change policy was a long shot. Given that the Rio sustainable development event coincided with the 2012 expiration of the Kyoto protocol, which had placed caps on greenhouse gas emissions in developed countries, businesses were understandably keen to address the uncertainty ahead (Engau & Hoffman, 2009). While a number of countries and subnational governments had made progress on constructing policies to combat climate change, the most notable being the 2005 European Union's Emission Trading Scheme, a global movement to enact climate change policy was unlikely. And, every day that policies were not in place, the effects of climate change were more evident. Motivated by images of glaciers receding, communities coping with sea level rise, and the increasing occurrence of severe droughts, and armed with knowledge of the impacts these events would have on global economic security, members of the UNGC initiated a concerted effort to promote global climate change policy.

These members' efforts were acts of environmental leadership. These actions were not those of the kind of leadership in which heads of state or heads of corporations exercise formal power and deign that particular actions will be taken, but rather committed partnerships with like-minded others engaged in joint problem solving. The existential global climate crisis motivated members to consider innovative approaches to leadership, in which personal, titular power would not be the sole source of change. These exercises of environmental leadership that occurred post-Rio were not sustained by personal charisma, motivated by desires to transform organizational relationships, or rooted in visions of heroic actions, but rather grounded in a sense that humility and collaboration are critical to the survival of the planet.

This chapter details the efforts of UNGC members to perform *collaborative environmental leadership* and engage in climate policy development at the global level under the auspices of the UNGC's Caring for Climate (C4C) platform. The findings and analysis are informed by participant observation and ethnographic methods (Spradley, 2016) in which the researcher immerses herself in an organizational setting to discern connections between individual member performances and the development and practice of organizational norms (Van Maanen, 1979). In this study, the author attended a series of United Nations Global Compact meetings from 2013–2015, interacting with attendees at Caring for Climate gatherings to uncover the ways in which environmental leadership practice evolved and to knit together a working theory of collaborative environmental leadership. The chapter begins with an overview of the history and structure of the United Nations Global Compact as a transnational public private partnership and agent of environmental leadership. The Caring for Climate platform is then detailed. This sets the stage for a larger consideration of how UNGC members engaged collaboratively in two C4C initiatives, Responsible Corporate Engagement in Climate Policy and Carbon Pricing Leadership, and were instrumental in facilitating the landmark 2015 Paris Climate Agreement.

The United Nations Global Compact: Transnational Public–Private Partnership

Private sector organizations have long partnered with public sector agencies and non-governmental organizations to address problems of common concern, such as response to natural disasters, support for education and the arts, and limited access to food and nutrition. Opportunities to engage in these issues through private philanthropy abound. However, multinational corporations motivated to confront problems like global climate change increasingly engage as active members of transnational public private partnerships (TPPPs). TPPPs are broadly defined as "multisectoral networks that bring together government, business and civil society ... as institutionalized transboundary interactions between public and private actors, which aim at the provision of collective goods" (Benner et al., 2005, as cited in Bäckstrand et al., 2012, p. 126). Corporate partners in TPPPs derive legitimacy by participating in joint problem solving and in the construction of procedural norms to address critical issues. By the same token, TPPPs such as the UNGC have long derived legitimacy for the project of creating a global green economy by focusing on market-oriented, business-based solutions to issues such as climate change and biodiversity protection. In this chapter, such a search for legitimacy within the marketplace is called into question as we consider opportunities for collaborative leadership.

Historically, multinational corporations participating in TPPPs have been motivated to more concretely fulfill responsibilities as global citizens and to learn new ways of functioning in a global society in which lines between sectors are increasingly blurred (Bromley & Meyer, 2014; Waddock, 2013). Members of TPPPs such as the UNGC work together to activate shared processes of organizational learning (Ruggie, 2002). Partnerships such as the UNGC, which place attention on addressing critical environmental problems, avail member companies with opportunities to enact leadership behaviors and influence global environmental policy change (Gallagher, 2013).

The United Nations Global Compact: Platform for Environmental Leadership

The 1992 Rio Declaration on Environment and Development declared, "The right to development must be fulfilled so as to equitably meet developmental and environmental needs of present and future generations," but did not lay out a specific role for private sector organizations to play. Recognizing this oversight, in 1999 at the World Economic Forum in Davos, Switzerland, UN Secretary General Kofi Annan called on private sector organizations "Individually through your firms, and collectively through your business associations – to embrace, support and enact a set of core values in the areas of human rights, labour standards, and environmental practices" (United Nations, 1999). This plea ultimately resulted in the creation of the UNGC as a network of leaders from business, non-governmental organizations, and labor organizations ostensibly focused on promoting a mission to spur sustainable development, educating each other about best practices, and on partnering to benefit the greater good.

Since 1999, the UNGC has increased its membership significantly via global marketing and direct outreach through the establishment of in-country and regional local networks. Local networks provide opportunities for members to participate in activism at ground level, for example by providing training to non-member companies on best practices in environmental stewardship or fair labor practices. The UNGC has employed increasingly sophisticated tools to gather information about best practices in combatting corruption, empowering women, alleviating poverty, managing water resources, protecting biodiversity, and adapting to the impacts of global climate change, and to disseminate this information around the globe.

UNGC members regularly gather in issue-oriented summits, local network meetings, global conferences, and webinars to share information on best practices and learn from each other. Compact members are encouraged to affiliate with initiatives that align with the UNGC's key themes of human rights, labor, environment, and anti-corruption. Members join and lead campaigns that address critical issues relevant to their organizations. For example, members may participate in the UNGC's Global Business Initiative on Human Rights (GBI), which offers opportunities to develop tools for integrating human rights into business practices and to join a global dialog on best practices. Alternatively, they may engage in an online "dilemmas" forum in which members discuss challenges and offer company case studies of how challenges were confronted.

Members are required to report each year on activities in service of the Sustainable Development Goals (SDGs). In annual communications on progress (COPs), UNGC member organizations must publicly disclose the progress made in both implementing the UNGC's ten principles[2] and in addressing the SDGs.[3] Failure to provide COPs results in termination of membership. While there are currently over 12,000 UNGC members in good standing, free-riding has long been a concern – annually the number of members terminated runs into the hundreds.

In the environmental arena, critical issues such as biodiversity, water resources, and climate change are addressed by UNGC members who participate in initiatives that offer opportunities for them to engage directly with one another under the guidance of UNGC professional staff. UNGC initiatives such as "Corporate Action on Biodiversity," "CEO Water Mandate," and "Caring for Climate" provide platforms for members to become involved in addressing these issues. However, while formal affiliation with specific environmental initiatives, evidenced by the number of signatory companies, generally runs into the hundreds on each initiative, in reality a small group of members actively work to advance corporate perspectives on responsible environmental behavior. As will be described below, these members are leaders who engage in non-traditional, post-heroic leadership practices such as working across organizational borders and transparently sharing information about organizational practices with a broad swath of stakeholders.

Caring for Climate

The Caring for Climate (C4C) Initiative was unveiled at the annual UNGC members meeting in Geneva, Switzerland, in 2007. At the launch, 153 companies pledged to take

> ... practical actions to increase the efficiency of energy usage and to reduce the carbon burden of products, services and processes, to set voluntary targets for doing so, and to report publicly on the achievement of those targets annually [... and participate in] urgent creation, in close consultation with the business community and civil society, of comprehensive, long-term and effective legislative and fiscal frameworks designed to make markets work for the climate, in particular policies and mechanisms intended to create a stable price for carbon.
>
> (United Nations Global Compact, 2007, p. 27)

Signatories also committed to dealing with the climate issue strategically and to building relevant capacity. They pledged to work collaboratively with other enterprises on a sector basis and along their global supply chains, promoting recognized standards and taking joint initiatives to reduce climate risks.

C4C offers its over 300 members from 60+ countries opportunities to "advance practical solutions, share experiences, inform public policy as well as shape public attitudes" on climate change. Members collaborate to tackle the impacts of climate change through several work streams – climate and development, sustainable energy for all, low carbon solutions, and transparency and disclosure. Before members are cleared to participate in C4C and its initiatives, firm CEOs must sign on to the "Caring for Climate Business Leadership Platform," a carefully negotiated and tightly crafted manifesto. The platform 1) declares that climate change is a critical global issue that requires actions by business, governments, and citizens, and further that the private sector must lead through energy efficiency, reduced emissions, and use of low-carbon technologies; 2) requires a commitment to specific actions, such as carbon-footprint-reduction target-setting, reporting on progress, capacity building, policy advocacy, setting standards in the production value chain, and serving as champions for climate action; and 3) declares that governments must work with the private sector to develop both legal and economic frameworks that focus on market-based policies and mechanisms aimed at constituting a global price for carbon, acknowledges that public-private partnerships are critical, and finally that "vigorous international cooperation" is required to support the private sector in investing in a low-carbon global economy (United Nations Global Compact, 2010).

In addition to signing the platform, members must report annually on progress in addressing climate change challenges, using the UNGC's Commitment on Progress, "COP-Climate" mechanism. The COP-Climate specifies that participants must declare continued support for the C4C initiative, describe actions, policies, and procedures taken to address each of the components of C4C, establish annual greenhouse gas emission reduction targets, and report actual reductions using frameworks such as the Carbon Disclosure Project (CDP) or the Global Reporting Initiative (GRI).[4] In the long run up to the 21st United Nations Framework Convention on Climate Change Conference of the Parties (COP 21) in Paris, C4C was one of the most prolific UNGC member initiatives. Two C4C initiatives, Responsible Corporate Engagement in Climate Policy and Carbon Pricing Leadership, described below, provided opportunities for members to engage in collaborative environmental leadership.

Responsible Corporate Engagement in Climate Policy

Much of the UNGC's Rio+20 side event agenda was focused on promoting the "global green economy," reflecting an optimism that such a focus would both create economic benefits to participants and mitigate the impacts of climate change. The global green economy discourse (Wanner, 2015), which promotes a neoliberal capitalist agenda to solve critical environmental problems, was in evidence throughout the meeting venue. For example, participants provided examples of practice in renewable energy and offered specific high-impact opportunity commitments to promote further progress in energy efficiency. The new "Sustainable Energy for All"[5] initiative was highlighted. Under this platform, UNGC member firms made tangible commitments to collaborate on practical solutions and support sustainable energy financing to double the global rate of improvement in energy efficiency by 2030. Expressed motivations for efficiency projects were notable in that they focused both on opportunities to address climate change and on providing prospects for the development of new markets and ensuring competition.

It should be noted that such a neoliberal approach, one singularly focused on markets as saviors of the Earth, is not without its critics. Some attendees at the Rio conference, most notably those from less developed countries in the global South and environmental non-governmental organizations unaffiliated with market-based solutions, began to cry foul. These critics were largely concerned about the dominance of corporations and markets in crafting solutions to climate change. A main target of these critiques was a type of policy described as "payments for ecosystem services (PES)." Under these policies, the market value of nature's services, such as forests, which take in carbon emissions, and wetlands, which purify water resources, would be estimated. Holders of these resources would be paid to protect them, thus creating new markets for ecosystem services, with attendant winners and losers.[6] While much of the criticism of PES was leveled at economists working to set up such markets (Kosoy & Corbera, 2010), a second critique focused broadly on leadership issues, worried that those intended to receive payments to conserve would not be treated fairly if they did not have a place at the negotiating table (Shapiro-Garza, 2013).

Nevertheless, support for a global green economy perspective to mitigate climate change continued to build in formal sessions. However, even as this approach moved "full steam ahead," a new collective discourse began to emerge in hallway conversations. UNGC members, affiliated researchers and staff began to consider whether a singular focus on climate change mitigation through the establishment of markets was ill-placed and that a new effort focused on promoting proactive public policies on climate would be more productive to address the "super wicked"[7] problem of climate change. These conversations led to the creation of a new UNGC member initiative, Responsible Corporate Engagement in Climate Policy (RCECP).

Responsible Corporate Engagement in Climate Policy: Collective Policy Leadership

Leaders of corporations hold that regulatory uncertainty presents a significant challenge to the development of effective strategy (Engau & Hoffman, 2011). Further, scholars note that when uncertainty is minimized by regulations, business response can be a source of competitive advantage through a process of innovation and institutionalization of industry compliance norms (Jaffe et al., 1995). Thus, for some firms, corporate engagement in policy development is seen as an important and effective strategy to guard against the risks of regulatory uncertainty (Hadani & Schuler, 2013). From this perspective, and fueled by a desire to make a difference in the fight against global climate change, UNGC staff and a select group of members launched RCECP in 2014. Their efforts were bolstered by the knowledge that only 62 percent of C4C's 350 members fulfilled their membership obligations as described in Caring for Climate's constitution, to "engage more actively with ... national governments, intergovernmental organizations and civil society to develop policies and measures to provide an enabling framework for business to contribute effectively to building a low-carbon and climate-resilient economy" (C4C, 2011).

The initiative comprised three phases: research into best practices in policy engagement, development of a generalizable engagement model, and development of case studies of best practices. UNGC members who participated in RCECP worked collectively with UNGC staff and researchers to design a process for companies to lobby for public policies that would slow the pace of global climate change and hasten global policy action to address the issue. As researchers reviewed the literature on procedures and ethics of policy engagement to develop the engagement model, RCECP leadership committee members reached into their firms to test components of the model.

The engagement model directed organizations to first connect with internal and external stakeholder experts to assist in naming company activities, including investments, which could both directly and indirectly influence climate policy and the opportunities and risks of these actions. For example, companies were encouraged to develop an inventory of trade associations or professional membership organizations in which positional company leaders and other employees may have encountered and participated in climate policy discussions and served as company spokespersons. The model then directed companies to audit their engagement activities and messages and flush out spaces within the organization in which a climate change policy message was not aligned with the overall message that company leaders desired to communicate. This step emphasized the need for corporations to focus on accountability and consistency of policy engagement practices across their organizations.

Many RCECP members found that a uniform and deliberate message was not being communicated, and that in some cases employees were acting as unofficial company spokespersons without truly understanding the company's official climate change policy position. Companies with extensive, global supply chain and product delivery networks, and those that employ myriad professionals from multiple disciplines such as finance, engineering, and marketing, found themselves most at risk from dissonant messaging. This is not surprising, as employees' identities and environmental values are not only tied to the organizations they work for, but also to the professions they affiliate with (Gallagher, 2007), which makes carving out a consistent message on climate change policy sometimes difficult to do. The RCECP participants described taking on this step as challenging but necessary, recognizing that environmental policy leadership requires all organizational spokespersons, regardless of position, to speak with one voice.

Finally, in the third step, company leaders developed a clear message and outlined procedures and processes to transparently communicate that message. A key component of this last step would be to report on progress toward addressing the organization's impacts on climate change (identified in the first step) and to publicly disclose climate policy positions. For RCECP leadership companies this step was complicated – multiple platforms are used to communicate corporate engagement in climate policy, from the UNGC's annual Communications on Progress and Carbon Disclosure Project[8] submissions to annual sustainability reports on company websites. Isolating a clear and consistent message on climate policy and wrangling data from disparate sources and platforms served to be a considerable challenge for many. However, most members reported it to be a valuable learning experience for all involved.

While a select group of RCECP leadership team members shared data on their firms' practices to inform the model and to develop case studies, it was necessary to reach a broader audience of UNGC members and stakeholders to catalyze extensive corporate engagement in climate policy. Thus, a series of meetings was held to test the draft model with a larger group of UNGC members and other stakeholders and to make modifications where needed. Various scenarios in which companies implemented the model were shared with attendees who offered feedback. Results of these interactions served to refine the model and provide larger context for a guidebook (United Nations Global Compact, 2013) intended to inspire UNGC members to engage in climate policy development and share their experiences.

The UNGC held its inaugural Business Forum at the 19th Conference of the Parties (COP 19) in Warsaw, Poland, with the overall objective of supporting partnerships for collaboration between business leaders and global policy makers. The RCECP guidebook was formally launched at COP 19, and lessons about how to responsibly engage in climate change policy were put into action there. For the first time, UNGC members acting as representatives of the Caring for Climate platform participated in direct talks with policy makers geared toward finding climate change solutions. This was an important step in the lead-up to the Paris negotiations, in which a global climate change framework was anticipated.

As Christiana Figueres, then the Executive Secretary of the United Nations Framework Convention on Climate Change (UNFCC), described it, this face-to face meeting of businesses and negotiators would "create the political space for more ambition in the UN climate process, which as part of a virtuous cycle can in turn catalyze more business action." She noted that on climate change, "all the bad guys are totally joined up" and that "everybody knows that governments are listening to the private sector." Before gathering to participate in the formal COP negotiations, company leaders described the need to "work together to get the policy right," and to "draw the conversations out of the shadows."[9] Members recognized that further work would have to be done to close the messaging gap between corporate executive suites and operational units. They noted that this would require additional leadership actions on the part of business professionals, who needed to "go inside the trade associations" and engage on the climate change issue, to exercise the "right to membership privileges and power." One member compelled others to engage, saying, "We need all businesses to participate. There is a 'silent majority' of businesses who are in agreement [on climate change]." UNGC members and C4C participants described their experience at the Warsaw COP 19 as critical and "game-changing," enabling businesses to articulate a more long-term perspective on climate action. In Warsaw, UN Global Compact members expressed a responsibility to backstop national political leaders who "need to sell a future for their society rather than the fear of the unknown" by moving from "climate negotiations to climate collaboration."[10]

RCECP participants' leadership behaviors focused on engaging in the challenging work of diagnosing organizational consistency problems and coming up with solutions to facilitate the communication of a concise, honest, and transparent policy perspective. As the first step in the engagement process called on leaders to audit organizational climate change messaging, which uncovered unwanted truths, leaders needed to be prepared to confront those within the organization who were not communicating shared values. These actions necessarily required leadership practice to be deeply embedded within the organization to serve a project of mutual meaning-making (Raelin, 2016). It required both formal and positional as well as informal and marginal leaders at multiple levels and organizational roles to expose "dirty laundry." It also required them to collaborate to carefully craft an organization-wide policy message that could be used in service of a greater good – to advocate for forward-thinking climate change policies. As described below, the final phase of the collaborative leadership effort, linking with others who had engaged in similar internal organizational journeys to publicly communicate a convincing message to global policy makers, took place in Paris at the 21st Conference of the Parties.

Carbon Pricing Leadership: Collaborative Policy Engagement on a Global Stage

Once the corporate climate policy engagement model was built, validated by participants, and piloted at COP 19 in Warsaw, UNGC members, researchers and staff embarked on a journey to put the model into practice on a larger scale. It was agreed that corporate engagement in climate policy up to and during the 21st Conference of the Parties in Paris, at which the global community hoped to reach a landmark climate accord, would be an important and invaluable positive influence on policy makers. The UN Global Compact catalyzed engagement around a single mission – to mobilize members to serve as Carbon Pricing Leaders (CPL). The goal was to recruit members to provide testimony on how they had initiated a price for carbon on activities within their organizations. These testimonies were intended to provide cover for policy makers who sought to develop a global price on carbon,[11] and had often been met with resistance from others who parroted the adage that climate change policies were opposed by business.

To ensure successful implementation of the carbon pricing leadership initiative, during the course of the two years between the Warsaw COP and the Paris COP, UNGC staff and researchers focused on three efforts: conducting a survey of leaders of member organizations, interviewing individual leaders, and benchmarking best practices.[12] In the survey, UNGC members were queried to gauge overall support for a global price on carbon and to understand company motivations for implementing an internal price on carbon.[13] Unfortunately, the survey was poorly designed and results were descriptive at best. Many respondents used the survey as an opportunity to share opinions, boast about environmental stewardship accomplishments both related and unrelated to climate policy, and to vent about existing regional, national, and subnational climate policies and regulations, rather than to offer useful data on interest and motivations for implementing global climate policies.

The second and third phases of pre-Paris research were more effective. Approximately 30 environmental leaders from companies identified as having implemented internal carbon pricing policies participated in lengthy interviews with staff and researchers. Information about the nature of their programs, how they were developed, leadership actions taken to support and encourage organizational acceptance and uptake, and impacts on the organization's carbon emissions was gathered. Leaders described lengthy processes both from the ground up designing the technical components of the programs, and from the top down catalyzing their use. Programs ranged from the implementation of highly technical and closely specified prices based on years of engineering and financial analyses, to rule-of-thumb prices offered as experiments in institution-building. Uptake was highly dependent on leadership messaging and internal collaboration structures. For example, companies that involved a larger range of organizational units in developing the pricing schemes quickly noted high levels of acceptance, as did companies whose top leadership were strong advocates. Overall, once pricing schemes became organizational norms, employees largely became advocates.

In parallel with conducting in-depth interviews, researchers developed benchmarking case studies to highlight challenges and offer pathways to successful implementation. For example, Statoil, an oil and gas producer based in Norway, developed a shadow price on carbon, which has been used to assess investments in technology. Alternatively, Microsoft, the US-based computer software company, implemented a small fee on carbon that was used to fund investment in research and development of carbon reduction technologies and renewable energy projects. Interview data and benchmarking information was shared in webinars and used to develop a guide for businesses seeking to engage as a carbon pricing leader in Paris and beyond (United Nations Global Compact, 2015).

By November 2015, prior to the Paris climate meeting, at least 65 businesses had aligned with the UNGC's leadership criteria on climate action by: 1) setting an internal price on carbon significant enough to drive decreases in greenhouse gas emissions, 2) publicly advocating the need for carbon pricing, and 3) transparently reporting on progress. Many had also joined the World Bank Group's Carbon Pricing Leadership Coalition.[14] These companies were among the over 400 representatives of businesses, governments, and civil society organizations who attended the UNGC's third Caring for Climate Business Forum in Paris in December 2015. Company positional leaders who committed to speaking publicly at the Forum (after all, a UN event on a global stage requires diplomacy undergirded by formal power and influence) provided motivation to others and offered examples of climate policy advocacy and internal initiatives. They also implored others to join their collaboration. For example, John Woolard, Vice President of Energy for Google, offered that, "we hope that other companies join in. We need this to become a much more forceful and formidable movement." Paul Polman, CEO of Unilever, went further, saying, "As CEOs we understand the important signals that are sent when climate leadership comes from the very, very top. Together we are committing to providing that leadership." But it was not lost on the attendees and hopefully will not be on future readers of UNGC guidebooks that not only positional leaders were involved in these collaborative leadership efforts. Much of the collaborative work was performed by employees without formal corporate leadership designations, but with critical knowledge of *how things work* and the motivation to make a difference.

Attendees of the Forum learned about responsible engagement in climate policy and how their individual and collective actions could contribute to national commitments on climate action, or Intended Nationally Determined Commitments (INDCs).[15] They discussed additional strategies to use in enacting collaborative leadership, such as setting science-based targets on greenhouse gas reductions, using big data on climate change to influence policy makers, calling for increased investments in renewable energy, implementing climate change adaptation strategies, and participating in UNGC Local Network efforts to hasten climate change action at the local level. In a subsequent meeting, carbon pricing leaders and others met in the official negotiation venue. The UN Secretary General, US Secretary of State, France Minister of Ecology Sustainable Development and Energy, and Executive Secretary of the UN Framework Convention on Climate Change listened as business leaders announced their actions and commitments to reduce greenhouse gas emissions and work within supply chains and described their experiences as members of the RCECP and CPL initiatives. An interactive discussion followed in which participants and dignitaries considered the relationship between a right price for carbon and the realization of INDCs and actions which could be taken to support global adoption of a price on carbon.

The leadership challenge for those who participated in the CPL initiative was focused on moving beyond internal transformations to engage in external outreach in service of a lofty goal – the curation and delivery of inspirational messages about business commitments to climate action. They worked in the frame of pluralized leadership (Denis et al., 2012), in which multiple leaders pool formal and informal influence structures to advance extra-organizational goals. These carbon pricing leaders worked together across organizational boundaries to develop clear messages of support for future-looking climate policies.

Lessons from Caring for Climate: Informing a Theory of Collaborative Leadership

United Nations Global Compact members participating in the Responsible Corporate Engagement in Climate Policy and Carbon Pricing Leadership initiatives worked beyond structural borders to engage in collective action with like-minded leaders in other organizations; they created innovative paths to exercise collaborative environmental leadership. While these leaders were informed by experiences and perspectives based in their home organizations, they were freed from those organizations to engage in collaborative work in the fight to address climate change.

UNGC member company leaders that participated in both Caring for Climate initiatives – RCECP and CPL – were engaged in a three-step process of first *grounding* and then *untethering* organization-based environmental actions, followed by *linking* with those participating in the collaboration to define an expanded sense of purpose. The first two steps, grounding and untethering, are critical to the practice of collaborative environmental leadership. Leaders were grounded in a sense of the environmental mission and the organizational challenge, in this case using business resources to address the wicked problem of climate change, but then became untethered from the organization so that they were free to join with others and act collectively as boundary spanners (Tushman & Scanlan, 1981).

In global organizations facing the impacts of climate change, such as those of the C4C participants, boundary spanners play a critical role in bringing knowledge from the external environment into the internal workings of the firm. That knowledge is used to alter practices within the organization. In this case, learnings from participation in the RCECP initiative enabled leaders to audit and align climate change messaging and focus on consistent, cross-organization external communication. But, in a departure from traditional practice, these boundary-spanning leaders did not remain organization-bound. Once they transferred and translated knowledge from the external environment and used it to transform the organization (Carlile, 2004), they turned their attention to problems beyond their organization. They became "untethered." They deployed their enlightened firms' resources in service of the existential challenge of climate change and linked with like-minded leaders of other global businesses as members of the CPL initiative.

Collaborative environmental leadership is post-heroic leadership. It is not the practice of a unitary empowered, titular leader at the top of an organizational structure. It is performed in stark contrast to transformational leadership that is mostly organization-bound and hierarchal in nature. Collaborative environmental leadership is performed by a collective of leaders, both positional and ad hoc, in service of the greater good, rather than in service of a single organization and its stakeholders. Collaborative environmental leadership, the process of grounding, untethering, and linking, is critically important, as Paul Polman, Unilever CEO, recently stated: "The global business community remains committed to delivering ambitious climate action, working in partnership with city mayors, governors, and nearly 200 country governments around the world, to ensure that together we capture the economic, public health and environmental benefits of a cleaner, more efficient and resilient global economy" (B Team, 2017).

The practice of collaborative environmental leadership, which is necessary and critical to address myriad crises facing Earth and her inhabitants, operates in stark contrast to heroic or managerial leadership. It does not view Earth's resources as organizational inputs to be managed or conquered. It takes its cue from the natural environment, from the way in which ecosystems depend on their members and operate within limits. It embraces the climate crisis as motivation for leaders to leave ego by the wayside and band together as collaborators safeguarding our common future.

Notes

1 "The Millennium Development Goals set time bound targets, by which progress in reducing income poverty, hunger, disease, lack of adequate shelter and exclusion – while promoting gender equality, health, education and environmental sustainability – can be measured. They also embody basic human rights – the rights of each person on the planet to health, education, shelter and security. The Goals are ambitious but feasible and, together with the comprehensive United Nations development agenda, set the course for the world's efforts to alleviate extreme poverty by 2015" (United Nations, 2008, p. 2).
2 The ten principles are: Businesses should support and respect the protection of internationally proclaimed human rights, and make sure that they are not complicit in human rights abuses. Businesses should uphold the freedom of association and the effective recognition of the right to collective bargaining, the elimination of all forms of forced and compulsory labor, the effective abolition of child labor, and the elimination of discrimination in respect of employment and occupation. Businesses should support a precautionary approach to environmental challenges, undertake initiatives to promote greater environmental responsibility, and encourage the development and diffusion of environmentally friendly technologies. Businesses should work against corruption in all its forms, including extortion and bribery (The Ten Principles, n.d.).
3 World Leaders come together at a United Nations Summit in 2015 to ratify the 2030 Agenda for Sustainable Development, which comprises 17 SDGs. These goals provide a practical framework for a global agenda to end poverty, attack inequality and confront climate change.
4 Companies that fail to report are delisted from C4C membership rolls.
5 Sustainable Energy for All is a United Nations-sponsored, ongoing, global movement to provide universal access to renewable energy. (See www.se4all.org/.)
6 One of the most well-known PES schemes is REDD+, or reducing emissions from deforestation and forest degradation in developing countries. (See http://redd.unfccc.int/.)
7 Climate change is often termed a super wicked problem because of four characteristics: It must be addressed before it's too late, those of us trying to find a solution are responsible for creating the problem, government structures are non-existent or timid, and the economics of discounting push the problem off the current agenda (Levin et al., 2012).
8 The Carbon Disclosure Project (CDP) is a global disclosure framework that enables companies to systematically self-report environmental impacts according to a well-defined protocol. (See www.cdp.net/en/info/about-us.)
9 Uncited quotes within this chapter are from observations of conversations and informal, unattributed interviews with participants at UNGC events.

10 As a postscript, since the initiative was launched, over 100 UN Global Compact companies have made commitments to formally engage in climate policy development action.
11 This could be done either through a global tax on carbon at the input or output to production or through the development of carbon emission trading systems such as those implemented in the EU, Canada, the Northeastern US, and California.
12 UNGC members also gathered in December 2014 in Lima, Peru, at COP 20 for the second Caring for Climate Business Forum, entitled *Innovation, Ambition, Collaboration.*
13 Companies implement an internal price on carbon within their organizations in a variety of ways. They could develop a shadow price, and use it to evaluate investments; create an internal tax, fee, or trading system; or describe an implicit price based on how much the organization spends to reduce greenhouse gas emissions.
14 The carbon Pricing Leadership Coalition is a voluntary partnership between leaders from government, business, and civil society dedicated to building an evidence base to use in communicating the effectiveness of carbon pricing as a means of mitigating global climate change. Coalition members work on policy development, implementation, and evaluation. (See www.carbonpricingleadership.org/leadership-coalition.)
15 INDCs are the individual measures that UNFCCC signatory countries committed to act upon to reduce greenhouse gas emissions.

References

B Team. (2017). The B Team Statement on U.S. Withdrawal from Paris Agreement. June 1, 2017. Retrieved from: http://bteam.org/press/the-b-team-statement-on-u-s-withdrawal-from-paris-agreement/.
Bäckstrand, K., Campe, S., Chan, S., Mert, A., & Schäferhoff, M. (2012). Transnational Public Private Partnerships. In F. Biermann & P. Pattberg (Eds), *Global Environmental Governance Reconsidered* (pp. 123–148). Cambridge, MA: The MIT Press.
Benner, T., Reinicke, W. H., & Witte, J. M. (2005). Multisectoral Networks in Global Governance: Towards a pluralistic system of global governance. In D. Held and M. Koenig-Archbugi (Eds), *Global Governance and Public Accountability* (pp. 191–210). Malden, MA & Oxford: Blackwell Publishing.
Bromley, P., & Meyer, J. W. (2014). "They Are All Organizations:" The cultural roots of blurring between the nonprofit, business, and government Sectors. *Administration & Society*, 49(7), 939–966.
C4C. (2011). Caring for Climate: The Constitution. Retrieved from: http://caringforclimate.org/forum/wp-content/uploads/C4C_Constitution_FINAL.pdf.
Carlile, P. R. (2004). Transferring, Translating, and Transforming: An integrative framework for managing knowledge across boundaries. *Organization Science*, 15 (5), 555–568.
Denis, J. L., Langley, A., & Sergi, V. (2012). Leadership in the Plural. *Academy of Management Annals*, 6(1), 211–283.
Engau, C., & Hoffmann, V. H. (2009). Effects of Regulatory Uncertainty on Corporate Strategy – An analysis of firms' responses to uncertainty about post-Kyoto policy. *Environmental Science & Policy*, 12(7), 766–777.

Engau, C., & Hoffmann, V. H. (2011). Strategizing in an Unpredictable Climate: Exploring corporate strategies to cope with regulatory uncertainty. *Long Range Planning*, 44(1), 42–63.

Gallagher, D.R. (2007). The Professionalization of Sustainability. In B. Husted and S. Sharma (Eds), *Organizations and the Sustainability Mosaic* (pp. 272–290). Northampton, MA: Edward Elgar.

Gallagher, D.R. (2013). The United Nations Global Compact: Forum for environmental leadership. In O. Williams (Ed.), *The UN Millennium Development Goals, The Global Compact and the Common Good* (pp. 271–291). South Bend, IN: Notre Dame University Press.

Hadani, M., & Schuler, D. A. (2013). In Search of El Dorado: The elusive financial returns on corporate political investments. *Strategic Management Journal*, 34(2), 165–181.

Jaffe, A. B., Peterson, S. R., Portney, P. R., & Stavins, R. N. (1995). Environmental Regulation and the Competitiveness of US Manufacturing: What does the evidence tell us?, *Journal of Economic Literature*, 33(1), 132–163.

Kettunen, M., & ten Brink, P. (2012). Nature, Green Economy and Sustainable Development: The outcomes of UN Rio +20 conference on sustainable development. *Nature Conservation*, 2, 1–6.

Kosoy, N., & Corbera, E. (2010). Payments for Ecosystem Services as Commodity Fetishism. *Ecological Economics*, 69(6), 1228–1236.

Levin, K., Cashore, B., Bernstein, S., & Auld, G. (2012). Overcoming the Tragedy of Super Wicked Problems: Constraining our future selves to ameliorate global climate change. *Policy Sciences*, 45(2), 123–152.

Raelin, J. A. (2016). Imagine There Are No Leaders: Reframing leadership as collaborative agency. *Leadership*, 12(2), 131–158.

Ruggie, J. G. (2002). The Theory and Practice of Learning Networks. *Journal of Corporate Citizenship*, 5(1), 27–36.

Shapiro-Garza, E. (2013). Contesting the Market-Based Nature of Mexico's National Payments for Ecosystem Services programs: Four sites of articulation and hybridization. *Geoforum*, 46, 5–15.

Spradley, J. P. (2016). *Participant Observation*. Long Grove, IL: Waveland Press.

The Ten Principles of the UN Global Compact. (n.d.). Retrieved from: www.unglobalcompact.org/what-is-gc/mission/principles.

Tesner, S., & Kell, G. (2000). *The United Nations and Business. A partnership recovered*. Basingstoke: Palgrave Macmillan.

Tushman, M. L., & Scanlan, T. J. (1981). Boundary Spanning Individuals: Their role in information transfer and their antecedents. *Academy of Management Journal*, 24(2), 289–305.

United Nations. (1999). Secretary-General Proposes Global Compact on Human Rights, Labour, Environment, in Address to World Economic Forum in Davos. Retrieved from: www.un.org/press/en/1999/19990201.sgsm6881.html.

United Nations. (2008). Committing to Action: Achieving the Millennium Development Goals. Background note by the Secretary-General. Retrieved from: www.un.org/ga/president/62/issues/mdg/backgroundmdg_sg.pdf.

United Nations Global Compact. (2007). Caring for Climate: A statement by the business leaders of the UN Global Compact. Retrieved from: www.unglobalcompact.org/docs/issues_doc/Environment/climate/Caring_for_climate_Tomorrow_07.pdf.

United Nations Global Compact. (2010). Caring for Climate: The business leadership platform. 15 June. Retrieved from: http://unglobalcompact.org/docs/issues_doc/ Environment/climate/ CARING_FOR_CLIMATE_STATEMENT_2010.pdf.

United Nations Global Compact. (2013). Guide for Responsible Corporate Engagement in Climate Policy: A Caring for Climate report. 15 June. Retrieved from: www.unglobalcompact.org/library/501.

United Nations Global Compact. (2015). Executive Guide to Carbon Pricing Leadership: A Caring for Climate report. 15 June. Retrieved from: www.ungloba lcompact.org/library/3711.

Van Maanen, J. (1979). The Fact of Fiction in Organizational Ethnography. *Administrative Science Quarterly*, 24(4), 539–550.

Waddock, S. (2013). The Wicked Problems of Global Sustainability Need Wicked (Good) Leaders and Wicked (Good) Collaborative Solutions. *Journal of Management for Global Sustainability*, 1(1), 91–111.

Wanner, T. (2015). The New "Passive Revolution" of the Green Economy and Growth Discourse: Maintaining the "sustainable development" of neoliberal capitalism. *New Political Economy*, 20(1), 21–41.

9 Climate Change Leadership

From Tragic to Comic Discourse

Benjamin W. Redekop and Morgan Thomas

Introduction

Amidst calls by the scientific community for help from social scientists (Nature Climate Change, 2014, 2015), climate change is increasingly gaining the attention of leadership scholars, who have begun to consider climate change and other environmental problems as *leadership* challenges that elicit specific forms, approaches, and styles of leadership in response (e.g., Gallagher, 2012; Redekop, 2010; Stober et al., 2013). It is not enough to apply well-worn leadership conceptions to environmental problems, since those conceptions emerged in the service of our current extractive and unsustainable industrial system (see the Introduction and Chapters 1 and 4 in this volume). Rather, we need to critically evaluate and rethink the form and content of leadership in this new and frightening "Eaarth" we are creating (McKibben, 2010).

When it comes to grand challenges like global climate change, such rethinking must not only be theoretical, but also grounded in real-world practices. It must take into account the lived experience and perspectives of activists and leaders working on this issue worldwide. It must also be grounded in the growing body of scholarly research into the relationship between human beings and the natural environment. Given the relative novelty of the concept of "climate change leadership," we believe that a broad perspective on the recent history of climate change leadership as it has evolved from the 1980s up to the present day is a useful starting point for further thinking and research on this topic.

Our analysis begins with an overview of the first-generation climate leadership of Al Gore, James Hansen, and Bill McKibben, who can be broadly characterized as propounding a "tragic" and "catastrophizing"[1] discourse. It then moves to analysis of in-depth interviews with 14 second-generation climate leaders from the United States, Canada, Mexico, the Philippines, Hungary, South Africa, Taiwan, and Australia, contextualized by recent academic research on this topic. We suggest that this second generation of climate leaders offers a more "comic" discourse that acknowledges the tragic consequences of inaction but tends to avoid catastrophizing rhetoric, appealing to a sense of hope and possibility despite limited progress on this issue. This part of the chapter is organized into topic areas that reflect the questions we asked our interviewees as well as emergent themes and existing research on this topic.

As we will show, despite significant variations in approach and emphasis, our interviewees generally lend credence to Simon Western's conception of an emerging Eco-leadership discourse (or paradigm) that eschews traditional forms of hierarchical, positional leadership in favor of approaches more congruent with the healthy functioning of biological systems, aimed at fostering the emergence of leadership at the margins and throughout the organization or social entity (i.e., "grassroots") rather than simply emanating from the center, and the flourishing of the social-environmental system as a whole rather than narrow economic or political interests (Western, 2008/ 2013; 2010; see also Wielkiewicz & Stelzner, 2010).

We do not mean to suggest that the eco-leadership paradigm is a totalizing discourse as much as a way to understand and interpret emerging approaches to climate change leadership. As Western (2010) suggests, previous leadership discourses are still with us, overlapping with eco-leadership rather than being entirely displaced by it. Our suggestion in this chapter is that over time, a perceptible shift can be seen taking place, away from more traditional approaches and understandings of leadership, toward an eco-leadership approach; and this shift has been characterized by a trend away from more tragic to more comic discourses of climate change.

First Generation Climate Leaders: Tragic and Catastrophic Discourse

This distinction draws on Foust and Murphy's (2009) suggestion that there are two variants of apocalyptic discourse about climate change in the US elite and popular press: tragic and comic. The tragic version points to a fallen social order and unstoppable catastrophic ending that limits human agency. In its extreme form, it is a polarizing discourse that invites skepticism and also exempts human beings from responsibility to take action on the issue. The comic discourse, on the other hand, "promotes humanity as mistaken, rather than evil. As such, comic discourse allows some space for bringing ideologically disparate communities together … Time is open-ended, with human intervention possible. Humanity is less likely to be resigned to its fate, and, as such, may be inspired to take steps to change" (pp. 162–163).

While we do not wish to suggest that first-generation climate leaders like Gore, Hansen, and McKibben present entirely negative and pessimistic perspectives, and that second-generation leaders are naively hopeful and optimistic, we believe that the distinction we are making helps to shed light on the general differences in form between first- and second-generation climate change leadership.[2] It is also important to note that McKibben, born in 1960 and leader of 350.org, a global, grassroots leader on climate change, should be counted a member of both first- and second-generation cohorts of climate leaders. Nevertheless, the tragic discourse seems more descriptive of the approach of McKibben and other first-generation leaders who felt – and continue to feel – compelled to communicate the awful truth that they have uncovered (e.g., McKibben 1989/2006; McKibben 2010), while the comic approach better characterizes second-generation leaders who have absorbed the tragic message but feel compelled to move beyond it. It is our contention that a conscious synthesis of both approaches may offer a way forward for leaders who seek to find creative avenues for leadership on this issue.

Al Gore

Al Gore (b. 1948) has been at the forefront of the climate change issue from the late 1980s, when he chaired Senate hearings on global warming. He deserves credit for recognizing the importance of this and other environmental issues and bringing them to mainstream attention. Gore has been at least partly responsible both for raising the climate change issue to public awareness, and inadvertently for the politicization and fracturing of the issue along party lines in the United States. As such he presents an example of both the strengths and pitfalls of political leadership on this issue.

Gore long ago recognized the entrenched nature of fossil fuels in American life and politics and has called repeatedly for leadership on global warming. His language has been highly apocalyptic from early on. In *Earth in the Balance* (1992/2006), he speaks in terms of an ecological crisis that is a threat to civilization, with the fight for environmental sustainability similar to the fight against Nazism and failure to do so as a form of appeasement, and of the need for a "global Marshall Plan" to save the environment. He critiques Western capitalist culture as materialistic and our ecological crisis as the result of a spiritual malaise. More recently, he has been speaking in terms of "ecological crisis" and "global planetary emergency" (Barringer & Revkin, 2007).

At the same time, Gore has always sought to work within existing political and economic structures, so much so that he has become wealthy from his investments in media and alternative energy: in 2013, he was reported to be worth around $200 million (Condon, 2013). He has long proposed international agreements that establish rules of acceptable environmental behavior. He helped to negotiate the Framework Convention on Climate Change and the Kyoto Protocol and has continued to be a player in international efforts to secure binding agreements on climate change. Gore is a founder of the Alliance for Climate Protection, The Climate Reality Project, Generation Investment Management, and Current TV; he has also served as a member of the Board of Directors of Apple, a senior advisor to Google, and a partner at the venture capital firm Kleiner, Perkins, Caulfield, and Byers.

Gore has in many respects played the role of both "prophet" and "explainer" of climate change (Traub, 2007). He has always been very well-informed and knowledgeable about the science of climate change, and tireless in warning anyone who will listen about the dangers of inaction. His slide show, film, and book about global warming have done much to publicize the issue and bring it to worldwide attention. Because of this work, he shared the Nobel Peace Prize in 2007 with the Intergovernmental Panel on Climate Change.

Despite his impressive résumé, we would suggest that Gore's efforts have brought mixed results. Without his stature as Democratic Senator, Vice President, and US presidential candidate, he would not have been able to bring as much attention to the issue; but at the same time, it seems clear that it helped to cement Republican opposition, supported by the fossil fuel industry, to taking action on climate change over the past few decades. The extreme polarization of American politics has meant in this case that "if he's for it, I'm against it," aided and abetted by fear among Republicans that regulations aimed at mitigating climate change will expand the scope and reach of the US government. Thanks to Gore's status as a grandee of the Democratic party, it has become all too easy to identify action on climate change with the Democratic party and supposed Democratic proclivities for "big government." Gore's recent sale of Current TV to Al-Jazeera (owned by the petro-state Qatar) has given further ammunition to his enemies and those who wish to stall action on climate change, and has seriously undermined his effectiveness as a public leader. He appears to have broken one of the fundamental rules of effective leadership: don't be a hypocrite. This is a truth of common sense and common experience, but also social science research (see for example Martin et al., 2013; Moorman et al., 2013; Palanski & Yammarino, 2007. For an example of critique of Gore along these lines, see Rapier, 2013).

Gore's putative hypocrisy and growing wealth also undermine one of his previous advantages as a climate leader. As communication scholar Denise Stodola (2010) has astutely pointed out, Gore's loss in the 2000 presidential election and subsequent reinvention as a global climate change leader helped to humanize him and foster audience identification with him and a similarly beleaguered natural world. It has, however, become increasingly difficult to view him as an "underdog." His separation from his popular wife Tipper also has not helped him maintain public affection. All of these issues do not negate the grim reality of climate change and the need to address it, but they have seriously damaged Gore's ability to lead on this issue, and arguably have caused some damage to the cause. Nevertheless, it is important to acknowledge the scope and impact of Gore's leadership on this issue over many decades.

James Hansen

Dr. James Hansen (b. 1941) is one of the preeminent climate scientists of his generation, and was one of the first and most vocal figures in bringing the science of climate change to public attention. He has been at the forefront of climate change research since the 1980s, and his Congressional testimony in 1989 (at Gore's behest) launched the modern climate change movement. Honored by *Time* magazine in 2006 as one of the world's 100 most influential people, Hansen served as Director of NASA Goddard Institute for Space Studies from 1981 until his retirement in 2013. Since then, he has continued to work tirelessly as a scientist, activist, and leader on this issue. He has become a fixture at major climate protests and has been arrested or cited a half dozen times as a result of nonviolent civil disobedience.

Some scientific colleagues have questioned his activism, saying it gives climate skeptics ammunition to say he is not being "objective" (Gillis, 2013). Hansen for his part has called repeatedly for strong political leadership on this issue (e.g., Hansen, 2006), and feels that political inaction means that scientists themselves need to start taking a leadership role. Although he would be the first to say that he is not a "born leader" – portraying himself as by nature a shy, nerdy scientist – he has most certainly become one, by most any standard of leadership, and is seen so by others (e.g., Abraham, 2013).

As Hansen makes clear in his book on climate change, *Storms of my Grandchildren* (2009), his emergence as a leader on climate change occurred only by necessity and not without a great deal of reluctance and anguish on his part. The book, part popular science and part memoir, can be read as a *bildungsroman* that chronicles Hansen's transition from innocent, shy scientist to public activist and leader, based on what he has learned about climate change. Despite his innate shyness, Hansen has not been reticent in clearly and forcefully communicating the realities and dangers of anthropogenic climate change: it is simply "the greatest threat civilization faces" (2009, p. 70); "We really do have a planet in peril" (p. 72); as such, "this is our last chance" (p. xii). Although "rational, feasible actions could divert dangerous consequences, anthropogenic forcing has created a ticking time bomb" (p. 74, 78). "If the world does not make a dramatic shift in energy policies over the next few years, we may well pass the point of no return" (p. 171).

Hansen presents himself as a "witness" rather than a "preacher": someone who has knowledge that is so terrifying he cannot remain silent (Hansen, 2009; Hansen, 2012). The birth of his grandchildren had much to do with his transition from bench scientist to vocal public activist and leader, and they are featured in photos throughout *Storms of my Grandchildren*. As a top NASA administrator during the Bush administration, Hansen faced tremendous pressure and even at times censoring. He proved himself to be indefatigable and fearless in stating the science above political interference by the White House (Bowen, 2007; Hansen, 2009). He started writing letters to public leaders in 2007 and since then has been deeply involved in policy discussions, with a moratorium on the building of new coal plants a major goal. Hansen has also recently been working on making a case for nuclear power as an alternative to the burning of fossil fuels (Kharecha & Hansen, 2013).

Hansen has begun studying Gandhi's concepts of civil disobedience, arguing that "We cannot give up" even if the democratic process fails us (2009, p. 246), and that "Civil resistance may be our best hope" (p. 277). He was arrested for the first time at Coal River Mountain, West Virginia, in 2009, and was subsequently arrested in civil protests in 2010, 2011, and 2013. Bill McKibben calls Hansen the "patron saint" of 350.org, and Hansen has served as a model to other climate scientists about "how to navigate a world where speaking truth about climate change guarantees vitriolic attack" (Abraham, 2013).

Although he has repeatedly offered solutions to the problem of climate change, including for example the idea of a revenue-neutral "carbon fee" on fossil fuels, Hansen's main discursive trope has been tragic: humanity is on a collision course with the laws of physics and seems unable to act in a rational manner in response, despite the best efforts of scientists to get the word out. It is his task to share the terrible truth that he and others have uncovered, before it is too late. As in Rachel Carson's *Silent Spring* (1962), there is a stealthy, spectral enemy in our midst, and it is us.

Bill McKibben

If James Hansen is the reluctant scientist/leader, Bill McKibben is the activist/leader intent on spreading Hansen's message that 350 ppm of CO_2 is the only "safe" level for the perpetuation of human civilization in its current form. McKibben has mobilized young and old worldwide, using the internet to carry out "distributed political action" that seeks to combat climate change (McKibben, 2010, p. 210). McKibben is a journalist and author who wrote the first book on climate change for a popular audience (The End of Nature, 1989), and is currently Schumann Distinguished Scholar at Middlebury College when not on the road campaigning for 350.org.

His recent book, *Eaarth* (2010), is a tough, unflinching look at global warming as it is already happening, while seeking to chart a way forward in sustainable living that leaves a lighter footprint on this new, transformed planet *Eaarth*. "Imagine we live on a planet. Not our cozy, taken-for-granted earth, but a planet, a real one, with melting poles and dying forests and a heaving, corrosive sea, raked by winds, strafed by storms, scorched by heat. An inhospitable place" (2010, p. 1). McKibben charts, in painful detail, all that is already happening on earth due to climate change, arguing that this was not an issue for our grandchildren, but for *our parents*. And he does so as a master of darkly humorous doomsaying: "We're not … going to get back the planet we used to have, the one on which our civilization developed. … We're like the guy who smoked for forty years and then he had a stroke. He doesn't smoke anymore, but the left side of his body doesn't work either" (2010, p. 16). McKibben laments the loss of "Earth" as we knew it, replaced by an "Eaarth" that we are only just beginning to understand. "We have traveled to a new planet, propelled on a burst of carbon dioxide. That new planet, as is often the case in science fiction, looks more or less like our own but clearly isn't. I know that I'm repeating myself. I'm repeating myself on purpose. This is the biggest thing that's ever happened" (2010, pp. 45–46).

McKibben goes beyond doomsaying in the book, however, to talk in practical terms about what in his view needs to change, including the fixation on economic growth; even the idea of "green growth," promoted by Al Gore, is criticized as wrongheaded, given the scope of the challenges faced by Eaarth (2010, pp. 49–52). Instead of growth, McKibben talks about "backing off": "So here are my candidates for words that may help us think usefully about the future. Durable, Sturdy, Stable, Hardy, Robust. These are squat, solid, stout words. They conjure a world where we no longer grow by leaps and bounds, but where we *hunker down*, where we *dig in*." They are words that imply maturity, and steadiness; "think husband, not boyfriend" (2010, pp. 102–103).

McKibben thus goes firmly against the grain of American optimism and youth culture. Yet he has been able to inspire grassroots action by all ages – including young people – via 350.org with a distributed international staff of (at last count) 56 people, most under the age of 35, many in their 20s. The approach has been to use the internet to organize local events and share them, rather than all gathering together into one place, which makes little sense given the resulting CO_2 emissions. This approach thus features a distributed leadership model, fostering leadership at the local level via organizing events to coincide with the global events that 350.org organizes. This is but one example of the ways in which conscious attention to the natural environment impacts leadership styles and approaches. The organization has been heavily involved in protesting completion of the Keystone XL pipeline via a variety of demonstrations and marches that have included civil disobedience and arrests. It has also been a leader in the fossil fuel divestment campaign, which is beginning to gain traction in various institutions, including universities.

Contemporary Climate Change Leaders: From Tragic to Comic Discourse

In order to move beyond the focus on paramount leaders like Gore, Hansen, and McKibben, and to gain a wider perspective, we conducted in-depth interviews with 14 second-generation environmental leaders from the United States, Canada, Mexico, the Philippines, Hungary, South Africa, Taiwan, and Australia, who are leading, in one way or another, on climate change. They ranged in age, at the time of the interviews, from their early 20s to mid-50s, with ten in their 20s and 30s, and four in their 40s and 50s. Their names and occupations/affiliations are listed at the end of this chapter. Our goal was to conduct in-depth conversations with second-generation climate leaders from around the world; we acknowledge that our sample is neither particularly large nor representative of all those who are leading on this issue. It was limited by a number of factors, including the difficulty of finding individuals willing to engage in a one-hour recorded interview. Nevertheless, we believe that our sample provides useful data on climate change leadership in a variety of settings, and that in-depth interviews provide the necessary nuance and context for such a complex, systemic issue as climate change.

We asked each interviewee the same basic questions and fully transcribed their answers. Responses were analyzed and correlated by question and topic for comparative purposes. What follows are some of the more salient questions we asked, followed by a representative sample of our interviewee's responses. Our goal in this section is to provide a sketch of some of the primary themes and issues that are emerging on the ground by a variety of climate leaders, put them into context – including the relevant academic research that has been done on this topic – and compare them to the themes and topics of first-generation climate leaders like Gore, Hansen, and McKibben. The first question we asked our interviewees acknowledged the tremendous challenges of climate change:

What do you see as the biggest obstacle for leaders when it comes to this issue?

Answers to this question were diverse and included: breaking through social-media dilettantism to get people actively engaged in their communities; lack of political will on the part of those in power; the difficulty of translating grassroots efforts into national-level policy, and vice versa; untangling the science from the politics; dealing with government harassment of NGOs; finding good role models people can relate to; discovering an appropriate leadership development model; the power of the fossil fuel industry; how to connect local impacts to the larger global phenomenon of climate change; overcoming fears that action on climate change will harm the economy; and overcoming apathy and the feeling of being overwhelmed by this issue. One interviewee said that his answer to this question "changes on a daily basis."

Most of our respondents did not say that lack of information was a major challenge; and indeed, most researchers are in agreement that simply communicating scientific data about climate change is not enough to motivate relevant behavior change (e.g., Chess & Johnson, 2007; Dunwoody, 2007; Kahan et al., 2012; Lakoff, 2010; Moser & Dilling, 2007; Nisbet, 2009; Whitmarsh et al., 2011). On the other hand, a number of our interviewees mentioned the utility of bringing attention to the local impacts of climate change, and one individual noted that bringing clear, objective, and actionable information to politicians is one of the best ways to influence them toward action on this issue.

Critics of the straightforward scientific approach to shaping public policy argue that if scientific data becomes the ultimate arbiter of action on global warming, then there will always be those who will deny or bend the science to suit their own interests, ideology, and partisan political affiliation, which can easily trump scientific data when it comes to beliefs about climate change (see for example the studies by Kahan et al., 2012, and Wolsko et al., 2016). Rather, the thinking goes, we need to focus on pragmatic arguments like energy security and efficiency, economic development, and national health policy, rather than science, to move forward on this issue. It might even be best not to mention "climate change" or "climate science" at all (Hampel, 2015; Nature Climate Change, 2017).

This viewpoint was reflected in the responses of many of our interviewees. For example, some indicated that instead of engaging climate change deniers directly on the science, they shift the ground to talk about known health benefits of lower fossil fuel emissions. Others suggested that they focus on local impacts or contributors to climate change that are not in doubt – e.g., air pollution from power plants. The point is to frame the problem in terms of shared environmental values and effects that are obvious and local. Yet even here there is a slippery slope, since scientific data plays a key role in deciding the nature of public health problems like the effect of coal plant emissions on respiratory problems, just as it does in providing guidance on climate change. This leads us to the next question we asked our climate change leaders:

What is your main approach to influencing others to act on climate change?

We also received a wide variety of responses to this question. Our interviewee from the Philippines focused on "naming culprits and calling for justice," and seeks to "get people enraged." One of the climate leaders from Mexico stated that "it depends on whom I am talking to." She uses simple language and provides basic information about climate change impacts and responses to local communities. A unique challenge in Mexico is to overcome fear of government corruption when dealing with local land use programs that are aimed at mitigating climate change. As indicated above, most interviewees stressed the need to connect global climate change to local impacts; this was one of the most commonly cited influence strategies, and is a finding strongly supported by empirical research (e.g., Dunwoody, 2007, pp. 93–95; Leiserowitz, 2007; Moser, 2007, p. 70; PRRI/AAR, 2014; Whitmarsh & O'Neill, 2011, p. 5). It seems clear that those who want to lead on climate change should familiarize themselves with data on local impacts and share it with others as a first step toward mobilizing support and action.

Younger-generation leaders focused on the need to stay positive (more on that in a moment); sincerity, authenticity, and personal connections were important to a number of our interviewees. Our Australian interviewee stated that it is very important to understand peoples' motivations and concerns, and to work with visceral and emotional responses, navigate them, and find "connection points" with people. He appeals to Australians' national pride and pride of place, their entrepreneurial spirit, and he works to create a space for dialogue rather than reinforcing a single point of view. This focus on dialogue and engagement at the grassroots level – rather than top-down information campaigns – is gaining increasing traction in the scholarly literature (e.g., Brulle, 2010; Regan, 2007; Whitmarsh et al., 2011) and will be discussed further below.

One interviewee spoke of trying to induce behavior change with small steps that can lead to changes in habits. Research shows that habits are powerful predictors of behavior and can override intentions and make us resistant to new information (see for example Verplanken, 2011). As such, it is useful to understand how habitual behaviors can be changed. Life-course changes can bring about changes in habits, for example; and some even argue that forced behavior change – for example via legislation – aided by cognitive and emotional reinforcement can lead to positive changes in habits (Verplanken, 2011, pp. 26–28). This latter viewpoint conflicts, at least on the surface, with the finding that intrinsic motivation tends to be superior to extrinsic motivation when it comes to spreading pro-environmental behaviors (Redekop, 2010a), pointing to a question for further research: what are the situational variables that predict the superiority of intrinsic versus extrinsic motivation when it comes to behavior changes relevant to climate change? One important contextual variable to consider is that of age, leading us to our next question:

Do you use different influence strategies according to age? Are there generational differences in awareness on this issue?

Most interviewees acknowledged that younger people – those still in school – are generally more aware and accepting of the science of climate change. Predictably, younger people are more easily activated on this issue, and more ready to challenge the status quo. A Taiwanese interviewee called it a "sassy issue" for young people. Our South African climate leader felt that those 55 and older were tired out from the fight against apartheid, and were looking to younger generations for leadership on climate change. One of our Mexican respondents feels that older generations did not grow up with the idea that global phenomena like climate change can affect their lives, in the way that younger generations have. However, although our Canadian interviewee felt that school-age children were more aware of the issue, she did not see much of a correlation between age and level of engagement. The climate leader from the Philippines felt that the older generation is more interested in achieving middle-class status and comforts than protecting the environment.

A 2010 national (US) survey that looked at generational differences in attitudes and beliefs about climate change reinforces the idea that while younger people – e.g., 18–34-year-olds – are in some ways more informed about the issue, there is "no predictable portrait of young people when it comes to global warming. While less concerned about and preoccupied with global warming than older generations, they are slightly more likely to believe that global warming is caused by human factors and that there is scientific consensus that it is occurring" (Feldman et al., 2010, p. 2). Statistics show that climate change, as an issue, becomes more concerning to people as they grow older. However, twice as many people aged 18–22 think global warming is "personally important" than 23–34-year-olds. The younger cohort is also more open to changing their mind about climate change than the somewhat older cohort.

In general, interview and survey data indicate that while there are some differences between age cohorts when it comes to beliefs and understandings about climate change, "generational differences on this question are modest" (PRRI/AAR, 2014). The main conclusion that we feel can be drawn is that younger people are the age cohort most open to education and influence on this issue, and developing a variety of ways to reach and engage younger people is of great importance.

The jury is still out on whether "new media" is a catalyst for change or a way to feel like one is engaged without really doing anything. New media certainly provides connections, but it does not replace the old-fashioned need to organize and inspire people on the ground and away from their computers (O'Neill & Boykoff, 2011). This was a common challenge highlighted by some interviewees – how to leverage social media to get people to actually do things in the 'real' world. One tempting approach is to heighten fears about the impacts of unchecked climate change. We asked our interviewees:

To *what degree is it useful to frighten people about the future, as opposed to projecting optimism about being able to meet its challenges?*

If there was one topic that seems to divide the generations, it is this one. If first-generation climate leaders like Al Gore, James Hansen, and Bill McKibben have often used catastrophizing rhetoric to bring the issue of climate change to public attention, younger-generation leaders are strongly averse to "doom and gloom" and the use of fear tactics. Our youngest interviewees – those in their 20s – were the most adamant that fear tactics were counterproductive and to be avoided at all costs. One interviewee stated that "it makes me cringe" to even think about frightening people; she and others felt that people need a "yes" to move forward. All but two of our interviewees were under 50 years old, and ten were under 40. Nearly all were opposed to fear tactics: information and understanding – yes; doom and gloom, no. The consensus is that fear is disempowering and "switches people off" – if overwhelmed, people will feel detached and helpless. They need a sense of hope and optimism and clear pathways toward making a difference on this issue, tied to local concerns and interests. One of the climate leaders from Mexico (aged 32) stated that although she does talk about "the bad perspectives on the future" when seeking to motivate people to act, "I always have to be very positive ... I'm always quite optimistic when I approach actors to highlight the roles [they] can play" in making a difference on climate change. One respondent spoke about the need to "enrage" people rather than frighten them. Although this was not a common response, it still reinforces the idea that people need to feel empowered rather than frightened.

There is in fact a growing body of research that supports the idea that "fear won't do it" when it comes to motivating people to act on climate change. Empirical studies show that "although [fear-inducing] representations have potential for attracting people's attention to climate change, fear is generally an ineffective tool for motivating genuine personal engagement. Nonthreatening imagery and icons that link to individuals' everyday emotions and concerns in the context of this macro-environmental issue tend to be the most engaging" (O'Neill & Nicholson-Cole, 2009, p. 355; see also DeLuca, 2009, p. 268; Moser, 2007). If this is the case, one might ask, how can we move beyond, and not simply between, the poles of debilitating catastrophism and blind optimism in attempting to influence others on this issue?

Narrative Approaches

This leads us to the topic of narrative approaches to climate change. This topic was not covered by our initial interview questions, but it emerged as a salient subject through our interviewees' responses as well as a survey of the literature on climate change communication. The Australian climate leader we interviewed indicates that he is "quite big" on narrative approaches. As part of his focus on "connecting" with people on a personal basis, he feels that public narrative bridges the emotional gap between people and that stories help to address emotional responses to the issue of climate change. He feels that you have to "give away" part of yourself, or find something in yourself that might be endearing to others. The ReCharge program, with which two of our interviewees are affiliated, includes storytelling as one of its four leader-development quadrants. One climate leader we interviewed uses Jonah Sacks' book *Story Wars* as a guide. He employs what he calls "narrative campaigning" that connects climate change to problems experienced by the most vulnerable, inserting messages that enrage and highlight injustice, and framing the audience as partaking in a "hero's journey" as described by Joseph Campbell.

One of our respondents quite naturally brought up the topic of narrative and storytelling in response to our question about fear tactics, saying: "There used to be so many [negative] stories that were so far away from me. ... Now I hear more and more sad stories that [have occurred] closer to me. ... So, I'm always trying to use these stories [to tell people] that climate change is not only happening at the North Pole with the polar bears, it actually is showing itself close to me or my family or around the world. It's a way to make it closer." Thus, although not all of our interviewees mentioned narrative and storytelling as a communication tool, a number of our respondents use very well-developed narrative approaches, and spoke about them in the course of answering other questions.

According to Nature Climate Change (2014a), "The stories we construct to contextualize climate change and formulate policy responses are not only important for their role in shaping our goals and objectives, but also have the capacity to inspire or demotivate." The editors argue that "Climate change is – perhaps because of its cross-cutting nature – particularly open to being interpreted within a multitude of different overarching frames, or narratives. Consequently, disagreements about facts and figures seem to be, at bottom, due to disagreements about the fundamental story into which these details fit, rather than facets of the details themselves" (n.p.). The communication theorist George Lakoff (2010) suggests that when it comes to complex issues like global warming, frames matter. "What is needed is a constant effort to build up the background frames needed to understand the crisis, while building up neural circuitry to inhibit the wrong frames." Leaders thus need to "provide a structured understanding of what [they] are saying. Don't give laundry lists. Tell stories that exemplify your values and rouse emotions ... find general themes or narratives that incorporate the points you need to make" (p. 74; pp. 79–80).

Nisbet (2009) provides a typology of eight narrative frames applicable to climate change: social progress; economic development/competitiveness; morality/ethics; scientific & technical uncertainty; Pandora's box; public accountability/governance; middle way; conflict and strategy. These frames can provide arguments both for and against taking action on climate change, and as such are "deductive mental boxes and interpretive storylines that can be used to bring diverse audiences together on common ground, shape personal behavior, or mobilize collective action" (p. 22). Nisbet notes that "One way to reach audiences is to recruit influential peers to pass on selectively framed information about climate change that resonates with the background of the targeted audience and that addresses their personal information needs" (p. 22). This latter point was raised by two of our interviewees. In both contexts (Hungary and Canada), they are involved in recruiting speakers on climate change for various audiences. Their task, as they see it, is to align speaker background and experience with appropriate audiences, thereby enhancing the credibility of the message or story about climate change that audiences will hear.

The storytelling theme resonates throughout the literature and research on pro-environmental influence strategies. For example, Hamilton (2011) describes "Open Homes" events in England designed to share eco-renovation projects with the public: "The greatest strength of the Open Homes events seems to be the power of real-life experience and the telling of a 'story' by an ordinary citizen about their own home, combined with the visitor's experience of being in, seeing and touching their home" (p. 175). In a study of the leadership shown by Small Island Developing States (SIDS) in climate change negotiations, the authors conclude that SIDS were most powerful and influential when telling a story about the existential threat of climate change to their communities and way of life (Corneloup & Mol, 2014, p. 293). In a quite different context, researchers suggest that when it comes to using social comparisons to promote public engagement with climate change, the evidence suggests two basic strategies will be most effective: either compare the ingroup's environmental behavior to underperforming or non-normative outgroups, or "inform the target group about its deteriorating performance in comparison with its past results" (Rabinovitch et al., 2011, p. 80). In other words, tell a story about how the in-group has fallen away from its own better self as it existed in the past.

Conclusion: Eco-Leadership at the Grassroots

Finally, a question that we asked our interviewees had to do with their views on the best or most appropriate forms of leadership to make progress on climate change. It was posed both as a specific question and as a thematic element of the interview as a whole:

What kind of leadership is needed to move forward on this issue?

Among the climate leaders we interviewed, the most common theme was the need for bottoms-up, grassroots approaches. None spoke of the need for powerful, charismatic, "transforming" leaders, although a few working at higher government levels cited the need for political will and the importance of leadership at the highest levels to get things done; but they too cited the importance of grassroots leadership coming from the bottom up as a key element in the process: "There are a lot of politicians who call themselves leaders, but if you analyze what they do, they are actually only giving good speeches." This climate activist/leader went on to praise local, "frontline" leaders like an individual she knows who is developing community greenhouses. Our climate leader from Taiwan suggested that in the United States, grassroots leadership was more salient, while in China it is the opposite – the Chinese government is like a father who provides leadership on issues that are of concern to his people. Clearly, the more authoritarian the government, the less likely it is that leadership will flourish at the grassroots. Yet, according to this interviewee, the anger of Chinese citizens about environmental issues "is definitely a reason why the government is doing SO much right now, going so fast right now. ... Maybe I shouldn't be positive but I think this is a very good sign, actually like the Chinese people have some voice being heard."

The general emphasis (with some exceptions) on grassroots, non-hier-archical approaches is no doubt due in part to the nature of our sample: we interviewed younger climate activists/leaders who are themselves for the most part working at the local level. But even those working among estab-lished political, social, and economic constituencies (Mexico, Hungary, Canada) emphasized grassroots leadership and/or education of children as key forms of climate leadership. One interviewee, who is himself clearly a leader on this issue, was hesitant to discuss "leadership" in a traditional positional sense, as a useful construct, and stressed the need to engage on a personal level with other individuals, and in general to make the issue of climate change less abstract and more personal. The only individual to mention charismatic leadership suggested that although people expect it, it "suppresses" the leadership of others and was to be avoided.

In general, the responses we received lend credence to Simon Western's contention of an emerging Eco-leadership discourse that rejects traditional forms of hierarchical, positional leadership in favor of approaches more congruent with the healthy functioning of biological systems: leadership aimed at fostering the emergence of leadership at the margins and through-out the organization or social entity rather than simply emanating from the center, and the flourishing of the social-environmental system as a whole rather than narrow economic or political interests (Western, 2008/2013, 2010; see also Wielkiewicz & Stelzner, 2010). According to Western, "While tradi-tional historical teaching points to the 'great man' theory of leadership, it is the marginalized, grassroots social movements that often lead and innovate change, and so it is with eco-leadership, which emerges from environmental social activism" (2010, p. 43). As such, "Eco-leadership shifts the focus from individual leaders to leadership – a radically distributed leadership – in an attempt to harness the energy and creativity in a whole system" (p. 43). It would seem to be no coincidence that leaders working on complex environmental problems like climate change tend to advocate an eco-leadership model. A systemic problem needs systemic forms of leadership to address it, and people who spend their time thinking about environmental problems are naturally more attuned to the workings of complex ecological systems.

Others argue that *both* "industrial" *and* "ecological" leadership approa-ches are needed to address complex environmental problems (Wielkiewicz & Stelzner, 2010), and it is indeed an open question as to whether any one leadership approach or perspective can on its own adequately address issues like climate change (Redekop, 2010b). Whatever the case, the climate leaders we interviewed, most of whom were under 50 at the time of the interview, articulated understandings of leadership that resonate with, and provide evidence of, an emerging eco-leadership paradigm. Their focus on bottom-up, grassroot approaches was also congruent with another related feature of the literature on environmental leadership: the need for public engagement on climate change. As stated by Whitmarsh et al. (2011), "Proponents of public participation in science and policy making argue that involving the public in knowledge production and decision making can lead to better quality and more acceptable decisions, improve relationships, and build trust" (p. 279; See also Regan, 2007).

Public engagement cultivates efficacy. According to Hőppner and Whitmarsh (2011), "Decades of research ... have established efficacy as one key foundation of human agency ... In the case of climate change as a collective long-term challenge, engagement fostering collective and political efficacy appears to be crucial, as such beliefs influence how much effort people put into actions, the persistence of their efforts even if they fail to produce quick results or meet opposition, and people's vulnerability to discouragement" (p. 60). There is thus a growing chorus of voices arguing that the public at large needs to be involved and engaged in policy discussions about climate change, if real and lasting change is to occur. Some refer to this as "a discourse of civic environmentalism" that challenges the dominant discourses of "ecological modernization" and "green governmentality" (Lassen et al., 2011; see also Wolf, 2011).

Reliance on mass information campaigns and political leadership at the highest levels has not yet led to substantial mitigation of climate change; the task, it seems, is much deeper and will require leadership at the local, grassroots level, just as it did in earlier campaigns for civil rights and against nuclear war (for an example of the latter, see Redekop, 2010c). As such, our interviewees are for the most part engaged in a long-term task of deep, substantive change that will, it is hoped, bear fruit in years to come. The tragic and catastrophizing discourse of first-generation climate leaders, arguably an important first step, is slowly being superseded by a more open-ended, "comic" discourse that seeks to encourage human agency at a deep and lasting level. Few people want to spend their daily lives as another act in an ongoing tragedy, and few return home after watching the performance of a Greek tragedy with a renewed sense of hope and optimism about the future. Comic narrative, on the other hand, tends to critique the powerful and empower the weak and marginal. As such, there would seem to be a natural affinity between it and Eco-leadership, and it is to be hoped that together they will help build a better world. It would be naïve, however, to assume that there is no longer any need or place for tragic discourse; as one of the oldest narrative forms, it remains compelling and deeply rooted in our "nature," and would seem to provide a realistic perspective on our current climate predicament. In the end, some form of synthesis between tragic and comic discourses may be the most productive way forward, and we encourage readers to consider just what such a "tragi-comic" discourse might look like.

Interviews

Transcripts of interviews in possession of the lead author. These were semi-structured interviews aimed at qualitative understanding of the main issues and approaches related to leadership on climate change. Responses were correlated thematically and by question using rubrics. The information given below was accurate at the time of the interview. The authors would like to thank these individuals for being part of this project and for their important work on climate change.

Ferrial Adam: Arab World Team Leader, stationed in South Africa for 350.org. Her campaigns focus on energy and climate change. Ferrial engages in climate change research, activism, and connecting the knowledge gaps between fossil fuel industries and the citizenry on climate change issues.

Ellie Angerame: Recent graduate of Wheaton College in Massachusetts and member of the 2013 Focus the Nation's ReCharge! Retreat. This program focusses on training students in environmental leadership and offers preparation for careers in environmental sustainability.

Chuck Baclagon: Digital communications specialist for 350.org in East Asia. Chuck has also engaged in activism with Greenpeace. Baclagon influences change in the East Asia region, working from his home base in Manila, Philippines.

Zsolt Bauer: At the time of the interview, Head of Communications and PR at Regional Environmental Center (REC) located in Szentendre, Hungary. Works on awareness-raising projects, educational campaigns for sustainable development, and climate change for MNCs in the region. Zsolt is a member of the board of the Hungarian Business Leaders Forum (HBLF) and a trained presenter of Al Gore's Climate Reality Project. He is at present Branch Manager for the Climate Reality Project in Europe.

Mariana Bellot: Ms. Bellot is Lead Coordinator for BIOFIN-Mexico, "a global partnership seeking to address the biodiversity finance challenge and to build a sound business case for increased investment in the management of ecosystems and biodiversity." She previously worked as Director of Climate Change Strategies for the Mexican National Commission for Protected areas (CONAMP), and as Director General of Institutional Development and Promotion for the same organization.

Marta Bonifert: Executive Director at Regional Environmental Center (REC) for Central and Eastern Europe 2003–2017. Responsible for leadership, fundraising, and management of REC, which is staffed by 200 employees from 30 employees; 300 projects in 17 countries. Worked with stakeholders, civil society, and businesses on creating sustainable environmental policy. She is scientific advisor to Agroinnova/University of Turin Scientific Committee and head of the environmental committee of the Hungarian Business Leaders Forum, and serves on many other boards and committees. She is also a trained presenter for The Climate Reality Project.

Garett Brennan: Executive director of Focus the Nation, a clean energy youth empowerment organization. In its ReCharge! Program, Focus the Nation selects 20 rising clean energy leaders from across the country for training and education.

John Canada: At the time of the interview (2013), Canada was a student at the University of Alabama and had served as American Chemical Society representative at COP 17 in Durban, South Africa. His leadership on Climate Change has mainly come in the form of blogs and social media activism.

Audrey DePault: National Manager of the Climate Reality Project in Canada. DePault facilitates climate leadership training and development to present information about the implications of climate change to businesses, policy makers, and the public.

Alexa Lee: Alexa Lee is a native of Taiwan and speaks Mandarin, Japanese, and Bahasa Indonesian. She is currently Manager of Environment & Sustainability for the Information Technology Industry Council (ITI), focusing on the Asia-Pacific region. In this role, Alexa coordinates information and advocacy efforts related to ITI members' energy and environmental policies in China, East Asia, Southeast Asia, and South Asia.

Sandra Guzman Luna: Sandra is founder and general coordinator of the Climate Finance Group for Latin America and the Caribbean (GFLAC). She works on climate finance, energy transition, sustainable mobility, and other issues related to climate change. Ms. Guzman has been representative of civil society in many international climate change meetings under the UNFCCC, since 2008, having an important participation as advisor of the Mexican and other latin American governments in conferences such as COP16, COP20, COP21, among others. She has worked for the World Wildlife Fund and the Mexican Center for Environmental Law.

Adam Majcher: Climate Reality Project Manager at the Conservation Foundation located in Melbourne, Australia. The Foundation strives to coordinate climate change leadership training in Australia and in East Asia. Majcher is a scientist by training; his organization educates local communities to empower citizens and to create an advocacy presence in his region.

Cecilia Simon: Simon works with the Climate Action Reserve in Mexico City on climate change and biodiversity issues. Previously, she worked as the Climate Change Program Director for Pronatura. Simon is primarily interested in the connections between forest biodiversity, carbon emissions, and climate change.

Erin Schrode: Co-founder of Turning Green, an organization that promotes global sustainability, youth leadership, environmental education, and conscious lifestyle choices. Since 2005, her youth-led nonprofit has worked to raise public awareness about environmental and social responsibility for individuals, schools, and communities through education and advocacy.

Notes

1 The notion of "catastrophizing" rhetoric or discourse emerges from cognitive psychology and psychiatry, but is highly relevant to environmental discourse, particularly when it comes to global threats like climate change, which can give rise to truly catastrophic scenarios.
2 This could change, however, as climate impacts become increasingly real and visible – the tragic discourse will likely become more salient as a tragic outcome becomes more visible and likely.

References

Abraham, J. (2013). What's Climate Scientist James Hansen's Legacy? *The Guardian*, 29 April. www.theguardian.com/environment/climate-consensus-97-per-cent/2013/apr/29/climate-scientist-james-hansen-legacy.

Barringer, F. & Revkin, A. (2007). Gore Warns Congress of 'Planetary Emergency.' *The New York Times*, 21 March. www.nytimes.com/2007/03/21/washington/21cnd-gore.html.

Bowen, M. (2007). *Censoring Science: Inside the Political Attack on Dr. James Hansen and the Truth of Global Warming*. New York: Dutton.

Brulle, R. (2010). From Environmental Campaigns to Advancing the Public Dialog: Environmental communication for civic engagement. *Environmental Communication*, 4(1), 82–98.

Carson, R. (1962). *Silent Spring*. New York: Houghton Mifflin.

Chess, C., & Johnson, B. (2007). Information is Not Enough. In S. Moser & L. Dilling (Eds), *Creating a Climate for Change: Communicating climate change and facilitating social change* (pp. 223–233). Cambridge: Cambridge University Press.

Condon, S. (2013). Report: Al Gore's Net Worth at $200 Million. *CBSNews.com*, May 6. www.cbsnews.com/8301-250_162-57583118/report-al-gores-net-worth-at-$200-million/.

Corneloup, I., & Mol, A. (2014). Small Island Developing States and International Climate Change Negotiations: The power of moral leadership. *International Environmental Agreements*, 14, 281–297.

DeLuca, K. (2009). Praxis Interview: Greenpeace International media analyst reflects on communicating climate change . *Environmental Communication*, 3(2), 263–269.

Dunwoody, S. (2007). The Challenge of Trying to Make a Difference Using Media Messages. In S. Moser & L. Dilling (Eds), *Creating a Climate for Change: Communicating climate change and facilitating social change* (pp. 89–104). Cambridge: Cambridge University Press.

Feldman, L., Nisbet, C., Leiserowitz, A., Maibach, A. (2010). *The Climate Change Generation? A survey analysis of the perceptions and beliefs of young Americans*. http://environment.yale.edu/climate-communication/files/YouthJan2010.pdf.

Foust, C., & Murphy, W. (2009). Revealing and Reframing Apocalyptic Tragedy in Global Warming Discourse. *Environmental Communication*, 3(2), 151–167.

Gallagher, D. (2012). *Environmental Leadership: A reference handbook* (2 vols.). Thousand Oaks, CA: SAGE Publications, Inc.

Gillis, J. (2013). Climate Maverick to Retire from NASA. *The New York Times*, April 1. www.nytimes.com/2013/04/02/science/james-e-hansen-retiring-from-nasa-to-fight-global-warming.html?pagewanted=all&_r=0.

Gore, A. (1992/2006). *Earth in the Balance: Ecology and the human spirit*. New York: Rodale, Inc.

Hamilton, J. (2011). Keeping up with the Joneses in the Great British Refurb: The impacts and limits of social learning in eco-renovation. In L. Whitmarsh et al. (Eds), *Engaging the Public with Climate Change: Behavior change and communication* (pp. 160–179). Abingdon & New York: Earthscan.

Hampel, M. (2015). Want to Convince People that Climate Change is Real? Stop talking about the science of it. *The Washington Post*, January 22.

Hansen, J. (2006). The Threat to Our Planet. *The New York Review of Books*, 53 (12). www.nybooks.com/articles/19131.

Hansen, J. (2009). *Storms of My Grandchildren: The truth about the coming climate catastrophe and our last chance to save humanity*. New York: Bloomsbury.

Hansen, J. (2012). Why I Must Speak Out about Climate Change. TED talk available at: www.ted.com/talks/james_hansen_why_i_must_speak_out_about_climate_cha nge.

Hőppner, C., & Whitmarsh, L. (2011). Public Engagement in Climate Action: Policy and public expectations. In L. Whitmarsh et al. (Eds), *Engaging the Public with Climate Change: Behavior change and communication* (pp. 47–65). Abingdon & New York: Earthscan.

Kahan, D., Peters, E., Wittlin, M., Slovic, P., Ouellette, L., Braman, D., & Mandel, G. (2012). The Polarizing Impact of Science Literacy and Numeracy on Perceived Climate Change Risks. *Nature Climate Change*, 2(October), 732–735.

Kharecha, P. A., & Hansen, J. (2013). Prevented Mortality and Greenhouse Gas Emissions from Historical and Projected Nuclear Power. *Environmental Science and Technology*, 47, 4889–4895.

Lakoff, G. (2010). Why it Matters How We Frame the Environment. *Environmental Communication*, 4(1), 70–81.

Lassen, I., Horsbøl, A., Bonne, K., & Pedersen, A. (2011). Climate Change Discourses and Citizen Participation: A case study of the discursive construction of citizenship in two public events. *Environmental Communication*, 5(4), 411–427.

Leiserowitz, A. (2007). Communicating the Risks of Global Warming: American risk perceptions, affective images, and interpretive communities. In S. Moser & L. Dilling (Eds), *Creating a Climate for Change: communicating climate change and facilitating social change* (pp. 44–63). Cambridge: Cambridge University Press.

Martin, G., Keating, M., Resick, C., Szabo, E., Kwan, H.K., Peng, C. (2013). The Meaning of Leader Integrity: A comparative study across Anglo, Asian, and Germanic cultures. *The Leadership Quarterly*, 24, 445–461.

McKibben, B. (1989/2006). *The End of Nature*. New York: Random House.

McKibben, B. (2010). *Eaarth: Making a life on a tough new planet*. New York: Times Books.

Moorman, R.H., Darnold, T.C., & Priesemuth, M. (2013). Perceived Leader Integrity: Supporting the construct validity and utility of a multi-dimensional measure in two samples. *The Leadership Quarterly*, 24, 427–444.

Moser, S. (2007). More Bad News: The risk of neglecting emotional responses to climate change information. In S. Moser & L. Dilling (Eds), *Creating a Climate for Change: Communicating climate change and facilitating social change* (pp. 64–80). Cambridge: Cambridge University Press.

Moser, S., & Dilling, L. (2007). Introduction. In S. Moser & L. Dilling (Eds), *Creating a Climate for Change: Communicating climate change and facilitating social change* (pp. 1–27). Cambridge: Cambridge University Press.

Nature Climate Change. (2014). Science that Matters. *Nature Climate Change*, 4 (September). doi:10.1038/nclimate2398.

Nature Climate Change. (2014a). What's Your Story? *Nature Climate Change*, 4 (September). doi:10.1038/nclimate2408.

Nature Climate Change. (2015). Using My Religion. *Nature Climate Change*, 5 (October). doi:10.1038/nclimate2821.

Nature Climate Change. (2017). Politics of Climate Change Belief. *Nature Climate Change*, 7(1). doi:10.1038/nclimate3198.

Nisbet, M. (2009). Communicating Climate Change: Why frames matter for public engagement. *Environment: Science and Policy for Sustainable Development*, 51(2), 12–23.

O'Neill, S., & Boykoff, M. (2011). *The Role of New Media in Engaging the Public with Climate*. Abingdon & New York, NY: Earthscan.

O'Neill, S., & Nicholson-Cole, S. (2009). 'Fear Won't Do It': Promoting positive engagement with climate change through visual and iconic representations. *Science Communication*, 30(3), 355–379.

Palanski, M. E., & Yammarino, F. J. (2007). Integrity and Leadership: Clearing the conceptual confusion. *European Management Journal*, 25, 171–184.

PRRI/AAR. (2014). Believers, Sympathizers, and Skeptics: Why Americans are conflicted about climate change, environmental policy, and science. Findings from the PRRI/AAR Religion, Values, and Climate Change Survey. Washington, DC: Public Religion Research Institute.

Rabinovitch, A., Morton, T., & Duke, C. (2011). Collective Self and Individual Choice: The role of social comparisons in promoting public engagement with climate change. In L. Whitmarsh et al. (Eds), *Engaging the Public with Climate Change: Behavior change and communication* (pp. 66–83). Abingdon & New York: Earthscan.

Rapier, R. (2013). Al Gore Profits from Fossil Fuels He Vilified. *Energy Trends Insider*, 5 February.www.energytrendsinsider.com/2013/02/05/al-gore-profits-from -fossil-fuels-he-vilified/.

Redekop, B. (2010). *Leadership for Environmental Sustainability*. New York & London: Routledge.

Redekop, B. (2010a). Challenges and Strategies of Leading for Sustainability. In B. Redekop (Ed.), *Leadership for Environmental Sustainability* (pp. 55–66). New York & London: Routledge.

Redekop, B. (2010b). Introduction. In B. Redekop (Ed.), *Leadership for Environmental Sustainability* (pp. 1–16). New York & Abingdon: Routledge.

Redekop, B. (2010c). 'Physicians to a Dying Planet': Helen Caldicott, Randall Forsberg, and the anti-nuclear weapons movement of the early 1980s. *Leadership Quarterly*, 21, 278–291.

Regan, K. (2007). A Role for Dialogue in Communication about Climate Change. In S. Moser & L. Dilling (Eds), *Creating a Climate for Change: Communicating climate change and facilitating social change* (pp. 213–222). Cambridge: Cambridge University Press.

Stober, S., Brown, T., & Cullen, S. (2013). *Nature-Centered Leadership: An aspirational narrative*. Champaign, IL: Common Ground.

Stodola, D. (2010). Communicating Leadership for Environmental Sustainability: The rhetorical strategies of Rachel Carson and Al Gore. In B. Redekop (Ed.), *Leadership for Environmental Sustainability* (122–132). New York & London: Routledge.

Traub, J. (2007). Al Gore Has Big Plans. *The New York Times*, 20 May. www. nytimes.com/2007/05/20/magazine/20wwln-gore-t.html.

Verplanken, B. (2011). Old Habits and New Routes to Sustainable Behavior. In L. Whitmarsh et al. (Eds), *Engaging the Public with Climate Change: Behavior change and communication* (pp. 17–30). Abingdon & New York: Earthscan.

Western, S. (2008/2013). *Leadership: A critical text*. London & Thousand Oaks, CA: SAGE Publivations, Inc.

Western, S. (2010). Eco-Leadership: Towards the development of a new paradigm. In B. Redekop (Ed.), *Leadership for Environmental Sustainability* (pp. 36–54). New York & Abingdon: Routledge.

Whitmarsh, L., O'Neill, S. (2011). Introduction. In L. Whitmarshet al. (Eds), *Engaging the Public with Climate Change: Behavior change and communication* (pp. 1–14). Abingdon & New York: Earthscan.

Whitmarsh, L., O'Neill, S., & Lorenzoni, I. (2011). *Engaging the Public with Climate Change: Behavior change and communication.* Abingdon & New York: Earthscan.

Wielkiewicz, R., & Stelzner, S. (2010). An Ecological Perspective on Leadership Theory, Research, and Practice. In B. Redekop (Ed.), *Leadership for Environmental Sustainability* (pp, 17–35). New York & London: Routledge.

Wolf, J. (2011). Ecological Citizenship as Public Engagement with Climate Change. In L. Whitmarshet al. (Eds), *Engaging the Public with Climate Change: Behavior change and communication* (pp. 120–137). Abingdon & New York: Earthscan.

Wolsko, C., Ariceaga, H., & Seiden, J. (2016). Red, White, and Blue Enough to be Green: Effects of moral framing on climate change attitudes and conservation behaviors. *Journal of Experimental Social Psychology, 65,* 7–19.

10 Followers' Self-Perception of Their Role in Addressing Climate Change

A Cultural Comparison

David J. Brown and Robert M. McManus

Introduction

Climate change is a compelling global leadership issue in the 21st century. Recent computer simulations indicate that global sea levels may rise as much as three feet by the end of this century, which would have devastating planetary consequences (Deconto & Pollard, 2016). The solution to this wicked problem is not simply the responsibility of world leaders; followers must also play a part. This is an issue that is the result of contributions from many sources, and as such it is critically important to have buy-in from the general population in order to address the issue effectively. In short, followers must play an integral part in creating and implementing solutions to climate change. Major questions addressed in this chapter are: "Do different cultures hold different understandings of the role of followers in addressing climate change?" and "What are the relevant cultural factors that impact followers' self-perception of their role in addressing climate change?"

The study of followership has increased dramatically in the past decade (e.g., Kelley, 1988; Kellerman, 2008; Riggio et al., 2008; Chaleff, 2009). In this chapter we will examine the role of followers in addressing environmental issues, in particular climate change. Because there is not one source of the problem, or one area that needs to be protected, it is difficult if not impossible for leaders to implement a solution to the problem from above without considering the followers. In order to obtain buy-in from the followers, it is important to educate them about the issue, show them how it is relevant to their lives, and convince them there is a solution and that they can have a role in addressing the problem.

Redekop (2010) likewise identifies these aspects of follower buy-in, issue relevance, and personal agency as being important specifically to leaders communicating to their followers in the context of environmental issues. Leaders cannot address the problems of climate change and their potential solutions on their own; they need followers to accomplish the monumental problems anthropomorphic climate change presents. These wicked problems require "all hands on deck" – i.e., both leaders and followers – to rally around the common purpose of environmental protection and sustainability. Mary Parker Follett called this sort of commitment to a common purpose the "invisible leader" for leaders and followers. "While leadership depends upon depth of conviction and the power coming therefrom, there must also be the ability to share that conviction with others, the ability to make purpose articulate. And then that common purpose becomes the leader" (Follett, 1933/2003, p. 172.). Leadership scholar Ira Chaleff echoes this observation in his study of followership, and identifies leaders and followers rallying around a common purpose as the central component of the leadership process (Chaleff, 2009).

Followers have more of an impact upon achieving a goal than leaders often realize. Kellerman (2008) makes this point in a typology of followership based upon a follower's engagement in achieving the common purpose. In Kellerman's typology, followers can be active or passive in pursuing a common goal. Active followers, of course, energetically pursue the common goal. These are the types of followers that environmental leaders need to recruit, develop, and groom for leadership positions of their own if they hope to achieve the common purpose of mitigating global climate change. However, this is not to imply that passive followers have no impact upon the leadership process. By their refusal or inability to act, passive followers tacitly support the *status quo* – in this case, the ongoing emission of greenhouse gases. Similarly, R. Kelley contends that effective followers are committed to a purpose outside themselves (Kelley, 1988).

In investigating these issues, we conducted surveys over the past four years as a part of a class we have taught on conservation and leadership in Central America. A major aspect of this class is collecting survey data in Costa Rica and Belize based upon a survey that was conducted in the United States in 2007 (Yale Environmental Poll, 2007). In what follows, we first examine three portions of the survey that are directly linked to followership and the role followers play in understanding and addressing the problem of climate change, before putting the findings into cultural, educational, economic, and media context. The relevance of climate change to followers, and the role of followers in addressing climate change, are then discussed, followed by our conclusions.

Survey Themes and Data

The central themes of the research and a summary of the data are as follows:

1 Education: "If I had to, I could explain climate change to someone I meet in passing."

In the United States, 67 percent agreed with this statement, while approximately 96 percent in Costa Rica and 81 percent in Belize agreed with this statement in our survey. In Costa Rica, global climate change is a topic that is brought up early on in grade school; thus, even though many people do not continue with their education beyond the 8th grade, they have been exposed to the topic. In contrast, in the United States there have been reports of uncertainty among teachers about what to teach as a result of the politicized nature of the topic (Plutzer et al., 2016). When people were asked what sources they trusted for information on environmental issues, it was interesting that the percentage that trusted scientists, business groups, and industry scientists was nearly identical in all three countries. In contrast, the level of trust in television news (United States – 50 percent; Costa Rica – 77 percent; Belize – 56 percent) and newspapers (United States – 45 percent; Costa Rica – 63 percent; Belize – 64 percent) was higher in the Central American countries.

2 Relevance: "I have personally been affected by climate change."

In Costa Rica and Belize more than 55 percent of the participants indicated that they had been affected by climate change. In conversations with those people being surveyed, they often referred to changes in climate affecting where animals were found or having effects on agriculture.

3 Role in the solution: "It is my responsibility to help reduce the impacts of climate change."

In the United States, 81 percent of those surveyed agreed with this statement, which is impressive considering the politicized nature of the topic (Yale Environmental Poll, 2007). However, in Costa Rica and Belize the percent agreeing with this statement was even higher; both were at 95 percent. The participants in Central America are looking to their leaders for encouragement and information on how to conserve energy (higher than 95 percent). Finally, in the most recent survey we found that many people are willing to make a personal sacrifice to address environmental problems. In both Costa Rica and Belize more than 80 percent of the respondents indicated that they would be willing to donate one hour of wages a month to protect forest and water resources.

The results that we obtained were not surprising and other studies, such as a survey conducted in 20 countries by Ipsos MORI, have shown that the United States has the lowest percentage of adults that believe climate change is caused by humans (Ipsos, 2014). With that in mind, the obvious next step is to look at these results and try to understand possible explanations for why these three countries are so different. As was stated previously, in order to motivate followers, it is important to educate them about the issue, show them how the issue is relevant to their lives, and help them see how they can have a role in addressing the problem. We are going to start the comparisons of these three countries by examining some of the historical, cultural, and educational factors that have impacted climate change education in each country.

Cultural Context

First, we will consider the cultural makeup of these countries. The United States of America (USA) was initially a British colony, although there were influences from other European countries. The USA became an independent country in 1776, and although there are multiple cultural influences the culture is generally considered to be "linear active." The terms "linear active" and "multi-active" used here are borrowed from R. D. Lewis (2006) to categorize a culture's preferences for their use of time, communication patterns, and mannerisms, as well as a culture's approach to leadership. Lewis synthesizes the work of Hall (1973), Hofstede (2001), Trompenaars and Hampden-Turner (2012), Tönnies (1887/2002), and Kluckhohn and Strodtbeck (1961) to identify cultural types, which he then groups into three broad categories: linear active, multi-active, and reactive cultures.

Lewis (2006) uses the term "linear active" to describe mostly English-speaking and Western European cultures and their individualism, use of monochromic time, preference for factual knowledge when making decisions, task orientation, small power distance between leaders and followers, and preference for progressing through decision making in a straightforward linear fashion. The United States is one of Lewis's prototypes of a linear active culture.

Lewis (2006) uses the term "multi-active" to describe mostly Latin American, Mediterranean, Middle Eastern, and African cultures. Lewis contends that multi-active cultures show a preference for collectivism, polychronic time, preference for relationships as well as factual knowledge when making decisions, relational orientation, greater power distance between leaders and followers, and preference for taking into account relationships and emotion when making decisions.

This chapter will use the terms "linear active" and "multi-active" as shorthand for these cultural types. Lewis uses the term "reactive" to describe mostly Asian and Southeast Asian cultures and their preferences in these same regards. However, this study does not address these cultures, so we will not develop this line of thinking here.

Belize was also a British colony until it became independent in 1981. However, the people of Belize have a more mixed cultural heritage than the USA, with the majority of people identifying as having mestizo (mixed European-American Indian) ancestry (53 percent), Creole (European-African) (26 percent), indigenous Mayan (11 percent), as well as significant populations of people with African ancestry (CIA, 2017). As such the culture in Belize is more of a mix of linear and multi-active characteristics. Finally, Costa Rica was a Spanish colony until it declared its independence in 1821. The population of Costa Rica mainly identifies as having either Caucasian or mestizo ancestry (83 percent), with smaller proportions of the population identifying as having African or indigenous ancestry than in Belize. Because of Costa Rica's higher standard of living and job opportunities, there is also a significant immigrant population (9 percent), with most of the foreign-born workers originating from Nicaragua (CIA, 2017). Because of the Spanish influence, Costa Rica tends to have a more multi-active culture. These cultural characteristics will be revisited, as they relate to several of the other perspectives that will be examined in this chapter.

Educational Context

One area where the difference between multi-active and linear active culture may be an important factor is in the area of education. In this section we will focus mainly on Costa Rica and the USA. The rationale for focusing on Costa Rica is two-fold. First, Costa Rica adopted the use of education to address critical environmental issues in the late 1980s when they were dealing with deforestation and the government wanted to educate the general population about the need to protect forested areas (Quesada, 1993). Those education efforts focused mainly on children (Sutherland & Ham, 1992), but since there was not time to wait for those children to grow up to be leaders, there also had to be efforts to educate adults (Medina, 1989). The second reason for focusing on Costa Rica is because there is more literature available on the outcomes of their educational efforts, partially because the population of Costa Rica is more than ten times larger than the population of Belize, and also because of these well-described, historical efforts to teach environmental issues.

There have been several studies that have examined the effectiveness of intergenerational transfer of information. Many of these studies have been conducted in Australia, a former British colony, and have documented mixed results. Ballantyne et al. found that whether the children talked to their parents about the environmental topics they were learning about in school depended on a number of factors (1998). Two of the most important factors were that students were more likely to initiate conversations with their parents if they enjoyed the educational program, and homework could be an effective strategy to get parents involved in the educational process.

A study conducted in Quebrada Ganado, Costa Rica, took this a step further by tracking the dissemination of environmental education from students to their parents; however, they also looked at whether community members that did not have children in the educational program were affected (Vaughan et al., 2003). The environmental program focused on conservation of the Scarlet Macaws, a threatened species of bird that was present near the village and therefore would be of interest to the students. Quebrada Ganado is a small village and 80 percent of the residents work in the tourism industry, so information about these birds would also be of interest to many of the adults. In the study, the individuals in each of the groups took a pre-test before the educational program began, then took two post-tests. One post-test was at the end of the course and the second post-test was after 8 months. The participants in the program were 3rd and 4th graders, and the students were given a coloring book that was associated with homework assignments. Homework involved the students reading the coloring book with their parents and answering worksheet questions based on the information in the book, and the parents had to sign the homework (Vaughan et al., 2003).

The education program in Quebrada Ganado incorporated the two factors that Ballantyne et al. (1998) found most important for intergenerational transfer of information: a topic that was interesting to the students and homework that engaged the parents. In the immediate post-test, they found that the students' knowledge about Scarlet Macaws had improved by 71 percent and the parents had improved by 38 percent, but the control group of adults that did not have children involved in the program did not change. On the second post-test 8 months after the program, the students' scores were still 67 percent better than their pre-test scores, the parents had improved to 52 percent better than the pre-test, and the control group of adults had improved 29 percent over their pre-test scores (Vaughan, et al., 2003). The authors theorized that the parents learned from the children and the neighbors learned from both the parents and the children. This transfer of information beyond the family seems much more likely to occur in a multi-active culture such as Costa Rica, where relationships are particularly important. If you have ever spent an evening sitting on a town square in Costa Rica or other Latin American countries watching conversations going on, you can appreciate how this transfer of information about environmental issues may have occurred.

When we conduct the course on leadership in conservation we stay at a field station in Costa Rica that is a perfect example of the impact that intergenerational dissemination of environmental information can have. The land was purchased by a man who runs a lumber company, with the intention of cutting the existing secondary and primary forest and replacing the forest with a tree plantation planted with fast-growing non-native trees. The purchase of the land was necessary because of legislation that stipulated that forest resources can only be harvested from privately owned land or indigenous reserves (Navarro & Thiel, 2007). The man had already started the process of clearing and replanting the land when his children learned in school about the importance of protecting the remaining forests in Costa Rica. Based on conversations he had with his children, he decided to look into other options for the land that did not require cutting the forest. Developing the field station was an option because of Forest Law 7575, which introduced the innovative concept of paying forest owners for environmental services if they apply sustainable practices in the management of their lands (Navarro & Thiel, 2007). Because of something that his children learned in school, a block of primary forest that backs up on a large area of protected forest was not cut for lumber and is now instead a field station where both local and international students and researchers learn about tropical rainforest ecosystems (I. Mesen, personal communication, 2015).

The Costa Rican environmental education about deforestation that started in the late 1980s provided a framework for teaching about forest conservation. This framework could then be used to address other environmental issues such as sustainability, energy conservation, and climate change. The fact that so many of the people that were surveyed for our course research project indicated that they understood how climate change occurs suggests that this framework has worked, and the Costa Rican population is educated about this current environmental problem.

In contrast, a study conducted in the USA in 2016 found that most students were exposed to the topic of climate change, but how the subject was taught was often less than optimal (Plutzer et al., 2016). They found that the median teacher only devotes 1–2 hours to the topic, less than is recommended (National Research Council, 2012). Plutzer et al. found that slightly more than half of teachers (54 percent) that teach about climate change emphasize the scientific consensus "that recent global warming is primarily being caused by human release of greenhouse gases from fossil fuels" (2016). Of the teachers that do not emphasize the scientific consensus, most (31 percent of the total) send a mixed message by both stating the scientific consensus but also indicating "that many scientists believe that recent increases in temperature are likely due to natural causes." This might result from teachers attempting to teach both sides of the issue in an attempt to accommodate beliefs brought to the classroom by the students, or because the teachers are not sure of the content for this relatively new topic (Plutzer et al., 2016).

One might expect that teachers who do not feel comfortable with a topic would rely on experts; however, most teachers were not aware of how extensive the scientific agreement on climate change is. When asked "what proportion of climate scientists think that global warming is caused mostly by human activities?" only 30 percent of US middle school teachers picked the correct answer, "81–100 percent," and high school teachers only fared slightly better at 45 percent (Plutzer et al., 2016). Since more than half of the teachers thought that a significant percentage of scientists disagreed that climate change is primarily caused by humans, it makes sense that they would be willing to teach both sides of what they perceived to be a two-sided issue (Plutzer et al., 2016). Finally, this study recognized that the solution to improving education about climate change might not be as simple as providing training for teachers to improve their knowledge of the subject. The best predictor of how a teacher approached teaching climate change was their political ideology, not their knowledge of the content (Plutzer et al., 2016).

So why is there so much confusion about the extent of the scientific consensus on climate change? In part this is a result of a campaign similar to the one used by tobacco companies to challenge the scientific consensus linking smoking tobacco to lung cancer in the 1970s. One of the organizations involved in both campaigns was the Heartland Institute, a conservative and libertarian public policy think tank whose mission is to "promote free-market solutions" (Heartland Institute, 2017). The campaign to challenge the scientific consensus on climate change gained momentum in the USA in 2008 and 2009. Public opinion was moving in the direction of addressing climate change, President Obama had been elected and a cap and trade bill had been passed by the House of Representatives, and it looked like there were 60 votes for the bill in the Senate (Upin & Hockenberry, 2012). The strategy became to attack the consensus and claim that there was enough uncertainty to require delay and more studies.

This strategy of attacking the cap and trade bill paired well with the anti-tax, anti-big government message of the Tea Party. This resulted in a lot of pressure being put on senators from their constituents. This pressure was reinforced by the economic downturn in 2008 and the cap and trade bill ended up being tabled in the Senate in January of 2009. One of the Heartland Institute's missions has been to promote doubt and confusion about the scientific consensus on climate change by organizing conferences and presenters and publishing books and pamphlets. Recently they have capitalized on the name recognition of the United Nation's Intergovernmental Panel on Climate Change (IPCC) and have titled their recent publication as "Why Scientists Disagree about Global Warming: The NIPCC Report on Scientific Consensus," where the acronym NIPCC stands for the "Nongovernmental International Panel on Climate Change" (Heartland Institute, 2017). This document has been professionally prepared to give the impression that it is authoritative, and as of June 2017 it has been sent out to 300,000 K–12 and college science teachers with a cover letter that encourages them to use the materials as a counterpoint to the IPCC reports so that teachers can teach "both sides" of the debate (Heartland Institute, 2017).

However, the NIPCC document primarily repackages old climate change skeptic arguments that have been discredited. The National Center for Science Education authored a critical review of the NIPCC document shortly after the first edition was sent out, pointing out the many shortcomings of the NIPCC document compared to the United Nations IPCC report (National Center for Science Education, 2014).

Economic Context

Part of the explanation for why there is a campaign to discredit climate change science in the USA, but not in Costa Rica and Belize, can be tied back to economics. The Heartland Institute has received funding from conservative foundations, individuals, and corporations, including fossil fuel companies. The United States has extensive fossil fuel resources and is home to powerful corporations that are involved in extracting those resources, whereas neither Costa Rica nor Belize have significant fossil fuel resources. Using crude oil as an example, in 2016 it was estimated that the USA has over 36 billion barrels of proven crude oil reserves, compared to 0.0067 billion barrels for Belize and 0 barrels for Costa Rica (CIA, 2017).

The availability of fossil fuels in these countries is also reflected in the way that electricity is generated. In the USA in 2012, 73.5 percent of electricity was generated from fossil fuels, while in Belize 46.9 percent of electricity was produced from fossil fuels, and in Costa Rica only 30.7 percent of the electricity was produced from fossil fuels (CIA, 2017). In Belize and Costa Rica the rest of the electricity was produced from renewable sources such as hydroelectric, solar, geothermal, and wind.

In fact, this data may understate the current situation, since in 2015 Costa Rica was able to produce 99 percent of its electricity from renewable sources and a new hydroelectric facility began operation in 2016 (Phys.org, 2015). In both Costa Rica and Belize, the historic reliance on importing fossil fuels resulted in a higher cost for electricity. This served as an incentive for consumers to conserve electricity and there were also programs in place as early as 2007 to encourage the use of compact fluorescent bulbs. We observed the widespread use of compact fluorescent bulbs in Costa Rica in 2009, well before they were commonly seen in the USA. The cost of generating electricity from fossil fuels also served as an incentive to the Costa Rican and Belizean governments and the electricity generating companies to pursue renewable sources, often partnering with foreign countries to obtain the capital needed to develop these facilities.

There is always resistance to change. In the cases of Costa Rica and Belize, the high cost of generating electricity using imported fossil fuels was enough of an incentive to offset resistance to change. In the USA, the availability of fossil fuels, and in particular the availability of coal and now cheap natural gas from hydraulic fracturing, have kept the cost of electricity relatively low, and there has been less incentive to adopt renewable sources of electricity. In fact, there has been active resistance from the corporations that would like to maintain the status quo.

Media Context

We would like to finish our examination of how followers learn about climate change in the three countries by looking at media as a source of information. As mentioned earlier, our survey found that the percentage of participants that trusted scientists, business groups, and industry scientists was nearly identical in all three countries. In contrast, the level of trust in television news was highest in Costa Rica (USA – 50 percent; Costa Rica – 77 percent; Belize – 56 percent) and the level of trust in newspapers was higher in both Belize and Costa Rica (USA – 45 percent; Costa Rica – 63 percent; Belize – 64 percent). The following information on freedom of the press in the three countries was obtained from Freedom House. This organization produces reports and we used the full annual reports that were closest to the year that we conducted the survey (the 2014 report for Belize and the 2015 reports for Costa Rica and the USA).

Freedom House assesses the freedom of the press in a country by scoring the legal, political, and economic environments as they relate to the media in the country. For each of these the lower the score, the more free the press, and the overall sum of the scores for these three categories is used to rate the overall freedom of the press (Freedom House, 2017). Scores for all three countries are listed below in Table 1. Using Costa Rica as an example, the legal environment received a low score of 4 because the Constitution protects freedom of the press, and although there was a 1902 printing press law that allowed for prison sentences for defamation, that law was struck down by the Supreme Court in 2010 (Freedom House, 2017). At 7 the score for the political environment was also low and the report noted that there might be some self-censoring by journalists as a result of the fear of possible legal reprisals, but journalists rarely faced threats or violence and there were no incidents reported in 2014 (Freedom House, 2017). The political environment score also takes into account the independence of news outlets and the ability of the populace to access information and sources.

The good score for Costa Rica's press in regard to the political environment may at least partially explain the high level of trust that we observed in our surveys for both print and broadcast media. If the press is viewed as being independent, it is more likely to be trusted. Finally, the economic environment for media was rated as 6 and the media sector of the economy was described as having numerous private and public newspapers and TV and radio stations. Under the economic environment the report also noted that approximately half of the population had access to internet, and although this was low compared to other countries, it was improving.

Freedom House defines countries with a free press as having a total score of less than 30, so all three countries have freedom of the press (Freedom House, 2017). For the purposes of this discussion, we will focus primarily on the scores for the political environment in comparing the three countries, since this is more closely related to the perceived trust in the media. In Costa Rica private media sources tend to be owned by individuals that are politically conservative, but the number of sources available in the market helps

Table 10.1 Freedom of the press scores from Freedom House

Country	Legal environment	Political environment	Economic environment	Total score	Year of report
Belize	8	9	5	22	2014
Costa Rica	4	7	6	17	2015
USA	6	11	5	22	2015

Note: The lower the score, the more free the media in the country is.

to offset this. In contrast, in Belize political parties are associated with newspapers and radio stations and many of these sources therefore have a partisan bias (Freedom House, 2017). The higher score for the media's political environment in the USA reflects the *appearance* of polarization. The report indicated that the popularity of mostly conservative talk radio, all-news cable channels, and blogs contributed to the perception of polarization, but that most newspapers and major news agencies avoided bias (Freedom House, 2017). Ironically, efforts to appear unbiased have probably contributed to the confusion associated with climate change. Even though the science is largely settled on climate change, the attacks on that consensus and the politicizing of climate change have resulted in many news sources opting to present "both sides" of the argument in the interest of balance, with conservative news sources often providing a platform for those who deny the existence of anthropomorphic climate change. Groups like the Heartland Institute have been happy to provide spokespersons to argue for the opposition.

After examining factors that could have an impact on the education about climate change of followers in Belize, Costa Rica, and the USA, it appears that the primary difference is related to economic factors, in particular the availability of fossil fuels resources. Unlike Costa Rica and Belize, the USA has extensive fossil fuel resources, so there has not been a comparable economic incentive to pursue renewable energy sources. More importantly, those individuals in the USA that were involved in fossil fuel industries had an economic reason to preserve the status quo. This led to efforts to question the science of climate change as a means of slowing down the response to it. The strategies used by groups such as the Heartland Institute have been to publicize any perceived controversy and attack the scientific consensus. This has had an impact on teaching climate change in schools, and they continue to attempt to influence teachers through publications such as the NIPCC Report. This has also likely impacted the perception of climate change in the media by promoting the impression that there are a significant number of scientists that disagree with the climate change science. Another aspect of the efforts to attack the science of climate change is that it has been conflated with the anti-tax and anti-big government orientation of conservative politics. This politicization of climate change will pose problems to any efforts to educate the US population about climate change, which we will discuss at the end of this chapter.

Other factors, such as Costa Rica's history of using education as a way to address environmental issues and the multi-active culture of Costa Rica, may have contributed to the successful education of the general population about the topic of climate change. The history of addressing environmental issues in grade schools provided a framework for teaching children about climate change. Costa Rica's multi-active culture and the importance of relationships in the culture may have then facilitated the distribution of that information to the children's parents and to other people in the community.

Relevance of Climate Change to Followers

In addition to educating followers about the issue, a second important factor that is needed to gain buy-in from followers is to show them how the issue is relevant to them. To get at whether climate change was relevant to the people we surveyed, we included a question about whether they have been affected by it in each of the surveys that we have conducted. In our survey in 2015, 77 percent of the participants in Costa Rica and 59 percent of the participants in Belize indicated that they had been affected by climate change. The Yale Environment Survey does not specifically ask this question, but in the 2016 version of the survey they asked whether "global warming is already harming people in the US," and 51 percent of the participants agreed with this statement. When asked more specifically whether "global warming will harm me personally," only 40 percent responded that they thought they would be affected in the future (Yale Program on Climate Change Communication, 2016). What are possible explanations for this difference? Why do the majority of people in Costa Rica and Belize claim that they are already being affected by climate change, while only 40 percent in the USA expect that they will be affected in the future? There are several possible explanations for this difference.

One difference that might make it more likely for people in Costa Rica and Belize to recognize that the climate is changing is related to the fact that both of these countries are tropical. Because they are closer to the equator than the USA, there is less seasonal change in temperature during the year and instead the seasons are more associated with precipitation, for example a wet and dry season. The average high temperature in San Jose, Costa Rica, varies from 75° F in January to 80° F in May. There is a little bit more of a range of high temperatures in Belize, but it is still only from 80° F in January to 87° F in May (Canty & Frischling, 2017). It could be argued that having more stable temperatures across seasons makes it easier for people in tropical countries to recognize slight increases in temperature from year to year. In temperate countries where there are large seasonal changes in temperature, it is more difficult to recognize small changes from year to year: for example, Chicago, Illinois' coldest month is January with an average high temperature of 31° F, and the warmest month is July with an average high of 84° F. However, this is unlikely to be the only explanation, since the European countries also have a temperate climate and have a much higher percentage of people that recognize that climate change is occurring.

Another possible difference between these countries is the proportion of the population that is involved in occupations that are dependent on the climate/weather, the argument being that people that are dependent on the weather for their livelihood would be more likely to recognize changes. In the USA in 2009, 0.7 percent of the labor force was in agriculture, forestry, or fishing jobs. In Belize an estimate from 2007 was that 10.2 percent of the labor force was involved in agriculture, and in Costa Rica 14 percent of labor was in agriculture in 2010. The estimate for Costa Rica is probably low, since it does not include immigrant workers that often work in agriculture, and it did not include figures for forestry and fishing (CIA, 2017).

One other possible explanation for why people in Belize and Costa Rica are more likely to claim that they have been affected by climate change is because they equate changes in the behaviors of animals with climate change. When students were conducting the survey, the subjects would often tell them about changes that they had observed. As an example, the Terciopelo (*Bothrops asper*) is a poisonous snake found in Costa Rica. Historically, it has only been found at lower elevations because locations like Monte Verde were too cloudy and cool. As the climate has warmed, Monte Verde has fewer clouds and it is warmer and drier than it was and Terciopelos have now been found in Monte Verde. Our students have also heard similar stories about changes in the distribution of scorpions, frogs, and birds. It may be difficult to recognize gradual changes in temperature, but if an animal or a plant starts to be seen someplace that it did not use to live, or its behavior changes, that tends to catch people's attention.

The fact that people in Costa Rica and Belize are more likely to recognize that they have been affected is probably the result of a combination of these factors. Because more people in these countries are involved in agriculture or know someone that is involved in agriculture, they have probably heard how changing climate has affected agriculture. As a result, they might be more observant and more likely to notice changes in temperature or biological responses to the changing climate. In any case, the fact that more people in Costa Rica and Belize believe that they have been affected by climate change indicates that this is an issue that is relevant for these populations.

Role of Followers in Addressing Climate Change

For complex global issues like climate change, it is easy for an individual to feel like what they do will not have an impact. If an individual doubts that what they do will have an impact, they are unlikely to be committed to doing anything to address the problem. Thus, in addition to educating followers and showing them the relevance of the problem, the third factor that is necessary for leaders to get buy-in from followers is being able to show them that there is a solution and they can contribute to reaching the goal. In the Yale Environment Survey there were two statements that addressed this factor. The first was "It is my responsibility to help reduce the impacts of global warming"; 81 percent of responses in the USA agreed with this (Yale Environmental Poll, 2007). When we used the same statement in our survey in Costa Rica and Belize in 2012, 95 percent or more of the participants in each country agreed with the statement. The second statement in the Yale Environment Survey was, "My behavior can help to reduce the impacts of global warming," and 75 percent of the responses in the USA agreed with this statement (Yale Environmental Poll, 2007). We used this statement in both our 2012 and 2015 surveys. In 2012, 96 percent of Costa Ricans and 93 percent of Belizeans agreed with the statement. In 2015, the proportion of people agreeing with the statement had decreased in both countries, to 92 percent in Costa Rica and 78 percent in Belize. It is not clear why the percentage of subjects agreeing with this statement dropped from 2012 to 2015 in both Belize and Costa Rica. We will be collecting survey data again in 2018 and we are interested to see whether this trend continues.

In both Costa Rica and Belize, the survey results indicate that the people have largely accepted that they are responsible for helping to address climate change and that they can have an impact. This success is likely at least partially the result of the way that short-term goals, such as saving money on electricity through conservation, and intermediate-term goals, such as benefits to the environment, have been linked to the long-term goal of shifting to renewable sources of energy as a way to reduce greenhouse gas production. Seeing positive results with respect to the short-term goals provides encouragement that the long-term goals can also be reached.

Although the percentage of positive responses to these comments was not as high in the USA survey, it was still encouraging that the results were as high as they were. Unfortunately, the groups that are opposed to making changes to address climate change realize that this is an important component of engaging followers. Arguments that are often heard are: What difference do our actions actually make? If we reduce carbon dioxide emissions, someone else will produce more, so why bother? In fact, this was one of the arguments that was used by the Trump administration to justify the withdrawal of the USA from the Paris Climate Agreement. One of the talking points cited a study done by a group at the Massachusetts Institute of Technology that estimated how much of an impact the agreement would have on global temperatures. The talking point was that there would be very little impact on temperature, with the implied message, "It will not have much of an impact, so why bother?" The group at MIT has issued a statement that explains how their data was used inappropriately and was presented in a way that was misleading (MIT News, 2017). The MIT statement clarified that their study predicted that the average temperature would be 1° Celsius lower in the year 2100 with the Paris Climate Agreement than it would be without a climate policy. In making their prediction, they also assumed that the commitments made by countries would not be strengthened after 2030, even though the agreement plans for annual meetings to revisit the goals and set more ambitious goals over time (MIT News, 2017).

Conclusion

Survey data has been used to assess whether populations in three countries are educated about climate change, understand how it is relevant to their lives, and believe that there is a solution and they can have a role in addressing the problem of climate change. All three of these are important in order for leaders to have engaged followers, something that is particularly important in order to address a complicated problem like climate change. Two of the countries, Costa Rica and Belize, are making progress in all of these areas based on the survey results and are likely to have engaged followers in their efforts to address this problem. These two countries have also made progress on converting to renewable sources of electricity – in particular Costa Rica, which has been able to produce most of its electricity from renewable resources for the past 2 years.

In the USA, fewer participants in the surveys demonstrated these characteristics. In particular, the percentage of participants that knew about climate change and that it was primarily caused by human activity was lower, and the percentage that realized that climate change either was impacting them in the present, or would impact them in the future, was also lower. The most recent Yale Climate Opinion Maps based on surveys collected in 2016 contain some data that is encouraging but also data that is troubling. The results for questions related to policies for responding to climate change were generally encouraging. Eighty-two percent of participants "supported funding research into renewable energy sources" and 75 percent "supported regulating carbon dioxide as a pollutant." There was also encouraging news in regard to whether the subjects "trust climate scientists about global warming," with 71 percent indicating that they do trust these scientists (Yale Program on Climate Change Communication, 2016). There have been a lot of ad hominem attacks on climate scientists, either attacking specific scientists or suggesting that scientists alter their data so that they can continue to receive grants. It is encouraging to see that these attacks have not had a larger impact on the general population's trust in these climate experts.

The last two data points are the most disturbing and point out the significant challenges that will need to be addressed by those wishing to show leadership on this issue. Slightly more than half of the subjects (53 percent) agreed with the statement that "global warming is caused mostly by human activities" (Yale Program on Climate Change Communication, 2016). So only half of the people surveyed accept the climate scientists' consensus that most of the observed increase in temperature is the result of human activity, in particular the release of greenhouse gases. This does not seem to make sense when you consider that 71 percent of the subjects trust climate scientists. This anomaly between how many subjects trust climate scientists and how many agree with the consensus on climate change is explained by the next data point. Only 49 percent of the subjects agreed with the statement that "most scientists think global warming is happening" (Yale Program on Climate Change Communication, 2016). This points out how effective the misinformation promoted by groups such as the Heartland Institute has been. These groups have provided a forum for a small group of climate change skeptics and have attacked the science and scientists involved in studying climate change. By doing this they have given more than half of the population the impression that the science is uncertain, when there is actually extensive agreement by scientists that climate change is occurring and what is causing it.

If the USA wants to become a leader in the response to climate change, the main follower characteristic that will need to be addressed is their education about climate change. Unfortunately, it will not be as simple as merely communicating information from the climate scientists to the general population (for further discussion and documentation of this point, see Chapter 9 in this collection by Redekop and Thomas). As has been stated earlier, the topic of climate change has been politicized and for many people has acquired the characteristic of a value or belief. And it is much more challenging to change someone's values or beliefs than it is to educate them on a "neutral" topic.

Environmental leaders often fail to take into full consideration the importance – and beliefs – of their followers. As argued at the beginning of this chapter, leaders cannot address the problems posed by global climate change on their own. They need effective, committed followers to achieve the common purpose of stopping global warming and mitigating its effects. Environmental leaders who fail to recognize this do so at the peril of this common purpose, but there is hope. Quoting Follett once again, "Loyalty to the invisible leader gives us the strongest possible bond of union, establishes a sympathy which is not a sentimental but a dynamic sympathy" (Follett, 1933/2003, p. 172). This is the type of bond, sympathy, and commitment leaders and followers must have to address the problems facing our environment. Leaders must realize that this common purpose is much bigger than themselves and they must rally their followers to this invisible leader if they hope to address the problem of climate change. In doing so, they must understand their followers, their beliefs and values, and the contextual factors that have an impact on them.

References

Ballantyne, R., Connell, S., & Fien, J. (1998). Factors Contributing to Intergenerational Communication Regarding Environmental Programs: Preliminary research findings. *Australian Journal of Environmental Education*, 14, 1–10.

Canty, J. L., & Frischling, B. (2017). *Weatherbase*. Great Falls, VA: Canty and Associates, LLC. Retrieved from: www.weatherbase.com.

CIA. (2017). *The World Factbook*. Retrieved from: www.cia.gov/library/publications/the-world-factbook/.

Chaleff, I. (2009). *The Courageous Follower: Standing up to and for our leaders*. San Francisco, CA: Berrett-Koehler Publishers.

Deconto, R. M., & Pollard, D. (2016). Contribution of Antarctica to Past and Future Sea-Level Rise. *Nature*, 31(531), 591–597.

Follett, M.P. (1933/2003). The Essentials of Leadership. In P. Graham (Ed.), *Mary Parker Follett: Prophet of management* (pp. 163–177). Washington, DC: Beard Books.

Freedom House. (2017). Freedom of the Press 2017. Washington, DC: Freedom House. Retrieved from: http://freedomhouse.org/reports/.

Hall, E.T. (1973). *The Silent Language.* New York: Random House.

Heartland Institute. (2017). *The Heartland Institute.* Arlington Heights, IL. Retrieved from: www.heartland.org/.

Hofstede, G. (2001). *Culture's Consequences: Comparing values, behaviors, institutions, and organizations across nations* (2nd ed.). Thousand Oaks, CA: SAGE Publications, Inc..

Ipsos. (2014). Ipsos Global Trends. London. Retrieved from: www.ipsosglobaltrends.com.

Kellerman, B. (2008). *Followership: How followers are creating change and changing leaders.* Boston, MA: Harvard Business School Press.

Kelley, R.E. (1988). In Praise of Followers. *Harvard Business Review*, 66(6), 142–148.

Kluckhohn, F.R., & Strodtbeck, F.L. (1961). *Variations in Value Orientations.* Elmsford, NY: Row, Peterson & Company.

Lewis, R. D. (2006). *When Cultures Collide: Leading across cultures* (3rd ed.). Boston, MA: Nicholas Brealey International.

Medina, G. (1989). *Campesinos and Conservation: Joining forces through environmental education.* Washington, DC: World Wildlife Fund.

MIT News. (2017). MIT Issues Statement Regarding Research on Paris Agreement. Retrieved from: http://news.mit.edu/2017/mit-issues-statement-research-paris-agreement-0602.

National Center for Science Education. (2014). Debunking the Heartland Institute's Efforts to Deny Climate Science: A message from the National Center for Science Education. Retrieved from: http://ncse.com/files/nipcc.pdf.

National Research Council. (2012). *A Framework for K-12 Science Education: Practices, crosscutting concepts, and core ideas.* Washington, DC: Board on Science Education, National Academies Press.

Navarro, G., & Thiel, H. (2007). Country Case Study 6: On the evolution of the Costa Rican forestry control system. Retrieved from: www.odi.org/publications/3401-evolution-costa-rican-forestry-control-system.

Phys.org. (2015). Costa Rica Boasts 99 percent Renewable Energy in 2015. Retrieved from: http://phys.org/news/2015-12-costa-rica-renewable-energy.html.

Plutzer, E., McCaffrey, M., Hannah, A.L., Rosenau, J., Berbeco, M., & Reid, A.H. (2016). Climate Confusion Among U.S. teachers: Teachers' knowledge and values can hinder climate education. *Science*, 351(6274), 664–665.

Quesada, C. (1993). *Estrategia de conservacion para el desarrollosostenible de Costa Rica.* San José, Costa Rica: Ministerio de RecursosNaturales, Energia y Minas.

Redekop, B. (2010). Challenges and Strategies for Leading for Sustainability. In B. Redekop (Ed.), *Leadership for Environmental Sustainability* (pp. 55–66). New York & London: Routledge.

Riggio, R.E., Chaleff, I., & Lippman-Blumen, J. (2008). *The Art of Followership: How great followers create great leaders and organizations.* San Francisco, CA: Jossey-Bass.

Sutherland, D.S., & Ham, S.H. (1992). Child-to-Parent Transfer of Environmental Ideology in Costa Rican Families: An ethnographic case study. *Journal of Environmental Education*, 23(3), 9–16.

Tönnies, F. (1887/2002). *Community and Society: Gemeinshaft and gesellschaft* (C.P. Loomis, Trans. and Ed.). Mineola, NY: Dover Publications.

Trompenaars, F., & Hampden-Turner, C. (2012). *Riding the Waves of Culture: Understanding diversity in global business* (3rd ed.). New York: McGraw-Hill.

Upin, C., & Hockenberry, J. (Writers), and Upin, C. (Director). (2012). Climate of Doubt [Television series episode]. In T. Mangini (Producer), Frontline. Boston, MA: WGBH/Boston.

Vaughan, C., Gack, J., Solorazano, H., & Ray, R. (2003). The Effect of Environmental Education on Schoolchildren, Their Parents, and Community Members: A Study of intergenerational and intercommunity learning. *The Journal of Environmental Education*, 34(3), 12–21.

Yale Environmental Poll. (2007). Yale Center for Environmental Law and Policy (undertaken by Global Strategy Group). In the authors' possession. For a summary see: http://climatecommunication.yale.edu/publications/american-opinions-on-global-warming/.

Yale Program on Climate Change Communication. (2016). Yale Climate Opinion Maps – U.S. 2016. Retrieved from: http://climatecommunication.yale.edu/visualizations-data/ycom-us-2016/.

11 Ending the Drought: Nurturing Environmental Leadership in Ethiopia

Fentahun Mengistu, Girma Shimelis and Vachel Miller

Introduction

Climate change has become a matter of global environmental justice (Selby, 2010). This is particularly the case in Africa, where countries that have contributed little to global carbon emissions face harsh consequences for impending climate disruption. In Ethiopia, those consequences involve persistent droughts, shorter growing seasons, shifting rainfall patterns, reduced agricultural production, and greater food insecurity. Climate change is also expected to result in intensified income inequality within the next 35 to 60 years (Hadgu et al., 2015; Mideksa, 2010; Siraj et al., 2014) as well as increased migration of youth to Europe and the Arab World. Such slow-creeping but pervasive impacts of climate change will surely make life in the Horn of Africa harsher than ever.

While climate change poses a long-term threat to Ethiopia, more localized and immediate environmental problems are also cause for alarm. Just one example: in early 2017, more than 100 people were killed in a landslide … a landslide of garbage, or "trash avalanche" (Ahmed & Fortin, 2017). What happened was this: a large landfill outside the capital city of Addis Ababa was home to hundreds of poor people with nowhere else to live. When a section of the landfill gave way, homes and human beings were crushed under a landslide of solid waste. This episode points directly to the nexus of environmental sustainability and social justice, as well as the vulnerability of extremely poor, marginalized urban populations to toxic environmental conditions.

In the past, environmental protection has sometimes been framed as a long-term concern that can be sacrificed in the short term for the sake of economic growth. However, the intensified severity of environmental problems and their social justice implications calls for a new kind of leadership that is attuned to the interconnections of ecology and social equity as integral to national development. In a country like Ethiopia where rapid economic growth has become a coveted (and often unchallenged) prize, we suggest that leadership – across the institutional landscape – should be reoriented toward concern for ecological responsibility and social justice.

However, we suggest that the expectations for environmental leadership should be contextualized in relation to cultural traditions and institutional constraints. We favor a locally grounded approach to environmental leadership, anchored in the limitations and possibilities of particular places. In this respect, we challenge a sometimes assumed ideal in environmentally oriented leadership discourse of an "eco-champion" leader who can operate fluidly in an unbounded (or undefined) cultural/geographic space. In other words, we suggest that the "where" of environmental leadership matters as much as the "why" and the "what."

The economic and social conditions in Ethiopia vary greatly from the conditions for leadership found in the West. For one, centralized control of institutional authority limits possibilities for local initiative. The government tends to monopolize strategic leadership and dictate solutions from the center, leaving little space available for alternative discourses or local initiatives to gain legitimacy. Another distinctive feature of Ethiopia is its deeply rural, agrarian character. In Ethiopia, more than 80 percent of the population live on the land and work in small-scale (often subsistence) agriculture. Thus, there is both an immediate dependence on local natural resources for survival and deep indigenous understanding of local ecologies. At the same time, though, we observe limited popular awareness of the causes of environmental deterioration. Strong cultural/religious traditions associate drought and climate change with divine punishment for wrongful action. Such traditions may limit critical understanding and motivation to address climate change, and should be taken seriously within any localized conceptualization of environmental leadership.

While broadly agrarian, Ethiopia defies geographic generalization. Ethiopia encompasses hundreds of unique microenvironments (culturally and geographically), ranging from the Danakil depression to Rift Valley lakes, farmlands, rugged canyons of the Nile, deserts, and the tangled urbanity of Addis Ababa. In light of such profuse diversity, environmental leadership may evolve differently across the Ethiopian landscape – but only if more generally favorable conditions for the emergence of environmental leadership can be created across the geographic, cultural, religious, and institutional landscape.

Little is known about environmental leaders in Ethiopia. In a recent study of 75 corporate sustainability leaders, Schein (2015) found that corporate sustainability leaders in the United States and Europe are often motivated by ecological worldviews rooted in their sense of relationship with the natural world. These individuals often developed early connections to nature as children. Schein also noted that corporate leaders' concern for social equity is often linked to eye-opening observations of injustice in the developing (majority) world. Such research, while valuable in exploring the origins of environmental leadership in the West, may not explain how sustainability leadership emerges in very different locations. We wonder about the origins of ecological awareness among leaders whose lives are grounded in rural environments, where the subsistence rhythms of agricultural life are close at hand. We wonder, too, about the social justice concerns of those whose personal experiences of race, ethnicity, and economic equity may be more visceral than for those in more comfortable circumstances in the West who grew up looking at injustice from a greater distance. In this chapter, we sketch our perspective on the challenges of environmental leadership in the Ethiopian context, mindful of both the real constraints and the urgency of change.

The Impact of a Changing Climate in Ethiopia

Before exploring the constraints and challenges of environmental leadership in Ethiopia, we briefly review the impact of climate change to highlight the urgency of environmental activism and leadership. In Ethiopia, agriculture supports 83–85 percent of the nation's population in both employment and livelihood (Bezabih et al., 2014; Iscaro, 2014). The agricultural sector produces 40–50 percent of the nation's GDP and around 85 percent of export earnings. Given its high level of dependence on agriculture, Ethiopia is extremely vulnerable to the impacts of climate change (Aragie, 2013). That vulnerability is heightened by low adaptive capacity at an organizational level and lack of a widely-accessible technology infrastructure (Robinson et al., 2013; Yohannes, 2016).

As suggested earlier, climate change is expected to alter traditional rainfall patterns and disrupt the seasonal patterns of agricultural work established over hundreds of years. In southern Ethiopia, climate change will likely affect the production of Arabica coffee due to increased temperature, reduced precipitation, and more pervasive crop pests. Coffee is the major source of foreign exchange that covers around 33 percent of Ethiopia's exports (Iscaro, 2014). According to Alebel et al. (2015), the textile and sugar sector also are key strategic export commodities. Climate change poses great risks to the production of cotton and sugarcane and may limit the foreign currency earning of the country. A recent analysis forecasts that Ethiopia could lose up to 6 percent of its agricultural output yearly due to reduced rainfall if current climate change trends continue (Aragie, 2013). Therefore, for a country whose economy is highly dependent on agriculture (especially crop production and livestock), the cost of climate change will be severe.

Moreover, climate change is expected to have negative public health consequences. According to a recent report issued by USAID (2016), Ethiopia has a high prevalence of climate-sensitive diseases. The report indicated that roughly 70 percent of the population lives in malaria-endemic areas and outbreaks that occur every five to eight years account for up to 20 percent of deaths for children under the age of five. With climatic change expected to increase temperatures – little by little, decade by decade – the geographic range of malaria will expand (Siraj et al., 2014). Rising temperatures will enable malaria-carrying mosquitoes to move up the mountains, affecting greater segments of the highland population. Forecasts also suggest that increased potential for flooding will facilitate the spread of waterborne diseases like diarrhea and cholera. In addition, as a result of greater food insecurity, NGOs have estimated that several million children in Ethiopia will be threatened by malnutrition (Save the Children, 2016). These predictions indicate the depth and breadth of the impact of climate change on human well-being and economic vitality across Ethiopia. Climate change has the potential to impede economic progress and reverse the gains made in Ethiopia's development unless measures are taken to alleviate the situation (Redda & Roland, 2016).

Government Initiatives to Address Climate Change

Over the past decade, Ethiopia has pursued turbo-charged economic growth, with rates of economic expansion hovering near 10 percent in recent years. This rate of economic growth is among the highest in Africa, if not the world, only falling below the growth levels of India and China (Federal Democratic Republic of Ethiopia, 2011). Ethiopia's capital city, Addis Ababa, now boasts multiple symbols of economic modernity, including a Chinese-engineered light rail system for mass transit and new cargo train link with Djibouti. A modern expressway extends from the capital city to nearby economic hubs, another expression of the nation's emerging economic power.

While pursuing accelerated growth, the Government of Ethiopia is well aware of the environmental challenges the country faces and appears to be taking active measures to move the country toward a more sustainable economy. Ethiopia already produces a large share of its electricity from hydropower, and the government has issued a number of policies and strategies to address climate change, including a "green economy strategy" that promises to enable Ethiopia to reach its ambitious economic growth targets while keeping greenhouse gas emissions low (FDRE, 2011).

The Ethiopian green economy strategy focuses on protecting and reestablishing forests, improving crop and livestock production practices for higher food security and farmer income while reducing emissions, expanding electricity generation from renewable energy, and shifting to energy efficient technologies in transportation and construction, among other sectors (FDRE, 2011). Overall, the strategy is intended to lower the current environmental impact of carbon emissions in the country and achieve economic development targets in a way that overcomes the potential conflict between economic growth and ecological protection.

Even though the components of the green economy strategy are sound, the government has made few significant achievements in implementing the policy over the past five years. Much of the expected work remains in the proposal or planning stage. On the ground, government activities focus on the protection of soil through planting of trees, terracing and building ditches, and preventing overgrazing. However, these efforts often seem driven by political interests in establishing the public appearance of environmental care more than establishing sustainable conservation practices at a community level. In some cases, farmers and other community members are forced to plant trees and prepare ditches and canals (usually once a year) in order for the government to produce media images of locally based environmental protection. In reality, such media-focused efforts are quickly abandoned until the next round of government visits.

Perhaps the central problem of environmental protection in Ethiopia is this: *Environmental policies and strategies are not fully owned by the larger community.* As a result, environmental protection efforts often appear artificial, shallow, and inconsistent. Such efforts tend to be top-down, government-sponsored agendas that lack local support. The government has made inadequate efforts to raise awareness among rural populations about environmental protection, including understanding of the causes and effects of climatic change or strategies for climate adaptation. Government has done little to mobilize environmental leadership at a local level or authorize and support locally driven environmental protection strategies. Strategy development remains highly centralized and bureaucratized (Gebissa, 2010). Within the government's green economy strategy document, for example, the only references to "leadership" are made in reference to the Prime Minister's office (and related government experts). From our standpoint, this is part of the problem: a highly centralized grip on leadership is a key cause of the drought of environmental leadership.

Contextual Barriers to Environmental Leadership

In Ethiopia, we have observed multiple obstacles to environmental leadership. We will identify and explore several of those barriers, including the following: 1) centralized control of leadership functions; 2) theological notions of climate disruption as a divine punishment for collective sin; 3) lack of systemic environmental awareness at the grassroots level.

By highlighting these barriers, our intention is not to argue against the possibility or the importance of environmental leadership. Rather, we suggest that environmental leadership must be understood in light of these constraints, so that they can be reshaped to leverage more conducive conditions for the emergence of local forms of environmental leadership. A contextually grounded, constraint-conscious approach to environmental leadership in Ethiopia (and Africa generally) can speak more authentically to emerging environmental leaders and generate more productive local dialogue about what environmental leadership looks like, how it works, and how it could contribute to the well-being of local communities over time.

1. Top-Down Centralized Control of Institutional Direction and Decisions

Since the fall of the communist regime in 1991, Ethiopia has been ruled by a single political party. In the 2016 national election, the ruling party won 100 percent of the seats in parliament, signaling its stranglehold on power to all potential political rivals (Arriola & Lyons, 2016). In a political environment of heavy-handed one-party rule, government is the central actor in all aspects of Ethiopian life. Institutional leaders receive their authorization from the government (either regional or central) and maintain their legitimacy through their ability to effectively implement government directives. In practice, leaders in Ethiopia are not encouraged to think independently and empower their followers to do the same. Rather, leaders in Ethiopia learn to make safe decisions that align closely with the strategies of the central government. A common phrase that middle-managers hear is "for your implementation." In our observations of educational institutions, it seems that mid-level leaders typically take directives from the top without questioning, and then pass the burden of implementation to lower-level officials and line workers. Ethiopians refer to this practice as *"tikus denich"* (passing the "hot potato"). This tradition affords little autonomy for middle managers to take alternative stances or pursue independent initiatives (Shimelis et al., 2017). At all levels, institutional leaders in Ethiopia are expected to hold instrumental views about the purpose of their work, aligned with normative national discourses, i.e., that the ultimate goal of leadership is advancing national economic development.

In this context, greater institutional attention to climate change and a thousand other local eco-justice challenges is unlikely, until there is greater openness to alternative viewpoints. In this respect, even the national "green economy strategy" may become a barrier to local dialogue and decision making, since it appears that the central government has found the solution to climate change and that the official strategy should be implemented as written, rather than critically examined and adapted to meet local needs.

2. Religious Traditions That View Climate Change as "Divine Punishment"

In the West, public debates about the nature of climate change often revolve around the quality or scope of scientific evidence. In a deeply conservative society as found in Ethiopia, however, attribution for the causes of climate change can also include religious concerns. Climate change in Ethiopia is often perceived, at a community level, as having both spiritual and scientific dimensions. In a recent survey of 60 local farmers in northern Ethiopia, most respondents pointed to local land use practices such as deforestation and overgrazing as contributing to climate change, with a small percentage (7 percent) also pointing to sinful action as the key cause (Tesfahunegn et al., 2016).

The theological attribution of climate change speaks both to the power of religious thinking in a traditional society as well as the relative thinness of scientific understanding of climate change from a global perspective among the broader population. With regard to persistent drought, famine, desertification, and depletion of soil fertility, people tend to hold fatalistic outlooks. Many people associate such hardships with divine punishments due to transgression of God's commandments.

Such beliefs are common to both Christian Orthodox and Islamic traditions (as well as indigenous traditions). Hence, many religious institutions admonish their followers to pray when there are prolonged droughts accompanied by famine, and even torrential rains followed by excessive and destructive flooding. Because environmental problems are frequently understood from a religious viewpoint as being caused by sinful action, religious followers may be asked to slaughter animals and pray together in nearby churches and mosques for divine intervention to reverse the situation.

In this respect, strong religious traditions position climate change as a problem to address through moral atonement and improvement, rather than policy action or adaptive organizational change. This is a vital consideration for environmental leadership in the Ethiopian context, since it must account for climate change as an issue sometimes interpreted as having a spiritual cause.

3. Lack of Environmental Awareness at a Grassroots Level

Most people of Ethiopia live an agrarian, subsistence lifestyle. Agrarian traditions hold rich understanding of local weather patterns, soil conditions, planting/harvesting cycles, and animal husbandry practices. Over generations, local farmers have developed highly contextualized working knowledge of how to sustain themselves where they live. Local farmers in Ethiopia have also demonstrated their own strategies for climate adaptation in certain areas (Gebissa, 2010). Nevertheless, local people are often ill-equipped to understand the broader patterns and implications of a changing climate. Due to limited access to media, there is limited popular access to scientific information about climate change and other environmental problems.

One of the authors had a discussion with local officials working in the agriculture sector. The discussion was about awareness of climate change, its impacts, and the role of leaders. One of the participants said the greatest challenge related to climate change is that people do not talk about it. At a village level, people might make observations about unseasonably high temperatures or uncommon rainfall patterns. A survey of farmers in northern Ethiopia found they were able to clearly identify changes in temperature and rainfall as indicators of climate change (Tesfahunegn et al., 2016). However, these observations often remain as localized snapshots. People do not have adequate access to information about climate patterns and the trajectory of incremental changes over time. As suggested above, popular thinking about climate change may also be influenced by religious explanations, associating drought or famine with divine punishment for wrongdoing, rather than providing explanations that reveal how human activity is altering natural patterns.

Land tenure in Ethiopia is a related barrier to local investment in the long-term quality of the environment. All land in Ethiopia belongs to the central government as a matter of law. This situation diminishes grassroots responsibility for environmental stewardship. Local farmers tend not to plant trees on government land because they do not feel a sense of ownership of the land and will not ultimately benefit from the trees. In this respect, central control of the land constrains longer-term thinking and limits efforts to preserve soil fertility over time.

Overall, practices of government control and discourses of divine punishment tend to remove agency from (and responsibility for) environmental leadership from ground-level leaders. We suggest that these constraints must be acknowledged as a starting point for fostering creative leadership in relation to local environmental challenges.

The Way Forward: Changing the Leadership Paradigm in Ethiopia

In nations like Ethiopia, local people can do little to limit the larger dynamics of global climate change or escape the consequences of climate disruption in the coming years. Thus, environmental leadership in Ethiopia must be attuned to resilience and adaptation. In this respect, such leadership is about strengthening the adaptive capacities of communities and organizations. That is the province of adaptive leadership, identifying the strengths of tradition and discerning (collectively) what aspects of tradition continue to serve the community and which aspects no longer serve, in order for the community to thrive in a changing environment (Heifetz et al., 2009).

In Ethiopia, resilience comes "built-into" cultural norms. Ethiopians have endured hardship and adapted to difficult conditions for hundreds of years. When faced with a physical or emotional challenge, people encourage each other through the exhortation of "*izosh/izoh*," (feminine/masculine) which means, literally, "be strong." Based on a widening body of research, it has become clear that climate change will bring intensified hardship to Ethiopia in terms of greater food insecurity, extreme weather, new vulnerabilities to malaria, etc. in the coming decades. Given this predicament, the cultural ethic of resilient strength amid adversity will be a key resource for Ethiopia's future. To affirm the indigenous tradition of resilience, we would like to suggest that leaders should take an appreciative approach to traditional capacities for endurance, rather than echoing or amplifying rhetoric of impending environmental catastrophe that is sometimes heard in the West. Such an approach fails to honor the Ethiopian capacity for endurance.

There is no question that Ethiopians will endure climate change. But how can the project of endurance become one of creative adaptation that minimizes the damage and maximizes the capacity for resilience of local communities? Perhaps the primary task of environmental leadership in this regard is framing intensified hardship as an adaptive challenge, calling forth indigenous capacities to act creatively and responsively – amplifying local agency, resilience, and responsibility – rather than framing intensified hardship as a divine curse or inexplicable event that must be endured passively. At this level, environmental leadership in Ethiopia is an epistemological and pedagogical project. That project starts at the top, in terms of loosening expectations for leaders to implement-solutions-as-planned and opening spaces for leaders to experiment with possible-solutions-at-hand, toward greater levels of well-being for human and nonhumans alike.

This project also involves focusing collective attention on the environmental problems that can be addressed with the tools and resources at hand. Because climate change is such a large-scale, global problem whose solution seems beyond the grasp of Ethiopians, it may be an ineffective focus for mobilizing local energies. Environmental leaders at a community level, while emphasizing local adaptation and resilience in the face of the inevitable changes in temperature and rainfall patterns, can also focus attention on the close-at-hand strategies for ecological well-being, such as the reduction/ elimination of plastic bags or the small-scale adoption of solar energy collection systems.

Leveraging Cultural Resources for Change

Ethiopia's rich religious heritage suggests that environmental leadership should consider ways to include religious leaders and religious ethics into their change efforts. After all, religious traditions and institutions can be allies in disseminating environmental messages. Historically, churches in Ethiopia have functioned as small-scale nature sanctuaries. By tradition, local people are not allowed to cut trees around churches; thus, churches often sit amidst old forests and abundant wildlife. In this respect, churches can serve as indigenous examples of effective microscale conservation. To our knowledge, there has been little discussion of the potential of religiously inspired conservation to inspire environmental leadership in other social sectors.

Given Ethiopia's strong religious traditions, another productive approach would be linking environmental leadership to notions of servant leadership. Originally inspired by the Christian religious tradition (Greenleaf, 2002), approaches to servant leadership call leaders to model a Christ-like service to others. As such, the discourse of servant leadership may find cultural resonance with traditional Orthodox religious teachings and speak to traditional religious values.

In this respect, servant leadership and environmental leadership have strong connections in that they emphasize the needs and interests of others over leaders' self-interests and needs. If a leader cares about human well-being in a context where the vast majority of people continue to rely on subsistence agriculture, then, by extension, the servant leader must care for the environment that people rely on to grow their food and make a living. Servant leaders become stewards of people and place, stewards of community well-being nested within the larger well-being of the community's natural support systems.

Adapting Global Leadership Discourses

A 2017 report from the Worldwatch Institute calls for "earth-centric" leadership, as part of a broader agenda of "earth education" (Assadourian,

2017). Such leadership helps organizations and communities build a sustainable future amid the disruptive consequences of climate change. According to Assadourian, earth-centric leadership involves critical consciousness, active civic engagement, and the freedom to act as a change agent. Earth-centric leaders empower others to address environmental problems and social injustice. While this approach makes sense in an open democratic environment, it can be difficult for people to act as change agents in a context where their civil rights have been constrained, as often happens in Sub-Saharan Africa and Ethiopia in particular. For that reason, we suggest that principles of environmental and "earth-centric" leadership must be adapted to fit local realities.

To enable a richly diverse expression of environmental leadership, what's needed at the macro-level is a full recognition of environmental problems and encouragement for local leadership – rather than treating environmental leadership as the prerogative of the central government or the tragic consequence of collective moral failure.

In education, Bottery's recent (2016) analysis of leadership for sustainability focuses on the capacities needed to address "wicked problems" of sustainability. Bottery suggests that wicked problems are often mistakenly framed as being "tame" in ways that promote simplistic, mechanistic solutions. Wicked problems cannot be solved by hierarchically driven implementation of mechanistic, centralized solutions. Wicked problems call from wicked approaches, pointing toward a "bricoleur" leader (p. 164) who experiments with multiple strategies, what Bottery refers to as "silver buckshot" rather than "silver bullets" (p. 171).

Bottery goes on to point out that a leader's role is not finding solutions: "they [leaders] need to understand that their role should be increasingly one of asking the right questions rather than providing the right answers" (p. 171). For Bottery, sustainability leaders also need an expansive tolerance of uncertainty and slow decision making: "In a wicked world characterized by too much concern with acting quickly, the strength and ability to remain comfortable with uncertainty, to resist the temptation to reify initial thoughts until further clarity is acquired, will be a vital quality" (p. 171).

Bottery's leaders do messy work to find their way to "clumsy solutions" (p. 172) in dialogue with multiple stakeholders. Such an approach to leadership is unlikely to flourish in an institutional environment that privileges, even demands, administrative compliance with centralized government directives. In this respect, central actors may do much to strengthen Ethiopia's capacity for climate change adaptation and ecological justice by holding greater tolerance for questions, for slow actions, and for the uncertainty that comes from loosened control over decision making.

Even though Ethiopia will be hit hard by climate change, most people don't know what's coming. The issue of climate change and its practical consequences are not earnestly communicated and understood (in scientific terms) by the majority population, particularly those with low levels of literacy and limited access to international media. Greater efforts to enrich environmental literacies and deepen ecological awareness will be critical for nurturing local support for environmental leadership. Broader public understanding of climate change and the urgency of adaptive work will build more supportive conditions for environmental leadership to take root.

Concluding Implications

What can other nations learn from Ethiopia's experience with environmental leadership? At one level, we applaud the fact that the Ethiopian government has raised the visibility of climate change and environmental issues, through discourses such as the Green Economy Strategy. Other nations can look to Ethiopian government leadership in framing economic growth in relation to long-term environmental protection. Nevertheless, we raise cautions about presumed environmental leadership from the top.

Due to the common-sense conflation of leadership with authority (particularly government authority), it's tempting to view Ethiopia as an environmental leader. Beneath the rhetoric, however, much of the government's efforts remain superficial and, sometimes, exaggerated for global audiences. In a one-party state like Ethiopia, the government tends to monopolize credit for environmental leadership and manage the environmental agenda. In this respect, environmental leadership from the center can mask, even limit, the vitality of environmental leadership locally. A caution about government-led environmental leadership is warranted in other settings with tight control on civil dialogue and citizen-driven initiative. Central governments have a key role in promoting environmental leadership but should not "own" that leadership role.

A second lesson: environmental leadership is practiced in specific cultural settings, and we recommend critical analysis of the cultural resources that both inhibit and promote environmental leadership. Like many other settings in Africa, rural Ethiopia is endowed with rich knowledge, gained from centuries of subsistence cultivation, of how people can sustain local soils and waters to meet human needs. Nevertheless, an industrializing economy, propelled by external investment and government ambitions to achieve rapid growth, has intensified urbanization and disconnection from place-based knowledge. How can nations like Ethiopia preserve traditions of environmental care and protection in the context of rapidly shifting aspirations and lifestyles?

In Ethiopia, traditional religions often play a dual-edged role in environmental leadership, attributing climactic catastrophes to moral failure, while also acting as agents of conservation through the protection of trees. We suggest that religious leaders have a particularly important opportunity to reframe climate change and cultural resilience as matters of human agency, problems that call forth moral responsibility rather than problems that have called down moral judgment.

Ethiopia has not yet integrated government policy pronouncements with traditional religious values to promulgate a common ethic of environmental stewardship at a community level. If environmental leadership could be infused with religious energy, environmental concerns might attract and mobilize a much broader audience. We would encourage religious, educational, civic, and business leaders to consider how they can model environmental leadership and nurture conducive conditions for such leadership to take root in local communities and institutions.

Ethiopians are widely regarded as a proud people. Ethiopians take great pride in their cultural heritage, their ethnic diversity, and the stark beauty of the land they inhabit. They have no desire for dependency on food aid as rains shift and crops wither due to climate change. Cultural pride and indigenous values of endurance can be a resource for animating environmental leadership. One of the key lessons we draw is that Ethiopia has not yet dug deep enough into its own resources to address its ongoing drought of environmental leadership.

At the same time, Western countries must better appreciate how their policy choices can push climate change and other forms of environmental degradation beyond peoples' capacity to endure. As people in the Horn of Africa migrate northward to escape drought and famine, environmental leadership – at a global, national, and local level – becomes a more widely shared concern.

References

Ahmed, H., & Fortin, J. (2017). As Trash Avalanche Toll Rises in Ethiopia, Survivors Ask Why. *The New York Times*, March 20. Retrieved from: www.nytimes.com/2017/03/20/world/africa/ethiopia-addis-ababa-garbage-landslide.html.

Alebel, B. W., Assefa, B., & Hagos, A. (2015). *Productivity and Welfare Impact of Climate Change in Sugarcane and Cotton Producing Regions of Ethiopia*. Addis Ababa, Ethiopia: Ethiopian Development Research Institute.

Aragie, E. A. (2013). Climate Change, Growth and Poverty in Ethiopia. Working Paper no. 3, Climate change and African political stability. The Robert F. Strauss Center for International Security and Law. Retrieved from: www.droughtmanagement.info/literature/CCAPS_climate_change_growth_poverty_ethiopia_2013.pdf.

Arriola, L. R., & Lyons, T. (2016). The 100 percent Election. *Journal of Democracy*, 27(1), 76–88.

Assadourian, E. (2017). EarthEd: Rethinking education on a changing planet. In E. Assadourian & L. Mastny (Eds), *EarthEd: Rethinking education on a changing planet* (pp. 3–22). Washington, DC: Worldwatch Institute.

Bezabih, M., Di Falco, S., & Mekonnen, A. (2014). Is it the Climate or the Weather? Differential economic impacts of climatic factors in Ethiopia. Centre for Climate Change Economics and Policy Working Paper No. 165.

Bottery, M. (2016). *Educational Leadership for a more Sustainable World*. London: Bloomsbury Academic.

Federal Democratic Republic of Ethiopia. (2011). Ethiopia's Climate Resilient Green Economy: Green economy strategy. Retrieved from: www.undp.org/content/dam/ethiopia/docs/ Ethiopia percent20CRGE.pdf.

Gebissa, E. (2010). Leadership from Below: Farmers and sustainable agriculture in Ethiopia. In B. Redekop (Ed.), *Leadership for Environmental Sustainability* (pp. 158–169). New York & London: Routledge.

Greenleaf, R. (2002). *Servant Leadership: A journey in the nature of legitimate power and greatness.* New York: Paulist Press.

Hadgu, G., Tesfaye, K., & Mamo, G. (2015). Analysis of CLimate Change in Northern Ethiopia: Implications for agricultural production. *Theoretical Applied Climatology,* 121(3), 733–747.

Heifetz, R. A., Linsky, M., & Grashow, A. (2009). *The Practice of Adaptive Leadership: Tools and tactics for changing your organization and the world.* Cambridge, MA: Harvard Business Press.

Iscaro, J. (2014). The Impact of Climate Change on Coffee Production in Colombia and Ethiopia. *Global Majority E-Journal,* 5(1), 33–43.

Mideksa, T. K. (2010). Economic and Distributional Impacts of Climate Change: The case of Ethiopia. *Global Environmental Change,* 20(2), 278–286.

Redda, R., & Roland, R. (2016). Becoming a Climate-Resilient Green Economy: Planning for climate compatible development in Ethiopia. Retrieved from: http://wlv.ac.uk/cidt.

Robinson, S., Strzepek, K., & Cervigni, R. (2013). The Cost of Adapting to Climate Change in Ethiopia: Sector-wise and macro-economic estimates. Ethiopia Strategy Supporting Program II Working Paper 53.

Save the Children. (2016). Ethiopia Food Crisis Reaches "Critical Moment," Warns Save the Children. Retrieved from: www.savethechildren.org/site/apps/nlnet/content2.aspx?c=8rKLIXMGIpI4E&b=9357115&ct=14894821&notoc=1.

Schein, S. (2015). *A New Psychology for Sustainability Leadership: The hidden power of ecological worldviews.* Sheffield: Greenleaf Publishing.

Selby, D. (2010). "Go, Go, Go, Said the Bird": Sustainability-related education in interesting times. In F. Kagawa & D. Selby (Eds), *Education and Climate Change: Living and learning in interesting times* (pp. 35–54). New York: Routledge.

Shimelis, G., Mengistu, F., & Miller, V. (2017). The Faces of Leadership in Ethiopia. In S. Western & E. Garcia (Eds), *Global Leadership Perspectives: Insights and analysis.* Thousand Oaks, CA: SAGE Publications, Inc.

Siraj, A. S., Santos-Vega, M., Bouma, M. J., Yadeta, D., Ruiz Carrascal, D., & Mascual, M. (2014). Altitudinal Changes in Malaria Incidence in Highlands of Ethiopia and Colombia. *Science,* 343(6175), 1154–1158.

Tesfahunegn, G. B., Mekonen, K., & Tekle, A. (2016). Farmers' Perception on Causes, Indicators and Determinants of Climate Change in Northern Ethiopia: Implication for developing adaptation strategies. *Applied Geography,* 73, 1–12.

USAID. (2016). Climate Change Risk Profile Ethiopia: Country fact sheet. Retrieved from: www.climatelinks.org/resources/climate-change-risk-profile-ethiopia.

Yohannes, H. (2016). A Review on Relationship between Climate Change and Agriculture. *Journal of Earth Science Climate Change,* 7(2).

12 We Don't Conquer Mountains, We Understand Them: Embedding Indigenous Education in Australian Outdoor Education

Shawn Andrews

Acknowledgement

I acknowledge the traditional custodians of our land; their Elders past and present and thank them for keeping my spirit safe as I travel across their lands. I also acknowledge my dear friend David Forsyth; without his help and guidance, this chapter would have never happened.

Introduction

I need to start this introduction by letting the reader know that this chapter is not focused on leadership theories. It is a chapter about leadership in practice, leadership for change, and leadership for a better world. I suggest that when a leader shares their story, and when they lead from a position of connection to the environment, that they connect the group to themselves and the environment around them.

There is always an internal struggle when I am writing anything academic. Traditional Western academia prides itself on research-driven, peer-reviewed, style-guided literature reviews. Although I have never found writing in this manner difficult, I do feel as though I am fighting against my very nature. As an Indigenous Australian (Aboriginal), my nature is to tell and listen to stories. I suppose that is why my life's work is built around presenting. In some ways everything we do is presenting, every conversation and every encounter with others is presenting. This is why we worry about how we look, what type of job we have, and what people think about us, and therefore we spend so much time and money on material things.

The more students I see, the more I realize that we as an Australian society are losing the very essence of storytelling, the basics of communication, and the ability to feel comfortable in new settings. Some of my peers say that it's the development of the mobile phones, and that technology is isolating us. I don't disagree with this idea; all one must do is have a look around at a local café and you will see many people with their eyes down scrolling through their phones. I certainly do it. I believe that we as educators and as a society have lost the ability to teach connection and this loss of connection is causing anxiety among our young people. They no longer know how to connect with others and the environment. This lack of connection is especially evident when we watch their interactions on school camps.

School camps (outdoor education) place young people in unfamiliar settings. They are often arranged into groups with young people that they normally don't associate with at school. This is the first time that they spend time with their teachers outside of the classroom, and for many this is their first time in the bush. If you are like me and love observing people and their behaviors, then school camps are a lot of fun. There are a lot of awkward conversations and a lot of personal growth. One of the key observations that I have made is young people struggling to make conversation with strangers and teachers. There is an obvious anxiety around sharing one's story and a fear of being judged. The question I ask myself constantly is, "Why do these young people struggle so much with their identity?" It's not just young people who struggle. I have witnessed many teachers and adults shirk questions about who they are and avoid conversations altogether.

As an Indigenous Australian I know how hard it is to discuss identity. For most of my life, I was told that being Indigenous was a bad thing. My own grandmother would often comment that we are better off telling people we are Maoris than saying we are Aboriginal. The strange thing about my internal struggle for identity was the observations I made when visiting Indigenous family or community events. Here were multiple clans of Indigenous Australians, all of which have suffered from colonization, all with trauma, yet here they are hugging and communicating with comfort about their identity and belonging. It took me many years to realize that there is great strength in Indigenous Australian ways of belonging and connection. That there is healing and comfort in knowing who you are and how you connect.

The setting for this chapter is an Indigicate school camp. Indigicate is a specialist outdoor education company that designs and facilitates outdoor education using Indigenous Australian pedagogies as the method of learning. I want you to imagine you are at camp with me as part of a group of university students. It is the start of a five-day hiking program and today's conversation is about connection, trust, unity, and change. You are here because you want to know more about Indigenous Australians and what they have to offer. Already you have heard that there are many negative problems associated with Indigenous Australians, but you don't know why. The aim of this chapter is to demonstrate how I teach connection through storytelling, how we have lost connection with ourselves and the environment, and that through our connection we can create a happier, stronger society.

This chapter is written as a story in first person. It is written in a traditional Indigenous Australian method that honors my ancestors. We are storytellers and our ways are old. As a book chapter, and due to this book being academic literature, I have added in the references as required. This is the internal struggle that I deal with, and it is tricky to honor both Indigenous and Western methods of academia. In my opinion, the best way to hear any story is on country (sitting on the land), from the very mouth of the storyteller. In the absence of that, this is the best I can do.

Getting to Know Each Other

You are with me on country now, out in the Australian bush on one of my programs. There are eight of us. We have walked a short distance to a cozy place among gum trees and kangaroo grass. It is warm. There is a slight breeze coming from the North. The breeze makes the trees ruffle, but they don't ruffle loud enough to drown out the sounds of the birds. In the distance, there is a small stream; those of you with good hearing can faintly hear it. Those of you with deep connection can feel it.

Can you all please sit and listen. I will introduce myself, and then you will introduce yourself. Can you please form a circle. This is an Aboriginal way of doing things. In a circle everyone is equal and no one can hide. We all sit in the circle in the Australian bush, sitting on what I like to call country. You ask me, "Why do you do what you do and why did you start doing this?" I look at you and for a short while I wait in silence. I am listening to my ancestors, waiting for them to direct me. With a warm tone, I introduce myself.

"I am Shawn Andrews, a Mununjali man with ancestral roots in Southern Queensland and Tasmania. My people have lived on this land for as long as there was wind. The soil, trees, waterways, and animals are my ancestors. I am an Echidna who does not sit still. I am the first in my family to make it past year nine at school, the first to go to university, the first to graduate, and the first to travel overseas. I come from generations of strong Indigenous women. Women who were stolen from their families, who were persecuted, called savages, and told their ways are uncivilized. I have struggled with my identity and for many years I felt it was wrong to be Aboriginal, that we are subhuman and that our ways are not as important as the Western ways. My struggle made me sick. I lived and studied with severe depression and anxiety, and formed a terrible addiction to gambling.

"In 2014, at age 32, I decided that I needed to change, that I must start to honor my ancestors and listen to them. I needed to listen to the wind and follow my calling. I needed to find out who I am and why I am here. I decided to stop gambling, to seek help for my depression and anxiety, and to start a business. I felt there was a better way to educate non-Indigenous Australians about Indigenous Australian history and culture. That we could create a sequential curriculum that taught the truth about Indigenous Australian culture and history. A curriculum taught in the outdoors on school camps. In February 2015, with only $20.00 in my pocket and no car, I started a company called Indigicate, an outdoor education company that aims to create unity between Indigenous and Non-Indigenous Australians. A business that teaches the beautiful things about Indigenous Australian culture, our connection to others, land, and spirit.

I sit in the circle, in silence for a short while. Looking directly at you I ask, 'Who are you? Where are you from?'"

A Fractured Country that Needs Unity

After a short reflection on each other's stories, I am asked, "Why did it take so long for me to become happy?" My reply is blunt. "Aboriginal people have lived in Australia for over 50,000 years, yet I always felt like a stranger in my own country. I was brought up believing that the English saved us with their medicines and food, that the European way of life was much better than ours, and that being an Indigenous Australian is a negative thing."

I pause again to gather myself when a kookaburra starts to laugh. It is as if he waited for us to stop talking before he laughed; maybe he is an ancestor or a creator. His laugh echoes through the bush and when he finishes he looks at us, possibly waiting for applause or maybe waiting for me to start.

There are many questions from the group. One person looks at me and says, "Surely things aren't that bad, I know the Indigenous Australians have a lot of problems today, but these are things you can fix. You just need to change yourselves." Another group member puts their hand up and asks if I can explain connection. Another asks, "Does Indigicate work, and what are its aims?" I look around the group and smile; the group doesn't realize that their learning journey is about to begin. That they, like many groups before them, will get a snapshot of the good and bad of being an Indigenous Australian. I close my eyes and listen; slowly I open them and say, "Before we can understand the future, we must learn about the past." With a deep breath, I start our history lesson.

"On January 26, 1788, the lives of Indigenous Australians were changed forever. On that day, the British invaded the Eora people's country (Sydney) and set up a colony that almost led to the total annihilation of the Indigenous Australians (Broome, 2010). After many frontier wars across Australia, then known as New Holland, the Indigenous Australians succumbed to disease and the eventual forced removal from their homelands to small parcels of land often known as missions. By the time of 1829, it was believed that less than 30 percent of Indigenous Australians' pre-1788 population still survived. In 1830, the Tasmanian Government decided to get rid of the entire Indigenous Australian population on the island. They formed the Black Line. Directed by Governor George Arthur, thousands of able-bodied men formed a human chain and marched across the island. Their objective was to kill every Indigenous Australian. It failed in the short term, as the Indigenous Australians had already moved to the smaller islands to the North. It succeeded in displacing Indigenous Australians and allowed the Europeans to take control of Tasmania (Macintyre, 2016). The myth that the Indigenous Australians from Tasmania had all died out was born from this event. This is not true. My family are descendants of both sides of this horrific policy. My English family, the Spotswoods, benefited from the new "free"

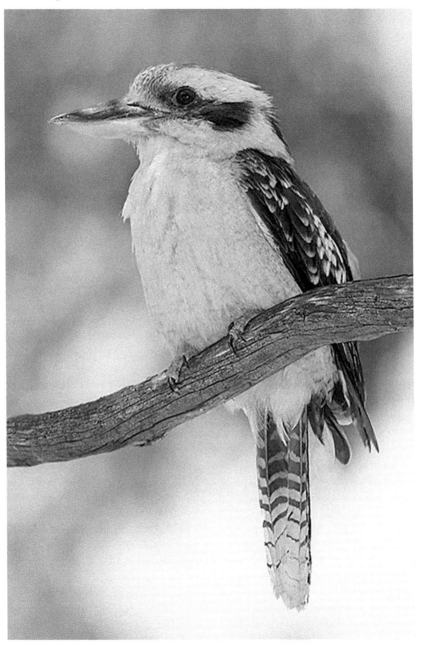

Figure 12.1 An Australian Kookaburra, known as a Kagaru in Mununjali Language
Source: Wikipedia, 2017. Taken by fir0002 flagstaffotos.com.au Canon 20D + Canon
400mm f/5.6 L (Own work) [GFDL 1.2 (www.gnu.org/licenses/old-licenses/fdl-1.2.
html)], via Wikimedia Commons.

and. Strangely, one of the Spotswoods, my great-grandfather four times removed, married one of the Tasmanian Aboriginal women.

"For Indigenous Australians, the 1800s was a horrific time. There were countless massacres, prolific disease, and catastrophic loss of culture. Clans were forced into missions and policies were developed to control Indigenous populations. In 1869, the Aboriginal Protection Act was established; protection boards were set up across the colonies, and the rights of Indigenous Australians became controlled by the state (Victorian Government, 1869). In 1886, the Half Caste Act was established (Victorian Government, 1886). This policy saw police, directed by the Aboriginal protection board, forcibly removing Indigenous Australian children of mixed race from their families. This led to a decline in the Indigenous Australian population on the missions and almost led to the destruction of the Indigenous Australians. The removal of the children is known in Australia as the 'stolen generations.' My family (like many Indigenous Australians) are descendants of stolen children. Often the children were stolen over multiple generations. The Australian government continued to remove Indigenous Australian children right up until the late 1960s. It was the government's opinion that our race would die out and that our people would assimilate into the white Australian population (Australian Human Rights Commission, 2017; Hill, 2008).

"During the early and mid-1900s, Indigenous Australians' rights decreased and their lives became increasingly difficult. Australia was formed in 1901 and along with federation came the white Australia policy. The basis of the policy started during the gold rush where it was determined that Chinese migrants were too good at mining and needed to be removed. 'The great white man's march for a great white country' occurred in 1885, and from here popular opinion was for the development of a country that was completely white.

This racist agenda did not impact the Indigenous Australians directly, as the white Australia policy only affected immigration. Indirectly, Indigenous Australians suffered as the general population became whiter and the general policy for immigration was for Australia to remain a white nation. All immigrants would need to submit to a dictation test, where they would need to read or write 50 words in a European language (Australian Government, 1901; National Archives of Australia, 2017).

"This policy was a huge 'success,' and in 1941 the Australian population was 99 percent white (ABS, 1941). It was only World War II that led to a change in immigration and the eventual disbandment of the white Australia policy in 1975 (National Archives of Australia, 2017).

"Adding to pressure of being the only colored people in a white nation, Indigenous Australians were additionally subjected to the historical opinion that they were savages and uncivilized, that without the help of the English we would have died out, we were primitive hunters and gatherers, without medicines, trade, social structures, and religion. History was rewritten and schools across the nation began to teach a negative view of Indigenous

Figure 12.2 A Poster for the Creation of a New Anthem for White Australia
Source: Naughton & Gyles, 1910.

Australians and that Australia's history began in 1778 when Captain Cook 'discovered' Australia (Pascoe, 2016).

"Obviously, Indigenous Australians knew that the 'white version' of our history was false and that we did have complex civilizations before and after the English invaded, but what could we do during this time? Our lands and children had been stolen. Our culture belittled and humiliated. Our people suffering and dying. To add insult to injury, the Australian Government decided to celebrate Australia Day on January 26, the day our suffering began: the day the British invaded the Eora people's country (National Australia Day Committee, 2017; Pascoe, 2016).

"Since the mid- to late-1990s, there has been a period of growth for Indigenous Australians and Australia. The Australian government, under pressure from the United Nations, began to address the 'Aboriginal Problem.' Working groups were established and studies conducted. In 2008, a report called 'Closing the gap on Aboriginal Australia: The challenge for Australia' was released. It made known some disturbing facts about Indigenous Australians (Australian Government, 2010; Katitjin, 2010). Indigenous Australians represent 2.5 percent of the population. On average, Indigenous Australians die 17 years younger than non-Indigenous Australians. Eighty-three percent of Indigenous deaths below the age of five occur in the first year of life. Infant mortality is 12.3 deaths per 1,000 births for Indigenous Australians compared to 4.2 for non-Indigenous Australians. There is a 25 percent difference in the minimum literacy and numeracy standards between Indigenous and non-Indigenous Australians; 43 percent of Indigenous Australians complete year 12 at high school; and 48 percent of the Indigenous Australian workforce-aged population are employed, compared to 72 percent of non-Indigenous Australians. Since 2008, there has been little improvement in these statistics. With improved reporting, the government has added the following alarming statistics: Indigenous Australians have 10 times the suicide rate of non-Indigenous Australians, 28 times more likely to be imprisoned, and have a 60 percent higher rate of mental health issues (Australian Government, 2010).

"Adding to these statistics are the issues that are not measured. Issues such as loss of identity, loss of family, and something that I experienced many times in my life, racism. There is a common myth that to be an Indigenous Australian you must be black or living in a remote Indigenous Australian community. When I identify as an Indigenous Australian, I am often asked what percentage or part me is Indigenous. There have been many times in my life when I have been asked to prove that I am an Indigenous Australian. To attend university and be part of an Indigenous unit, I was asked to provide written proof from a registered community that I am Indigenous. This process is humiliating and I imagine it is incredibly difficult for Indigenous Australians who are of the stolen generation and yet to find their ancestral home.

'In 2012–13 the Australian Government spent $30.3 billion on Indigenous Australian services, approximately 6 percent of general government expenditures' (Commonwealth of Australia, 2014). The money is spent on providing education, medical services, employment services, and recreation facilities. Even with this money going to services, the gap of Indigenous Australians' disadvantage in Australia grows. Prime Minister Malcolm Turnbull in his Close the Gap report (2017) says that we have made some small gains in closing the gap, yet we still have a long way to go with key targets not being met and statistics worsening in areas of health and employment. He speaks about there being a great optimism in Indigenous Australian communities and that we should work with Indigenous Australians more to help address their concerns. His words are echoed by Indigenous Australian academic Chris Sara who says, 'Do things with us not to us. Bring us policy approaches that nurture hope and optimism; and acknowledge, embrace and celebrate the humanity of Indigenous Australians'" (Turnbull, 2017, p. 1).

The Importance of Connection

I give the group a moment to reflect. It's hard to comprehend the brief history of Australia, and I sense there are many questions. I make one more statement before I take questions: "If you had questions as to why there are problems in Indigenous Australian communities, I hope that you understand that we have these issues due to loss of culture and from the inhumane treatment of our people." There is a somber feeling among the group. The person who stated that "Indigenous Australians need to change themselves" says "I didn't realize it is so bad, yet the Australian Government is spending billions on fixing Indigenous Australians, why is it not getting any better?" "There are many reasons as to why it is not getting any better," I answer. "The two key issues are the lack of understanding of Indigenous Australians' culture and the misrepresentation of Australian history."

"Indigenous Australians' culture, in my opinion, is a beautiful thing. Our songs, dance, art, and connection are highly visible pillars of our culture. The one thing that is overlooked or misunderstood is our connection. Karen Martin talks about her connection in her journal article 'Ways of Knowing, Ways of Being, and Ways of Doing: A theoretical framework and methods for Indigenous re-search and Indigenist research' (2003). Her method of explaining connection is experiential-based and demonstrates a spiritual connection with the land. For me connection with the land and my community is everything. Without it I become sick, I become lost, and I become unhappy. Understanding my connection to myself, my community, and my land gives me peace. For many years, I did not have connection and it was my lack of connection that caused my depression, anxiety, and gambling addiction. I did not know who I was and the sense of loss made me unwell.

"Many times in my life, I have heard the saying, 'Aboriginal people do not own the land, the land owns us.' This statement conflicts with Western views of ownership and land management, as we see ourselves as equals to the land, the animals, and each other. Indigenous Australians' connection is our greatest asset. Our connection to each other was what I witnessed as a child when people from different clans came together. They told their stories, good and bad. There was honor and respect in sharing one's story. It gave the storyteller a sense that they are real, they are trustworthy, and they are connected. They can share stories of their country, their totem animals, and their people. There is great healing in story sharing. I have witnessed this when sharing my story. There is great healing connection. I have witnessed this when I have traveled Australia: everywhere I went Indigenous Australians welcomed me, hugged me, and shared stories with me. All I had to do was explain my connection. From our connection comes our art, dances, and stories; they are intrinsically connected to each other and based on our connection to the environment and everything in it.

"Historically, Indigenous Australians' connection, history, and culture has been misrepresented. Especially in the context of Australian Curriculum. *Dark Emu*, a book written by Indigenous elder Bruce Pascoe (2016), debunks the myths that Indigenous Australians are hunters and gatherers and demonstrates that we have highly sophisticated agricultural systems, laws, religion, and trade. He writes about the deliberate and extraordinary lengths to which the Colonists and the Australian Government went to remove any knowledge of Indigenous Australians as sophisticated societies. If the world found out how sophisticated we are, then they would see that colonization was not a settlement of uncivilized people but rather a deliberate genocide of many cultures. A genocide that occurred so that the British could profit from our lands.

"Many of my conversations with non-Indigenous Australians suggest that it is still a popular belief that Indigenous Australians are uncivilized. It is not their fault that they believe this, since they, like me, are a product of the education we received at school. My own school education on my people was scarce. I was taught we lived here before the English discovered us. That we were poor souls more closely linked to apes than humans. I was taught that if the British had not arrived, we would have died out anyway. My year four teacher once shook her head as she said to our class 'We gave them (Indigenous Australians) everything, and now they thank us by being drunks and sniffing petrol.' When I returned home from school that day I asked my mother why she doesn't drink and if she ever sniffed petrol. Her laugh told me that she knew exactly what they were talking about. Her words were, 'When there is no hope, people drink too much and sniff petrol. It is a real shame.'

"It is only in recent years that there has been a significant improvement in debunking myths about Indigenous Australians. The drive behind this change has been made possible by the implementation of Indigenous Australian history and culture as a cross-curriculum priority for all schools in Australia. This was led by a shift in government policies and from government leaders wanting to close the gap of Indigenous Australian disadvantage by 2020.

In 2005, the Ministerial Council on Education, Employment, Training and Youth Affairs (MCEETYA) met to discuss a range of issues relating to Indigenous Education. The meeting led to the development of a working party that would investigate and identify key areas where improvement in Indigenous Australian education outcomes could be developed (Australian Curriculum Assessment and Reporting Authority, 2014). During 2005–2008, the working party established the Australian Directions in Indigenous

Education study, which outlined a number of key recommendations that would lead to better educational outcomes for Indigenous Australians (MCEETYA, 2006). In 2009, the Australian Directions for Indigenous Education study was reviewed and it was recommended that there needs to be significant changes if Australia wants to improve the educational outcomes of Indigenous Australians (Buckskin et al., 2009).

"The review was released shortly after former Australian Prime Minister Kevin Rudd gave an apology to the stolen generations, which coincided with the Council of Australian Governments (COAG) push to close the gap in Indigenous disadvantage (Council of Australian Government, 2008; Rudd, 2008). It was the aligning of Rudd's apology, with the review of the Australian Directions for Indigenous Education, and COAG's push for closing the gap, which led to significant changes in Indigenous Australian curriculum and the education of Indigenous Australians.

"The Australian Curriculum and Reporting Authority was formed in 2009 to investigate and implement a national curriculum, and on the advice of review of Australian Directions for Indigenous Education, implemented Indigenous Australian Education as a cross-curriculum priority in Australia's National Curriculum (Lowe & Yunkaporta, 2013). The implementation of Indigenous education as a cross-curriculum priority changed the education landscape and allowed us to finally move toward unity between Indigenous and non-Indigenous Australians."

Indigication

Having sat for a while, I ask the group if they would like to go for a short walk, of which there is a resounding yes. During our walk, I stop the group to point out the various animal tracks, the first of which is a Buneen. I explain that "Buneen" is the word for Echidna in my language. We walk and see many tracks and have many small conversations about the animals. Rain starts to gently fall and one of the group, looking concerned, asks "If the government made changes to improve education, and money is being spent on improving the lives of Indigenous Australians, then why did the prime minister say in his 2017 report that things haven't improved?" I ask the group to sit again. We create our circle under the shelter of a gum tree and begin my explanation.

"In my opinion, the key issue is that the Australian Government is focused on fixing Indigenous Australians. They presume that Indigenous Australians are the problem, so let's direct our spending on fixing them. The problem with this concept is that Indigenous Australians are not the problem. We don't need to be fixed; what we need to do is educate non-Indigenous Australians about us, they are the ones that need to be fixed. They often know little about Indigenous Australian culture and what they have been taught is incorrect. We need to shift the focus onto educating them and that is exactly what I aimed to do when I set up Indigicate.

"The concept of Indigicate started when I was studying Outdoor Education at University. I felt that there the outdoor education industry spent too much time focusing on journeys and activities in the outdoors and not enough time on connection and curriculum. The majority of the outdoor education I had worked with were hiking and canoeing journeys, and it was a popular belief among my peers that students should be kept busy and that the journey should be physically challenging. They believed that the challenge increased resilience and that resilient students became happier and healthier adults. I felt differently. I wondered why we didn't stop to investigate and spend quality time connecting with each other and with the bush. I queried my lecturers about it and was told that during the down time would be a good time to talk about connection and maybe even introduce some Indigenous education.

"Two issues arose from this suggestion. The first issue was the amount of down time available in this type of program. The group had hiked a long way, they were tired, and now had to cook dinner. The second issue was the type of Indigenous content that schools wanted to be taught. They want boomerang throwing and bush tucker (eating food from the forest) lessons, both of which turned out to be surface-based lessons and did nothing to work toward closing the gap of Indigenous Australian disadvantage. I remember during one of the lessons a student asked me why I was wearing clothes. Indigenous people don't wear clothes, she said. It was during these camps that I noticed the lack of communication between the students. They were scared to share their stories and I didn't know why. I decided to teach an open session around a campfire. The concept was simple. Talk about my story and then answer questions. The first lesson was a huge success and the feedback from the school and the students was that they wanted more. When I reflected on what made the lesson work, I realized that it is the Indigenous Australian method of educating and sharing that made it work, and that this was an opportunity to change the way we educate our young people.

"The journey to starting the business and working with schools was a difficult one. The first thing I had to do was strengthen my own connection. I was scared to do this, but when I did, it changed my life. I had learned that when I was connected I was happy. Sharing my story made the difficult parts seem a little less difficult and gave others the courage to ask difficult questions about Indigenous Australian history. The participants would connect with me and the connection gave our conversations depth and meaning.

"As the business grew slowly, we began to realize that we could teach curriculum-based lessons in the outdoors on school camps. We learned that when a leader shares their story, and when they lead from a position of connection to the environment, that they connect the group to themselves and the land around them. The students began to develop stronger connections to peers and their teachers, much stronger than we had experienced before. There was no shame in discussing one's past and one's story. The connection we developed allowed us to delve deeply into curriculum and we started to teach real Australian history. History that is telling the truth about the deliberate attempt at genocide of Indigenous Australians, told from our perspective, not the perspective of the colonists. Our camps became slow pedagogy, nonlinear journeys built around connection lessons such as whole body listening, local creations stories, finding your totem animal, and 'being ok being me.'

"The business is now in its third year. The growth has been phenomenal. We work with over 43 schools and multiple companies across Melbourne and Victoria, Australia. Some of our greatest achievements include the development of sequential school-wide Indigenous Australian curriculum that is driven by experiences on school camps. One of the programs has elders coming out to visit the students on a nightly basis, and the journey starts with traditional ceremonies and finishes with a visit to one of the missions where Indigenous Australians were once forced to live. The lessons from camp teach unity through understanding and connection through meditation, animal totem creation, and shared stories. The students on these journeys complete a graded project when they return to school. The projects' content comes from what they have learned at camp."

The sun is now starting to set; the rain has disappeared. In front of me are a group of hungry students who are torn between eating and wanting to know more. I know it is time to finish this part of today's lesson. I can see a distressed look on one person's face. I ask, "Is everything ok?" and she replies, "I am scared of sharing my story." I smile and say, "Your story isn't scary; it is your lack connection that makes you scared, and don't worry: we have already made a connection, so I suppose the rest is easy."

Conclusion

There is real value in looking at change and leadership through the lens of Indigenous Australians. We endured the invasion of our countries, the genocide of our people, and the deliberate destruction of our culture. We are still here and our knowledge systems still exist. The time has come for us to consider how we want to use them and if we can use Indigenous Australian knowledge systems to heal the pain and create unity.

There is great depth and beauty in Indigenous Australian culture. The key to sharing the beauty of culture is to continue to drive change in education and leadership. We need strong leaders who focus on creating change for the better, change with us, not for us. To achieve this, we need to ensure that Indigenous Australian education is continually driven by Indigenous Australians. We need to ensure that history is taught correctly, even if it is uncomfortable. Australia needs to provide adequate and appropriate cultural training for our teachers and our leaders. Training that is connection based and empowers them.

What I have created with Indigicate demonstrates that unity between Indigenous and non-Indigenous Australians can be established through inclusive, engaging, connection-based education. When leaders share their story and lead from a position of connection to self, community, and the environment, they are able to immerse groups in that connection. Their connection-driven leadership opens the senses and provides a platform for the individual to engage in new sights, sounds, and feelings. We need more connection-centered leadership powered by leaders who understand that the strongest thing they can do is share their story and the connection that they have. Leaders who do this will change the very fabric of education and forge new paradigms of the study of leadership.

It won't be easy to right the wrongs of the past. It will take considerable time and effort. It is important to know that what we are doing now in terms of Indigenous Australian education could not happen ten years ago – our nation and its people were simply not ready. Now we are entering a period of growth and change. The generation coming through schools now are a tidal wave of change makers and thought leaders. They are compassionate and want a world with more equality. As educators and leaders, we must harness the energy from this tidal wave and direct it toward the future we all want. Let's start the conversation and strengthen our connection. Let's share our story.

References

ABS. (1941). Chapter XII Population. Canberra: Australian Government. Retrieved from: www.ausstats.abs.gov.au/ausstats/free.nsf/0/8EBF8762C1A5976ECA257AF3 0011E323/$File/13010_1941%20section%2012.pdf.

Australian Curriculum Assessment and Reporting Authority. (2014). National Report on Schooling in Australia 2009. Part 7, Aboriginal and Torres Strait Islander education. Retrieved from: www.acara.edu.au/reporting/national_report_ on_schooling_2009/aboriginal_and_torres_strait_islander_education/aboriginal_an d_torres_strait_islander_education1.html.

Australian Government. (1901). Immigration Restriction Act 1901. Retrieved from: www.foundingdocs.gov.au/item-did-16.html.

Australian Government. (2010). *Closing the Gap*. Canberra: Government of Australia. Retrieved from: www.healthinfonet.ecu.edu.au/?gclid=CIOE1aLrxqIC FcIvpAod3Tb_Gw.

Australian Human Rights Commission. (2017). Track the History: The stolen generation. Retrieved from: www.humanrights.gov.au/track-history-timeline-stolen-generations.

Broome, R. (2010). *Aboriginal Australia: A history since 1788* (4th ed.). Melbourne, Australia: Allen and Unwin.

Buckskin, P., Hughes, P., Price, K., Rigney, L.-I., Sarra, C., Adams, I., & Rankine, K. (2009). Review of Australian Directions in Indigenous Education 2005–2008 for the Ministerial Council for Education, Early Childhood Development and Youth Affairs. Retrieved from: http://scseec.edu.au/site/DefaultSite/filesystem/documents/ ATSI percent20documents/review_of_aust_directions_in_indigenous_ed_2005–200 8.pdf.

Commonwealth of Australia. (2014). 2014 Indigenous Expenditure Report. Retrieved from: www.pc.gov.au/research/ongoing/indigenous-expenditure-report/indigenou s-expenditure-report-2014/indigenous-expenditure-report-2014.pdf.

Council of Australian Government. (2008). COAG meeting 29 November 2008. Retrieved from: www.coag.gov.au/node/294.

Hill, M. (2008). *Stories of the Stolen Generation*. Sydney: Pearson Education Australia.

Katitjin, K. (2010). What is Closing the Gap? *Australian Indigenous Health Infonet*. Retrieved from: www.healthinfonet.ecu.edu.au/closing-the-gap/key-facts/what-is-c losing-the-gap.

Lowe, K., & Yunkaporta, T. (2013). The Inclusion of Aboriginal and Torres Strait Islander Content in the Australian National Curriculum: A cultural, cognitive and socio-political evaluation. *Curriculum Perspectives*, 33(1), 1–14.

Macintyre, S. (2016). *A Concise History of Australia* (4th ed.). Port Melbourne: Cambridge University Press.

Martin, K. (2003). Ways of Knowing, Ways of Being, and Ways of Doing: A theoretical framework and methods for Indigenous re-search and Indigenist research. Paper presented at the New talents21C: Next Generation Australian Studies.

MCEETYA. (2006). Australian Education Systems Officials Committee Officials Working Party on Indigenous Education Directions in Indigenous Education 2005– 2008. Retrieved from: http://scseec.edu.au/site/DefaultSite/filesystem/documents/ ATSI%20documents/Australian_Directions_in_Indigenous_Education_2005–2008. pdf.

National Archives of Australia. (2017). Immigration Restriction Act 1901 (commonly known as the White Australia Policy). Retrieved from: www.naa.gov.au/col lection/a-z/immigration-restriction-act.aspx.

National Australia Day Committee. (2017). History. Retrieved from: www.australia day.org.au/australia-day/history/.

Naughton, W., & Gyles, H. (1910). White Australia: The great national party song. Retrieved from: https://collections.museumvictoria.com.au/items/1326028.

Pascoe, B. (2016). *Dark Emu: Black Seeds: agriculture or accident?*Broome, Australia: Magabala Books Aboriginal Corporation.

Rudd, K. (2008). Motion of Apology to Australia's Indigenous Peoples. Retrieved from: www.australia.gov.au/about-australia/our-country/our-people/apology-to-a ustralias-indigenous-peoples.

Turnbull, M. (2017). Closing the Gap Report Statement to Parliament. Retrieved from: www.pm.gov.au/media/2017-02-14/closing-gap-report-statement-parliament.

Victorian Government. (1869). Aboriginal Protection Act. Retrieved from www. foundingdocs.gov.au/item-sdid-22.html.

Victorian Government. (1886). *The Aborigines Protection Act*. Victoria, Australia: John Ferres Government Publisher.

Wikipedia. (2017). Laughing Kookaburra. Retrieved from: https://en.wikipedia.org/ wiki/Laughing_kookaburra.

13 Critical Internal Shifts for Sustainable Leadership

Kathleen E. Allen

Introduction

John and Paul are both CEOs of manufacturing businesses. John is proud of his business and is focused on maximizing profits for his shareholders. He considers himself a self-made man. He uses the river that his business is located by to dispose waste from his manufacturing process. He abides by the legal limits of the contaminants. He wishes the federal government would have less regulation because meeting these standards is costly and decreasing his profits. His business is his and is designed to optimize his income and profits. His employees are expected to be productive and serve his and his business's needs.

Paul is also the owner of a manufacturing business located on a river. He realizes that his business is impacted by local and global businesses and political, environmental, and social dynamics. He watches the turbulence of the external environment to learn how to adapt to disruptions in his business. He is grateful for all the people in his life who have helped him achieve success. He also uses the river to dispose of waste from his manufacturing process. He abides by the legal limits and even sets higher standards because he understands protecting the environment is how he can ensure his great-grandchildren will have a better quality of life. He sees regulations as feedback that current practices are creating harm and the businesses that are affected by these regulations need to redesign their manufacturing processes.

Paul studied how other manufacturing plants up and down the river were disposing their waste and decided to follow it downstream to see what the combined impact was of all these individual businesses decisions. He found that while all were abiding by the law, the combined effect of their disposal processes was creating a cesspool downstream. This caused him to start a coalition of business owners on this river to change their cumulative impact on the quality of water. Paul is proud of his business and treats his employees well. He knows that nothing can be done in his company without the active support of the people in it. John and Paul's choices and actions are all shaped by the way they see their world.

Much of environmental leadership focus has been on the level of strategies, structures, and business operations (Schein, 2015). In contrast, there has been little focus on critical internal shifts such as value systems and deep motivations for integrating sustainable leadership practices into our personal and organizational lives. The purpose of this chapter is to explore the interior work of environmental leadership.

Environmental leadership is defined as the choices positional leaders or individual agents of leadership make that result in environmentally sustainable solutions or decisions. In my consulting practice, I focus on the intersection of leadership and change. I have found that there are different levels of intervention that a consultant or individual leader can use to trigger organizational or personal change (Meadows, 2008; Scharmer, 2009).

Levels of Intervention

The first level is like the squeaky wheel. The focus is on stopping the squeak and anything that works is the solution. If you throw water on a squeaky wheel, the sound will go away. However, the solution doesn't last and when it comes back it is louder. This level of intervention doesn't have the reflective practice that looks for the root of the problem; rather, it focuses on a quick fix.

When we began to see domestic violence in our communities the first response was at this level. Individuals who cared about this issue began to open their homes to victims of domestic violence. This worked in the short term, but as more people came forward with the need for shelter, it wasn't sufficient to solve the problem.

The second level of intervention focuses on patterns of behavior that helps identify tactics. It is one step deeper than the first level. If a leader looked at patterns of behavior with a sustainability focus, they would look for solutions that would shift or create a new pattern. This focus would create some shifts but wouldn't reach a sustainable long-term solution because the shift in practice doesn't go deep enough.

Over time, a pattern of need by victims of domestic abuse emerged. The next level of response to increased demand for help by domestic violence victims was to increase the number of people who would open their homes to help shelter them. A network of people was linked together to provide a coordinated response. This was a good tactic but didn't meet the rising need and wasn't sustainable.

The third level of intervention focuses on the systemic structures and processes and how they can help or hinder the direction an organization wants to go. If an organization wanted to recycle and upcycle a carpet manufacturing business, the leaders would change the processes and structures to strategically achieve this goal (McDonough & Braungart, 2002). However, changing structures and processes can just as easily help an organization become more efficient, increase profit, or be more innovative. By itself, structure and processes don't necessarily lead to a sustainable orientation by positional leaders – that requires a shift in worldview.

In the domestic violence movement, the third level of intervention is when organizations were formed and shelters were built. Building shelters and providing additional help to the victims was a strategic response to the need. However, it only focused on responding to the victims and creating a safe refuge for them.

The fourth level of intervention focuses on an individual's mindset and worldviews. When an individual changes the way they view the world, all their relationships, thought patterns, behaviors, and insights shift. There are patterns of thought that align with sustainable leadership and others that drive actions and behaviors that don't. When a person's worldview changes in specific ways, the individual integrates their worldview and actions intentionally to support environmentally sustainable decisions (Kuenkel, 2015).

In the evolution of thought in the domestic violence movement, staff eventually started to look "upstream" to what was causing the problem. This shift in focus caused them to realize that if they wanted a sustainable solution to the problem, they would have to start influencing the larger system in their communities. It was at this point that leaders in the field began to build collaborations and partnerships with local law enforcement, the judicial system, legal aid, psychological services, and prevention programing. They created outreach and engaged their communities to build a culture of zero tolerance for domestic violence. These strategies expanded their relationships in their communities, built trust in the system, and helped them influence the larger systems and how they responded to this issue. For the first time in this movement, the people who built and ran the shelters were not alone. They had lots of company in their communities helping them with this issue. New strategies and solutions were generated to help create a more sustainable solution to domestic violence.

Worldviews and Deep Background Assumptions

Worldviews are the way an individual views the world. Worldviews often reflect the deep background assumptions that we hold. An assumption is a belief, supposition, conjecture, or theory that we hold that impacts our reactions and responses to a life event. The event could be how to handle a relationship or an organizational decision, respond to a disruptive challenge, or feel about a situation. Most often, deep background assumptions exist in the subconscious or unconscious mind. If a person becomes aware of their assumptions, it gives them great opportunity to consciously evaluate if they are of service to them. Given the dynamic shifting occurring in the world, reexamining deep background assumptions and worldviews are a powerful way to become more adaptive and effective. When worldviews shift, change can be achieved rapidly, and these shifts can open us up to new ways of thinking and to see different possibilities.

Four Worldview Shifts Needed for Sustainable Leaders

Based on my own research and consulting practice, I suggest that there are four internal worldview shifts that occur when an individual chooses an environmentally sustainable framework to lead from (Schein, 2015).

The first shift is from a seeing our organizations and communities as closed systems to seeing them as open systems. Closed systems are bounded, and dynamics outside the system do not change the dynamics inside a closed system. In a closed system, control is possible because the number of variables remains static (Allen, 2012). In an open system, dynamics from other systems can permeate and create an expansion of the number of variables. This creates a dynamic complex system. Leadership in an open system focuses on influence and patterns. To understand the leverage points that can influence the system, open systems thinkers learn how all the elements, ties, interconnections, and relationships impact the system as a whole (Capra & Luisi, 2014; Meadows, 2008; Miller, 2010).

A closed system worldview doesn't see or ignores the meaning of the connections between an organizational system and the broader external environment. They see solutions that are good for the organization alone. A closed system worldview inhibits an individual from seeing the connections between their system and other systems. This makes it difficult for them to see a world filled with networked relationships and connections (Ramo, 2016).

Open systems are complex and dynamic. In resilience science, sustainable solutions are always viewed from a linked systems perspective (Walker & Salt, 2012). If community leaders want to avoid overfishing, they know that they can't approach it from an environmental perspective alone. To get the active support from fishermen, the strategy also needs to consider how changes in their fish catch impact their ability to carry a loan on their boat. A sustainable strategy also needs to consider the social impact that can result in their family or community. Resilient solutions see systems as linked and look for sustainable solutions that work within social, environmental, and economic systems. Their solutions are more sustainable because their worldview accepts that systems are open and linked and changes in one system will ripple across other systems.

When a person shifts their worldview from a closed to open system, they realize that their choices will impact other individuals, organizations, and systems. In open systems, we realize that others' actions will affect us and our actions will impact and affect others. The stock market is an open system. Political destabilization in one part of the world will affect the economies in another part of the world.

The shift to open systems leads to the next worldview shift. Once we see our systems as open and linked, we begin to see connections that have been hidden but were always there. We start seeing the connections between ourselves and our organizations to the environment and the people in it.

The second worldview shift is thus from separation to connection. Separation is based on the perception that we are separate from each other and our environment. If one believes that one stands alone, then predominant self-interest is the logical choice. Serving yourself first and holding on to your power and resources regardless of its impact on others flows directly from a separate worldview. John's belief that he is a self-made man is an example of this belief that we all stand alone. The problem with self-interest, however, is that when unbridled, it oppresses others and the environment.

The belief that people are driven by self-interest is anchored in another myth – the myth of survival of the fittest (Hutchins, 2014; Kohn, 1992). If our individual survival depends on our ability to defend ourselves and be stronger than the next person, then self-interest becomes tightly linked to survival. This belief scales up into our organizational behaviors and justifies actions that can hurt communities and the environment. The fiscal crisis in 2008 would be one example where individual and organizational self-interest was used to justify actions that nearly took down the global economy and created great pain for many people.

A culture of separation and self-interest has misquoted Darwin's research as "survival of the fittest." Rather, he said survival of the best fit within the larger environment (Hutchins, 2014; Kohn, 1992). One of the ways to fit best into a place and thrive for the long haul is to be sensitive to the context and form mutually beneficial relationships. Researchers have found that mutuality and cooperation are widely present in nature (Baumeister, 2014; Benyus, 2002). Weather systems are complex, dynamic, and interdependent, which is why changes in the temperature of the Pacific Ocean can change the winter weather pattern in the Upper Midwest in the United States. Nature and weather are examples of systems based on connection.

When a worldview shifts to connection, everything changes. We see ourselves in relationship with others, our environment, and our future. This worldview shift helps us to see the hidden connections in our world and networks and interdependence become obvious. Connection shifts hierarchies to networks, changes the power dynamic in relationships, and recognizes new dynamic feedback loops (Allen et al., 1998; Brafman & Beckstrom, 2006; Capra, 1996; Capra, 2002; Satterwhite, 2010).

Connections shift self-interest to enlightened self-interest. Enlightened self-interest is defined as people who act to further the interests of others to ultimately serve their own self-interest. In nature, as ecological systems become more complex, species develop specializations. This specialization eventually shifts interspecies relationships. As a system becomes more complex, open, and connected, species begin to depend on other species in an ecosystem to provide key nutrients because other species can do it more effectively than they can for themselves (Kiuchi & Shireman, 2002). Connections and interdependencies create a shift in the nature of our relationships. Instead of standing isolated and alone, we see how our actions help others and in turn how others help us. This interdependent relationship occurs between people, organizations, and the environment – to see it, we must shift our worldview from separation to connection.

If we shifted our worldview to one that recognized our connection and interdependence, a natural result of increasing complexity, would what we see and how we think change? For example, can anyone succeed over time if another fails in an interdependent system? This question stimulates reflection about the nature of interdependence and connection. It also suggests that the way we can serve ourselves best is to ensure that the larger systems thrives and remains healthy.

The shift from closed to open systems helps us see how systems are linked, influence each other, and create complexity. The open system worldview causes us to see interconnections between our global economy and ourselves, others, our organizations, and the environment. In a connected worldview we begin to see how actions continue to ripple throughout linked systems. Paul reflected a connected worldview when he investigated how the combined impact of everyone's waste from manufacturing plants along the river affected the quality of water downstream. This leads us to the third shift, the need to see how actions impact systems over time.

The third critical internal shift is from short-term to long-term thinking (Brand, 2008; Satterwhite et al., 2015). Different feedback loops with different criteria show up when success is defined over the long term instead of just the short term. Long-term thinking extends the time horizon beyond quarterly profits and the next election cycle. Longer feedback loops shift decision making from short-term gain to long-term investment based on the higher purpose of the organization, which is to thrive over time. (Baumeister, 2014; Benyus, 2002; Capra & Luisi, 2014; Wielkiewicz & Stelzner, 2005).

Short-term thinking rests on a series of unexamined assumptions. The first is that events are discrete. Each problem is separate from another. As our world becomes more complex, being *temporally blind* causes us to see events as discrete. When we learn to connect time between the past, present, and into the future, we see events as streams flowing through time horizons (Oshry, 1995). We understand that how we solve problems in the past creates the agenda for current problems, and how we solve problems in the present creates the agenda of problems in the future. For example, if a CEO solves a current problem that serves a short-term goal in a way that diminishes trust with his employees, the next time a big problem needs to be solved, it will be more difficult to gain active cooperation because less trust exists in the organization.

In short-term time horizons, the focus is on the completion of a project instead of what effect this action or decision will have on the whole system. If the goal is to maximize profits, the focus and the measure is on the accumulation of profit. This serves the short-term goal, but there may be unexamined consequences over time. For example, if a company raises prices and disproportionately distributes profits, it can weaken the buying power of its customers, and over time cause the company to be less resilient.

Short-term thinking also causes us to be blind to the impact of our actions on the entire system over time. The North Dakota pipeline conflict is a disagreement based on time frame. One side is focused on getting the pipeline finished to fulfill the need to get oil to market and the other is looking at the risk to water quality if there is an accident in the future. Water quality is the introduction of another criterion and feedback loop that reflects longer-term thinking in the oil pipeline debate. An example of where both short- and long-term time horizons are being considered is in the field of investment. Financial investment strategies have now designed mutual funds that optimize both short- and long-term investments. They balance the mix of investments to extend beyond short-term profit to include stocks that will provide long-term returns.

Long-term thinking and action increases the number of variables that a company needs to consider in making decisions. In Paul's story, he shifted from dumping waste from his plant that met the federal regulations to raising his company's standards and eliminating harmful waste, even though it cost more to make this shift. His focus wasn't just on profit; he chose to reduce profit to ensure higher quality of water for the people downstream. Adding water quality as a criterion shifts the feedback loop to water quality as a measure of success as well as profit.

Long-term thinking also shifts our focus from a narrow range of factors to the entire system. Over time things don't stay in one place; events in an open and connected system start affecting other things. If everyone does the minimum, the emergent pattern can be devastating for the larger system. For example, if we choose to deny climate change because it disrupts the business model of the oil and gas industry, the short-term result is stability in those industries for employment and the economy. However, the long-term time horizon would look at the risk of air quality, climate disruptions in raising sea levels, increased natural disasters, and the social health and economic impact for our great-grandchildren. In a long-term time horizon, health of future generations, resilience of ecological systems, and sustainability of air and water quality becomes a meaningful criterion in addition to profit.

In a connected open system world, actions continue to ripple throughout the system. And those effects can only be truly understood over time and through a holistic view.

The fourth shift is from inert to living systems. When we see organizations or the environment as inert, we create a subject-to-object relationship with them. An object is something we own and can move at will. I don't have to ask my coffee cup's permission to move it to a more convenient place nearer my hand. Traditional worldviews see nature as an object. This means that the resources in nature can be exploited for a company's purpose and profit. We don't need to consider how to extract resources in a way that minimizes damage to the ecosystem the resources are found in. Inert objects don't need this consideration. Opening up national parks to extraction of natural resources reflect a subject-to-object relationship. The resources represent profits to companies. Their short-term purpose is to make profits and this drives the economy. Therefore, these parks' resources should be accessible to businesses who could profit from them. They aren't seen as a living system; rather, they are objects to be used by others.

When we shift to seeing our organizations and our environment as living systems, we shift our relationship to subject–subject. This shift changes the nature of our relationship. Living systems require consultation with each other. Each living entity needs to recognize its reciprocity and equity with each other. Living entities have decision-making rights in any negotiation, even though they can't speak for themselves. Living systems help us see all life as sacred including national park resources, the employees in our organizations, the communities we live in, and our customers and supply lines (Allen, 2012; Allen, 2015; Baumeister, 2014; Capra & Luisi, 2014).

Nature is a living system. It continually adapts and adjusts to allow for the future flourishing of life on earth. With a 3.8-billion-year history, we can say that the design of nature is successful since we still have life on this planet (Benyus, 2002). Nature is structured as a complex, dynamic, interdependent network. There is reciprocity and mutuality in its relationships. Shifting to a worldview of living systems causes us to see each other as unique living beings who make up living communities and organizations who are embedded in a larger living system called nature. This shift to seeing living systems requires leadership practices to become more skilled at leading collectively, a process that recognizes multiple stakeholders and decision-making rights (Kuenkel, 2016).

Implications

When a person assumes that they exist in an open system filled with connections, where actions can only be fully understood over time, and that systems are living, it changes the way they approach everything. For example, Al and Lois Steuter own the Sandhill and Sun Ranch in the Sandhills of Nebraska. It is a sustainable ranching business by design.

Al is an example of how these four worldviews shifts impact how he thinks about ranching and how his worldview has influenced how he ranches. "The Sandhill & Sun Ranch is conservatively stocked to insure long-term sustainable grazing for the cattle herd on standing perennial forage on a year-long basis" (http://sandhillandsunranch.com/). Al sees his ranch as an *open system* impacted by weather and the grassland's ecology. He is committed to maintaining healthy populations of native plant and animal species on his ranch. His decisions aren't just based on the relationship between his cattle herd and the grasslands. They also consider the other plant and animal species that use the same landscape. The ranch is linked to natural, social, and economic systems. He designed his ranch in a way that sees and uses his *connections* to the land and all the species in it, including the size of his herd. Finally, he considers his acreage in the Sandhills as his grassland endowment. It is a *living system* that he treats with respect. If he ran more cattle for a short-term economic gain, he would be hurting the *resilience of the long-term ecology* he depends on, much like spending down the principle of an endowment instead of using only the interest. He chooses to maintain the number of cattle in relationship to what is going on with his grasslands. If there is drought, he will maintain a smaller herd. I have even heard him ask, "what does the grassland need?" to ensure its resilience as an ecosystem. Al represents how these four worldviews can create an integrated framework that shapes one's behavior, thinking, and decision making.

These four worldviews are linked and together create an integrated approach to an individual's choices. If positional leaders held these world-views, they would lead in a sustainable way. If the worldviews became con-scious, a positional leader could articulate how they influence the definition, thinking, and practice of environmental leadership for sustainability.

However, there are people who see the world as a closed system where things are separate. They see nothing wrong with short-term time horizons or viewing their organizations as objects they control. There are reasons why people don't shift their worldviews as the world around them changes. The first is that people who have succeeded in the old paradigm of worldviews hold on to their perspectives (Kuhn, 1970; Ramo 2016). They have been rewarded for their mental models and see no reason to change. I suggest in response that there are three strategies that can be used to help an individual shift their worldviews.

The first strategy is to help people to become more aware and conscious of the worldview they are holding (Senge et al., 1994). When deep back-ground assumptions are named, they can be analyzed to see if they continue to serve the individual. For example, if one believes that they are separate from others and that protecting their self-interest is paramount, they can examine that belief to see if it has made them happier and more fulfilled in their life.

The second strategy flows from the first. As we become more aware of our worldviews, we can examine the external environment to see if our *internal map* fits the territory we are living in, or if it helps us explain dynamics we see in our life. For example, a colleague of mine recently became a grandfather. This resulted in a shift to a longer time horizon. Time became more visible to him and he began to see how his choices and the organizations he led could help or hinder the quality of life for his grand- and great-grandchildren.

The third strategy uses painful or frustrating experiences to trigger a reflective practice that causes a shift in worldview. Ramo in his book *The Seventh Sense: Power, fortune, and survival in the age of networks* tells a story of working with one- and two-star generals at the War College after the Iraq War (2016). The generals thought they had superior intelligence, equipment, strategy, and soldiers. What they found was they were fighting a war that used the rules of networks instead of hierarchies. This was a painful experience and triggered an intentional learning practice that led them to see the world as networked instead of separate. It also helped them to develop new strategies that fit this new worldview.

What Changes

When we shift our worldview, everything changes. Behaviors, actions, and decisions that made sense in a closed system that assumes separation, short-term timelines, and inert systems are very different when viewed with a different worldview. Once we see open systems, we realize that our actions affect others and other events will ripple throughout our organization. We understand that we can influence many things but control very few. Power is no longer a zero-sum game.

Connectedness opens us up to being in relationship with each other and to see how our actions impact others and how others impact us. We see ourselves in relationship with others and the world around us. We see our interdependence and how one person's success is built on relationships with others and our communities. We can no longer stand aside while various parts of our population struggle. Their struggle hurts them and ourselves. When we connect to nature, we notice how our decisions impact the environment and we can no longer make decisions based solely on how it will benefit ourselves alone.

When we extend our time horizon, we notice how actions and decisions might unfold over time. We look at short-term criteria and add longer time horizon questions that need to be asked before a decision can be made. We are no longer naive about the ramifications of choices over time. We become temporally competent. Choices we used to tolerate become intolerable.

Finally, we look to the livingness of all our systems. We see the sacredness of our relationships to each other and the larger environment. This shapes the way we think and treat each other. Our worldview and assumptions help us move toward leadership that is sustainable for our businesses, relationships, and the environment.

This chapter started with two stories that reflected different worldviews. If a person becomes aware of their assumptions, it gives them a wonderful opportunity to examine their assumptions and worldviews consciously and to evaluate if they still serve themselves and our world. It also gives us a way of influencing people to lead sustainably. Conversations that reveal deep background assumptions have the power to shift individuals toward sustainable leadership.

References

Allen, K.E. (2012). Dancing on a Slippery Floor: Transforming systems, transforming leadership. In C. Pearson (Ed.), *The Transforming Leader: New approaches to leadership for the twenty-first century* (pp. 64–74). San Francisco, CA: Berrett-Koehler Publishers.

Allen, K.E. (2015). Leading Living Systems. TEDX talk. Retrieved from: www.you
tube.com/watch?v=DAwHiM-1FnM.

Allen, K.E., Stelzner, S.P., & Wielkiewicz, R.M. (1998). The Ecology of Leadership:
Adapting to the challenges of a changing world. *The Journal of Leadership Studies*, 5(2), 62–82.

Baumeister, D. (2014). *Biomimicry Resource Handbook: A seed bank of best practices.* Missoula, MT: Biomimicry 3.8.

Brand, S. (2008). *The Clock of the Long Now: Time and responsibility.* New York:
Basic Books.

Benyus, J.M. (2002). *Biomimicry: Innovations inspired by nature.* New York: Harper
Collins.

Brafman, O., & Beckstrom, R.A. (2006) *The Starfish and the Spider: The unstoppable power of leaderless organizations.* New York: The Penguin Group.

Capra, F. (1996). *The Web of Life.* New York: Anchor Books Doubleday.

Capra, F. (2002). *The Hidden Connections: Integrating the biological, cognitive, and
social dimensions of life into a science of sustainability.* New York: Doubleday.

Capra, F., & Luisi, P.L. (2014). *The Systems View of Life: A unifying vision.* Cambridge: Cambridge University Press.

Hutchins, G. (2014). *The Illusion of Separation: Exploring the cause of our current
crises.* Edinburgh: Floris Books.

Kiuchi, T., & Shireman, B. (2002). *What We Learned in the Rainforest: Business
lessons from nature.* San Francisco, CA: Berrett-Koehler Publishers.

Kohn, A. (1992). *No Contest: The case against competition* (2nd ed.). Boston, MA:
Houghton Mifflin.

Kuenkel, P. (2015). *Mind and Heart: Mapping your personal journey towards leadership for sustainability.* Berlin, Germany: Collective Leadership Institute.

Kuenkel, P. (2016). *The Art of Leading Collectively: Co-creating a sustainable,
socially just future.* White River Junction, VT: Chelsea Green Publishing.

Kuhn, T. (1970). *The Structure of Scientific Revolutions* (2nd ed.). Chicago, IL:
University of Chicago Press.

McDonough, W., & Braungart, M. (2002). *Cradle to Cradle: Remaking the way we
make things.* New York: North Point Press.

Meadows, D.H. (2008). *Thinking in Systems: A primer.* White River Junction, VT:
Chelsea Green Publishing.

Miller, P. (2010). *The Smart Swarm: How to work efficiently, communicate effectively, and make better decisions using the secrets of flocks, schools, and colonies.*
New York: The Penguin Group.

Oshry, B. (1995). *Seeing systems: Unblocking the mysteries of organizational life.* San
Francisco, CA: Berrett-Koehler.

Ramo, J.C. (2016). *The Seventh Sense: Power, fortune, and survival in the age of
networks.* New York: Little, Brown and Company.

Satterwhite, R. (2010). Deep Systems Leadership: A model for the 21st century. In B.
Redekop (Ed.), *Leadership for Environmental Sustainability* (pp. 230–242). New
York & London: Routledge.

Satterwhite, R., Miller, W.W., & Sheridan, K. (2015). Leadership for Sustainability
and Peace: Responding to the wicked challenges of the future. In M. Sowcik, A.C.
Andernoro, M. McNutt, & S.E. Murphy (Eds), *Leadership 2050: Critical challenges, key contexts, and emerging trends* (pp. 59–74). Bingley: Emerald Group
Publishing Limited.

Scharmer, C.O. (2009). *Theory U: Leading from the future as it emerges.* San Francisco, CA: Berrett-Kohler Publishers.

Schein, S. (2015). *A New Psychology for Sustainability Leadership: The hidden power of ecological worldviews.* Sheffield: Greenleaf Publishing Limited.

Senge, P., Kleiner, A., Rovarts, C., Ross, R., & Smith, B. (1994). *The Fifth Discipline Fieldbook: Strategies and tools for building a learning organization.* New York: Doubleday.

Walker, B., & Salt, D. (2012). *Resilience Practice: Building capacity to absorb disturbance and maintain function.* Washington, DC: Island Press.

Wielkiewicz, R., & Stelzner, S. (2005). An Ecological Perspective on Leadership Theory, Research, and Practice. *Review of General Psychology, 9*(4), 326–341.

14 From Peril to Possibility: Restorative Leadership for a Sustainable Future

Seana Lowe Steffen

Introduction

A Declaration: Women of the World Call for Urgent Action on Climate Change & Sustainability Solutions

We are the mothers and the grandmothers, sisters and daughters, nieces and aunts, who stand together to care for all generations across our professions, affiliations and national identities. ...

We are gathering to raise our voices to advocate for an Earth-respecting cultural narrative, one of "restore, respect, replenish" and to replace the narrative of "domination, depletion and destruction" of nature.

International Women's Earth and Climate Summit (WECAN, 2013)

When Casey Camp-Horinek of the Ponca tribe invoked blessings from the four directions at the International Women's Earth and Climate Summit, she declared it to be a historic moment. The Summit – convened by the Women's Earth and Climate Action Network (WECAN) – gathered 100 women from the global North and South including Dr. Jane Goodall (Great Britain), former President of Ireland Mary Robinson, Dr. Vandana Shiva (India), Nobel Laureate Jody Williams (United States), Executive Secretary Christiana Figueres (Costa Rica), and many grassroots and indigenous leaders from areas such as the Democratic Republic of Congo, Maldives, and Sarayaku/Ecuador. To launch unified campaigns, the declaration *Women of the World Call for Urgent Action on Climate Change & Sustainability Solutions* was ratified and signed by all delegates, declaring in its Preamble:

Climate change threatens life as we know it on our one and only home planet. Our children, our grandchildren and all future generations are in danger. Natural systems upon which all living things depend are in jeopardy. We have a choice: between a path of continued peril and a path towards climate justice and a safe and clean energy future. We can and must join together as women to take action with common but differentiated responsibilities for achieving sustainability. We must act now for ourselves, for future generations, for all living things on Mother Earth.

(WECAN, 2013)

The declaration, together with a co-created *Women's Climate Action Agenda* of solutions, was then distributed to world governments throughout the United Nations network. Names continue to be collected to this day, with initial delegates' and additional grassroots signatures delivered regularly to global leaders.

While the arc of the choice between peril and possibility will be known by 2030, the story itself is being written today by the collection of individual acts and leadership choices made moment by moment. As a result of efforts by countless individuals and organizations, ranging from grassroots to global visionaries such as those assembled at the Summit, humanity has made great progress toward sustainability. We now have the scientific knowledge that reveals the awesome interplay of chemical and biological processes that have maintained the precise conditions to sustain human life (Lovelock, 2003). We also have the technological knowledge and skill to live sustainably (Hawken, 2017). We even have a comprehensive plan of action to chart a sustainable future in the form of the universally adopted United Nations *Transforming Our World: 2030 Agenda for Sustainable Development* (2015). What we do not yet have, however, is an understanding of how to mobilize the collective will to sustain and thrive as a whole. This question, which falls within the domain of leadership science, has yet to be sufficiently answered. Achieving a sustainable and peaceful coexistence for all living beings in the biosphere will require that we answer this ultimate leadership question: *How do we bring out the best of our diverse humanity to ensure a sustainable future?* The emergence of "restorative leadership" offers a response (Steffen, 2012).

Methodology

The guiding framework of *restorative leadership* has been discerned through a grounded theory process analyzing data from structured interviews, field observations, and primary and secondary source materials from over 45 individuals, organizations, and communities. Cases were chosen for the nature and degree of impact advancing measures of global sustainability and collective well-being. Data collection has spanned seven years, and the project appears to be the most extensive comparative analysis of its kind to date. The study draws from public, private, not-for-profit, and civil society sectors with foci on areas of business, development, ecology, and spirit. The full study includes active participation from recognized leadership such as: Her Excellency Gro Harlem Brundtland of Norway who chaired the first World Commission on Environment and Development and introduced the concept of sustainable development globally (WCED, 1987), as well as a lead negotiator of the *2030 Agenda for Sustainable Development*; the renowned development organization Tostan that empowers African communities to advance their visions of sustainable development, as well as the Skoll Foundation that funds innovative social entrepreneurs like Tostan to scale impact; and business leaders that changed corporate law to establish benefit corporations across a majority of the United States, as well as the leadership team that launched the B Corp movement, to name a few study cases.

What do those that have significantly advanced global sustainability and collective well-being have in common, and what distinguishes their leadership from that of others? What can they tell us about how to bridge the gap between vision and the necessary progress for a sustainable future? This chapter illustrates findings on *restorative leadership* demonstrated by a subset of cases reflecting underrepresented voices across a range of geographic and sector engagement. In addition to the international women's coalition WECAN and its members such as Amazon Watch (an indigenous rights advocacy organization), insights are illustrated by a rural community in the United States (Greensburg, Kansas), scientific leadership representing the voiceless interests of nature (biologist Janine Benyus and oceanographer Sylvia Earle), and the INGO Tostan. Findings illuminate the paradigm of restorative leadership and highlight a few practices that translate to remarkable outcomes such as establishing marine protected areas, arresting deforestation, evolving sustainable design innovation, and thriving out of natural disaster.

Emergence of Restorative Leadership

> We are at a tipping point. This is a turning point.
> We have a chance to get our act together.
> Celebrate, because if you choose a time to be influential,
> to make a difference in all of history, this is the moment!
> Dr. Sylvia Earle (personal communication, August 6, 2013)

The historical crossroads for humanity to choose between peril and sustainability calls forth the emergence of restorative leadership. At this great turning (Macy & Johnstone, 2012), some are numbed by fear of the future as they continue business and leadership as usual, some are preparing underground lairs to flee, yet others like the Earth and Climate Summit delegates are daring to envision and champion a sustainable future for life on Earth as they act now for future generations and for all living things. Orienting toward all and future generations is a distinction of restorative leadership. First introduced for its power to cultivate resilient communities, *restorative leadership recognizes the interconnectedness of all life and acts for the highest benefit to all. Striving to do no harm and to heal the Earth, our communities, and ourselves, restorative leadership cultivates collective well-being as a balanced expression of universal values and natural laws* (Steffen, 2012).

Restorative leadership emerges at the intersection of an ancient paradigm of wholeness with modern scientific and technological knowledge. The ancient paradigm is reflected by Chief Seattle's statement that, "All things

are connected. Whatever befalls the earth befalls the children of the earth"
(2015). Modern life sciences now confirm that interconnection and interdependency. Earth is a living and self-regulating system (Lovelock, 2003): we
have evidence of humanity's impact on the system, and that impact is
changing the conditions that have sustained the viability of life on Earth for
billions of years. Just as scientific theory affirms ancient wisdom, restorative
leadership captures the distinction of a phenomenon with deep roots.
Because it is evolutionary, engaging in restorative leadership naturally
reflects elements of existing theory and co-emergent leadership models.
Restorative leadership is fundamentally community leadership, inclusive in
nature and aligned with principles of multicultural leadership (Bordas,
2007). By being grounded in dynamically networked relationships and the
participatory nature of life, restorative leadership also reflects systems
thinking and systems leadership (Capra, 1996; Meadows, 2008; Senge et al.,
2015; Wheatley, 2006), and eco-mind and eco-leadership (Lappe, 2011;
Western, 2013). Akin to transformational leadership with a focus on purposeful outcomes and uplifting process, restorative leadership elevates leadership engagement beyond servant to transcendent levels (Burns, 1978;
Downton, 1973; Gardiner, 2006; Greenleaf, 1977). Restorative leadership
also extends adaptive leadership (Heifetz et al., 2009) by addressing what
could be considered the ultimate adaptive challenge – the existential threat
that humanity faces in the 21st century. A holistically integrated and multi-
dimensional approach, restorative leadership taps the best wisdom about
ways of being and doing to fulfill humanity's potential in response to the
21st century sustainability imperative.

Restorative Leadership Principles in Practice

Imagine the ocean teeming with life and vibrant with color. That is the
world Dr. Sylvia Earle first saw in 1979 when she made history as the first
human to dive solo and untethered to a depth of over half a mile. A literal
"living legend" according to the Library of Congress, Earle is a woman of
firsts beyond that dive, including the first female chief scientist of the U.S.
National Oceanic and Atmospheric Administration, and the first Time
Magazine Hero for the Planet (National Geographic, 2017). With insight
that extends to the deep-time perspective of the origins of life, Earle works
tirelessly to help others see that the "Earth generally and certainly the ocean
is not too big to fail" (personal communication, August 6, 2013). She warns
that we are altering the nature of nature itself, as evidenced by global
warming hazardously tipping the temperature and pH balance of the oceans,
waste disorienting and suffocating marine wildlife, and overfishing pushing
species and coastal cultures to extinction (Steffen, 2016). She is dedicated to
growing "awareness in people everywhere that their lives depend on maintaining the systems, the natural living systems, (and) protecting what
remains and restoring what we can as if our lives depend on doing that,

because they do" (Steffen, 2013). Through her perseverance, National Geographic Explorer Earle is credited for catalyzing the collective will to add the Ocean to Google Earth and to expand the Papahānaumokuākea Marine National Monument to be the world's largest marine protected area, among other leadership feats (Dell'Amore, 2009; Morelle, 2016).

Progress like that demonstrated by Earle and delegates from the International Women's Earth and Climate Summit reflects a qualitative distinction of restorative leadership. Fundamentally, leadership is an art and science that can be thought of as a collection of ways of being and doing that create the conditions for envisioned success to arise. In the case of restorative leadership, there are four principles underlying the distinct ways of being and doing that result in significant advancements toward global sustainability and collective well-being: *1) leadership is an innate and universal capacity; 2) the world is an interdependent and integrated whole; 3) genius, goodness, and generosity abound;* and *4) everything is possible.* These principles in turn give rise to a number of practices that are key to exceptional levels of positive impact, some of which will be illustrated below.

Leadership is an Innate and Universal Capacity

Individuals, communities, and organizations that practice restorative leadership have a holistic worldview. From a restorative leadership perspective, *leadership is an innate and universal capacity.* With roots in Old English, the word leadership in its original sense is the ability to influence others within a given context (OED, 2017). Being actors in the interconnected web of life is the universal context that all of humanity shares (Capra, 1996). Leadership is an innate and universal capacity because human beings cannot help but have influence on the web: each individual action and inaction impacts the interconnected unfolding of life itself. Liberating the power of our leadership potential and elevating the nature of our influence start with embracing the innate capacity to shape our world moment by moment. Naturally, the leadership question that follows is: What impact do we intend? With the power to shape the world comes the responsibility to do so with intention. Acting without intention risks being complicit with a harmful path. Choices matter and leadership matters. This fundamentally constructivist and ecological perspective translates to core restorative leadership practices such as *being highly intentional with life's leadership influence; awakening and authorizing;* and *advocating and empowering.* Awakening and authorizing, advocating, and empowering will be highlighted below.

Restorative leadership affirms and aligns with emerging Critical Leadership Studies insights that are pluralistic, participatory, and inclusive in perspective (Collinson, 2011). Consistent with critical theory (Horkheimer, 1972), power is implicit in all relationships. To engage in restorative leadership is to operate from power with others, recognizing that having influence is inherent within the web of interconnection and even marveling at such vast potential for beneficial impact throughout the web. Ecology and living systems science (Wheatley, 2006) help us to see that as ecological actors, each of us is in a position of power to play a distinct coevolutionary role in charting the future of humanity by virtue of the participatory nature of our inter-connected reality. Life is a coevolutionary flow; "Each of us has a capacity to actually make a difference and it starts with knowing" (S. Earle, personal communication, August 6, 2013). Restorative leadership is transformative in its ability to awaken and empower, and with that, to help humanity overcome the existential crisis now faced as a result of the dominant leadership paradigm. The state of the world is a reflection of the quality of our leadership.

Awaken and Authorize, Advocate and Empower

The moral courage to act boldly on behalf of all and to dedicate oneself to collective well-being starts, for most, with awakening – listening deeply to oneself and to ecosystem signals – and then self-authorizing individually and collectively for positive engagement. When Osprey Orielle Lake envisioned the Summit and co-founded WECAN, she intended "to engage women worldwide to take action as powerful stakeholders in climate change and sustainability solutions" (WECAN, 2013). This was in response to failure by the world's governments to act to avert a global rise of two degrees Celsius during climate treaty negotiations in Copenhagen. Lake self-authorized to advocate for women's and indigenous wisdom to influence global policy, and as a result WECAN allies now include Global Greengrant Fund, the National Wildlife Federation, Social Venture Network, and the Women's Environment and Development Organization, among others, championing positive change. The Declaration and subsequent campaign efforts among WECAN allies helped advance the Paris Agreement and compelled DNB of the Norwegian Oil Fund to fully divest their $331 million credit line of the Dakota Access Pipeline (Lake, 2017), in addition to other successes.

Because the dominant leadership paradigm is failing the planet and her people, humanity's diversity has been emboldened to engage. In the case of the Summit and WECAN, for example,

> Women around the world are rising with fierce resolve, because what is happening at national and international policy levels on climate change is not equivalent to the urgency we are facing...as we engage and take action we are part of social and environmental movements that are much greater than ourselves, greater than our communities or our countries. We are part of our planet's immune system that is rising up against injustices that are destroying our Earth and all life as we know it.
>
> (O. Lake, personal communication, July 17, 2014)

Restorative leadership advocates for diverse actors being heard and claiming their leadership as co-creative life forces. Local knowledge and lived experience are valued and imparted with authority and expertise. With the restorative leadership embrace of universal capacity comes the personal and collective responsibility to exercise what Paolo Freire – a renowned practitioner and scholar of critical pedagogy – described as our creative capacity to act to transform the world as permanent re-creators (Araujo Freire & Macedo, 1998). However, beyond traditional liberatory praxis that focuses on human discovery of oneself "to be a maker of the world of culture" (Bell et al., 1990, p. 85), restorative leadership awakens us to being ecological actors determining the future of life itself. As biologist Janine Benyus explains, there is an awakening that humans "are part of the redesign of everything on this planet. That they are agents of natural selection essentially …" (J. Benyus, personal communication, July 23, 2010).

The World is an Interdependent and Integrated Whole

Named one of the "World's Most Influential Designers" by *Businessweek* (Biomimicry Institute, 2017), Janine Benyus is a science writer best known as the author of *Biomimicry: Innovation inspired by nature* (1997). Benyus co-founded the world's first bio-inspired consultancy and launched the certified B Corp Biomimicry 3.8. Biomimicry brings the genius of nature's designs to sustainable solutions by emulating nature. For the impact of her restorative leadership transforming the field of design for highest-benefit outcomes, Benyus was named a Champion of the Earth in Science by the United Nations Environment Programme. Both Benyus and Earle have made very intentional restorative leadership choices to leverage the authority of their positions as scientists on behalf of nature, using their credentials and voices through spoken and written word to inspire the collective will to value nature from a holistic perspective. Engaging in restorative leadership reflects a return to the paradigm of wholeness, and demonstrates qualities of reverence and respect for the ever-evolving experience of life on Earth. Whether grounded in local knowledge or based in scientific fact, those practicing restorative leadership grasp the integrated and interdependent nature of the whole of life. Earle explains:

> All creatures depend on how the planet as a whole functions – not land here, ocean there, polar areas here, desert areas there. It's all connected in ways so that if any part suffers or changes, it resonates throughout the whole system. And as the creatures unique on Earth who can observe, document, [and] anticipate the consequences, we also have the responsibility to take this knowledge to heart while we still have time.
> (S. Earle, personal communication, August 6, 2013)

Restorative leadership orients vision and effort within that larger whole and acts from the implications of interdependence at multiple levels. Those who practice restorative leadership place preeminent value on relationships. Such a relational orientation is common to the organic solidarity of indigenous cultures like many allies of WECAN, and of place-based communities like the rural town of Greensburg, Kansas. As James Lovelock said, "[C]ountry people still living close to the earth often seemed puzzled that anyone would need to make a formal proposition of anything as obvious as the Gaia hypothesis" (Lovelock, 1979, p. 10), which is science explaining that the Earth is a complex, interdependent system. Such holism gives rise to core restorative leadership practices such as *taking the long view, persevering through learning,* and *leveraging the interconnection for cascading benefit.*

Take the Long View

Key to the level of impact possible through restorative leadership is the practice of taking the long view. Sylvia Earle explains that, "We need leaders who get the big picture, who are looking beyond their own time in office, or their own time in whatever role they are in ... to use that special gift that humans have to anticipate what their impact is going to have on the next decade, the next century, the next millennium, and to realize that we have a unique place in history right now" (personal communication, August 6, 2013). The age-old insight and scientific fact that the world is an inter-dependent web of life is grounded in a life cycle on Earth that extends into deep time (J. Macy, personal communication, July 28, 2010), both past and future. The past that we have to learn from is what Janine Benyus describes as "3.8 billion years of brilliant, time-tested solutions through life's evolu-tion" (personal communication, July 23, 2010). The future that we have to consider is best illustrated by the cultural practice of the Haudenosaunee Confederation, or Iroquois tribe, who "consider the impact on the seventh generation" when making decisions (Haudenosaunee, 2017).

Atossa Soltani, who is the founder, 20-year executive director, and now board president of WECAN ally Amazon Watch, describes taking the long view for collective well-being among indigenous peoples in the Amazon Rainforest:

> It's that everyone in their community is having access to a better life, but that better life does not jeopardize future generations. ... They get together, and it might take three years, but they get together and they articulate their true north or this idea of evolution ... they are looking at a circular frame around: "Okay in seven generations we want there to be forests standing with lots of wildlife and rivers that are running clean, with access to our medicinal plants, with our language still intact, with our cultural ceremonies and stories still alive, and with youth feeling proud to carry on this identity of our culture". That becomes their vision for their future and everything else, whether they are going to grow corn or do a fish farm or develop an educational program, has to serve the larger vision.
>
> (A. Soltani, personal communication, April 24, 2015)

Amazon Watch is one of the world's foremost advocacy organizations helping indigenous peoples to defend the forest for themselves and safeguard life's biodiversity for all of humanity. Soltani, recipient of the prestigious Hillary Laureate Award for Leadership in Climate Equity, guided the organization to forge cross-sector partnerships and longstanding relationships of trust while at the same time building local capacity throughout the Amazon basin of Brazil, Colombia, Ecuador, and Peru. As a result, indigenous voices have been present at forums like the United Nations COP21, and violators of indigenous and nature's rights have been held accountable, as with the verdict against Chevron Oil for $18 billion in penalties. Soltani illuminates deep understanding of interdependence and speaks to taking the long view organizationally: "When I look back at our successes, almost all of them took something like eight, 10, 12, 14 years. ... Generally, it's rare to have anything significant without spending at least ten plus years in a place committed to a long-term strategy. I think that that's been one of the lessons: it takes time, and we have to have the long-range view to think long-term and to think about our staying power in that place" (personal communication, April 24, 2015).

Genius, Goodness, and Generosity Abound

Restorative leadership empowers communities to come together in shared vision on common ground and orchestrates collective intelligence for collective action. An evolutionary paradigm, restorative leadership demonstrates a fundamental belief in human potential and the wisdom of human and natural communities, and therefore tends to co-create and facilitate rather than command and control (Steffen, 2012). Answering the 21st century call to evolve requires a combination of humility and confidence, and the courage to swim with others in unknown waters. For some in leadership it requires what Meg Wheatley calls a "conversion moment ... when you realize that it's not all up to you, and that other people are as competent and capable and creative as you are" (M. Wheatley, personal communication, May 11, 2011). For Janine Benyus, it's not only people that are competent: "If I could reveal anything that is hidden from us, at least in modern cultures, it would be to reveal something that we've forgotten that we used to know as well as our own names, and that is that we live in a competent universe, that we are part of a brilliant planet, and that we are surrounded by genius" (Benyus, 2009).

Intending to bring the highest benefit to all, restorative leadership recognizes the inherent value and goodness of the collective and utilizes a community-centered approach, engaging social networks to forward and sustain hopeful possibilities (Steffen, 2012). Also, asset-based and participatory, restorative leadership empowers diverse actors to see and apply their knowledge and skills, and to recognize their collective assets as valuable and relevant to addressing diverse community and global priorities. With deep faith in the resources of genius, generosity, and goodness that abound, key restorative leadership practices such as *ask and listen, align and co-create; bridge differences and scale across shared values;* and *act net generous* advance a world that works for all. Deep listening is the prerequisite to transformative progress. Through participatory process rooted in local knowledge and lived expertise, collective intelligence and wisdom can be revealed, amplified, and applied to resolving the world's most pressing problems.

Ask and Listen, Align and Co-create

Recognized as one of the world's leading social enterprises addressing complex global problems, Tostan is an INGO based in Senegal whose mission is to empower African communities to bring about sustainable development and positive social transformation based on respect for human rights. The rural regions across Sub-Saharan Africa where Tostan works could be considered ground zero for climate change. Restorative leadership as practiced by Tostan reveals the potential to chart a sustainable future when diverse actors are empowered to exercise their innate leadership potential and restore balance: to date, over 8,000 villages that have participated in the Tostan Community Empowerment Program (CEP) have self-organized and chosen to publicly abandon female genital cutting (FGC). With a vision of human dignity for all, Tostan provides human-rights based non-formal education to those that have not had access to formal schooling. The CEP utilizes active facilitation techniques and expressive arts to do so. Progress is co-produced, illuminating community assets and validating collective genius in process. During the three-year CEP, Tostan hosts weekly dialogues that explore and analyze community health, hygiene, environment, and education aligned with the community's development priorities. Tostan founder Molly Melching explains, "You have to start by getting people coming together around what is really important to them. Once they define that, it becomes much easier for them then to look at what they are doing and decide together." Melching calls it "an approach that unifies rather than divides" (M. Melching, personal communication, April 19, 2011).

Fundamental to restorative leadership, participatory practice is highly accessible: *ask and listen, align, and co-create.* This begins with starting where the community is. In the case of Tostan, for example,

> You start with why people are doing what they are doing, and see that the social constructs were decided upon and then became an integral part of the society over 200, 300, in the case of female genital cutting, 2,000 years ago. It became an integral part of that system in order for a respected woman to have that status, in order to prove that you were worthy of marriage. ... Then we look at the end result and ask, Why do we do this? Why is this necessary? Let's look at this now in terms of, What are our real values?
>
> (M. Melching, personal communication, April 19, 2011)

Melching clarifies that seeking to understand harmful practices like FGC does not mean excusing them. Rather, it empowers critically thoughtful dialogue, self-authorizing, and self-organizing in a nonjudgmental space consistent with core human values. As Skoll Foundation CEO Sally Osberg explains, "For people to change, they need some permission and they need some safety" (S. Osberg, personal communication, May 1, 2016). With participatory engagement, the process itself is transformative. The participatory approach liberates participants from internalized blocks or oppression, as well as acculturated patterns of silence or submission that perpetuate disengagement, disenfranchisement, and denial of personal and collective responsibility. In that space, communities feel freedom to revise their behavioral norms to more accurately reflect their values and vision for themselves.

In large part, participatory engagement is so effective because the process is the change and the means are the end (Steffen, 2012). Melching explains that, "If you don't go through the process, you lose so much of the meaning that comes with change" (M. Melching, personal communication, April 19, 2011). For example, the personal and collective actions involved in dialoguing about female genital cutting (FGC) represent change because the taboo of discussing FGC is being altered in the process of talking about it in public space. In addition, making inclusive decisions and choosing collective action in a deliberative way, particularly in cases that include men and women, organically evolves social norms of equity. For rural African women, the increase in confidence is evident as their voices grow from being barely audible in circle, to being projected while standing in front of their community, to being globally resonant when publicly abandoning the 2,000-year-old tradition of FGC.

Everything is Possible

From a restorative leadership perspective, everything is possible and we have infinite evolutionary potential to activate. Indeed, as Benyus says, "This is the era of demonstrating that it's possible" (J. Benyus, personal communication, July 23, 2010). We now know the state of the world as we have never known it, which calls us we to act as we have never acted – in concerted effort to yield unprecedented results like those of Tostan's rural African communities and the rural U.S. town of Greensburg, Kansas. During a historic storm in the spring of 2007, the people of Greensburg emerged from their shelters to discover that their town had been obliterated by the largest tornado in recorded history. Greensburg transformed total loss to renewal by rebuilding sustainably through a participatory process that considered the well-being of future generations and catapulted them to a global leadership role as a model of disaster recovery in a world facing increasingly extreme weather events.

Orienting from a paradigm of possibility, restorative leadership like that demonstrated by Greensburg navigates unknown waters while sustaining vision and charting breakthrough progress to yield previously unimaginable results. With a balance of humility and conviction to co-evolve for the highest benefit to all, there is deep commitment to and faith in the possible. To engage in restorative leadership is to have an empowered relationship to context and to choose possibility, which is consistent with liberatory praxis and constructivist facility. For example, Freire illustrated this mindset: "I had the possibility to experience hunger. And I say I had the possibility because I think that experience was very helpful to me" (Bell, et al, 1990, p. 24). Daniel Wallach, a community leader in Greensburg credited by many for effective post-disaster organizing that helped chart a sustainable future for the town, explains:

> I think that anything is possible. I mean, as trite as that sounds, we do forget the truth of that sometimes and we look at problems and think they're insurmountable, and they never are. We have incredibly profound creative spirits and what we're capable of doing individually is astonishing, but what we're capable of doing together is magical. ... So to be proactive in relation to problems instead of being reactive is key, because when we're proactive we feel a power and it makes us rise up.
> (D. Wallach, personal communication, July 23, 2013)

Proactive, possibility-oriented practices key to the transformative power of restorative leadership include *possibilize and create eddies of possibility by example; transform circumstances to aligned momentum;* and *live the guiding questions.*

Transform Circumstances to Aligned Momentum

Situated in the middle of everywhere or nowhere depending on who is talking, Greensburg is a politically conservative town in a conservative state, although for folks in Greensburg, ideology is irrelevant in disaster recovery. On May 4, 2007, the 120-year-old town of approximately 1,400 settled in for the night just as the sirens sounded. It took the first recorded EF5 tornado that was 1.7 miles wide with winds at over 200 MPH just eight minutes to reduce Greensburg to 388,000 tons of debris (Fox, 2013). Resourceful and resilient, Greensburg framed the disaster as an opening to honor lost lives and serve future generations. "Blessed with a unique opportunity to create a strong community, devoted to family, fostering business, working together for future generations," as the Greensburg Community Vision statement post-disaster reads (Fox, 2013, p. 21), Greensburg transformed the circumstance of utter devastation and the threat of ghost-town extinction to strengthening identity and becoming a model of what is possible. Mayor Bob Dixson illustrates this: "This is part of my healing process. (In) post-disaster recovery, if anything, you have two options: you can be humbly grateful or you can be grumbly hateful, and we as this community chose to be humbly grateful and we've had the opportunity to build for a better future" (B. Dixson, personal communication, July 20, 2013). Greensburg rebuilt itself through a highly visionary and participatory process, becoming one of the first cities to be 100 percent wind-powered and the first city in the United States to require that all city buildings be built to LEED platinum standards. The town now has the most LEED buildings per capita in the world (Greensburg, 2017).

In the first town meeting following the tornado, sitting mayor Lonnie McCollum, a former state patrol officer sensitive to the hardship, modeled the restorative leadership proclivity to *transform circumstances to aligned momentum* by declaring that recovering from the disaster was an opportunity to address systemic problems in the area. Local citizens like Daniel Wallach came with a concept paper envisioning a model green community and established the not-for-profit GreenTown to help facilitate the rebuild. City administrator Steve Hewitt was a consistent voice in a chorus of many championing the idea that Greensburg could and should rebuild with a bold vision. And they did. Dixson states:

> We did everything as a community, everything … we would have four and five hundred people show up at those community meetings under the big tent. We hugged together, we laughed together, we cried together, we worshiped together, and we planned together. So everything came from us.
>
> (personal communication, July 20, 2013)

Likening it to a barn raising, Wallach highlighted the restorative leadership distinction in process:

> The new model, which is really the old model, is … "Let's shepherd our resources and come out of this stronger and better," and again painting the picture of: If this succeeds, how good does this feel to be a model, to take this loss and to make a tribute to those that we did lose by doing this thing that is paying it forward in a really powerful way?
>
> (D. Wallach, personal communication, July 23, 2013)

To successfully transform the circumstances to aligned momentum, Greensburg returned to their foundational understanding of interdependence and core practice of taking the long view. One church leader explained:

> As pioneers, sustainability is not something new. It's old and familiar for us to be good stewards, making the most of what we had and taking care of those scarce resources. We already reused materials, what is now called recycling. We already placed our chicken coops facing south to prolong the laying of eggs. We already planted our crops on the north side to protect them. We were conservative with water because it

comes from our own lakes and streams or we had to pump it by hand. It's not something new, it's something old. We were called to be good stewards of our land.

(Woman Church Leader, personal communication, May 3, 2017).

And so, Greensburg mobilized the collective will to chart a sustainable future because, as this leader said with simple clarity,

It's the responsible thing to do. When the community was first built in the late 1800s, we built the best we could with what we had. It's the same thing now with new technology. Why would we build to the technologies of the 19th century and not build with the best we have now? It uses less energy, less resources, and is built to last 100 years or more. It's the right thing to do. ... We are doing it for the next generation. We are doing it for the future.

(personal communication, May 3, 2017)

Building upon a tradition of knowledge that respects the Earth and natural laws, while integrating modern scientific and technological advancements, Greensburg took the noble restorative leadership path of acting for the highest benefit to all in the most dire of circumstances.

Conclusion

With the future of life on Earth at stake, it is the collection of individual acts and leadership choices made moment by moment that can transform the risk of peril to previously unimaginable possibility. The extraordinary examples of Greensburg, Tostan, Amazon Watch, Janine Benyus, Sylvia Earle, and the Women's Earth and Climate Action Network illustrate the power of restorative leadership to chart a sustainable future where all life can thrive. It is possible. Drawing on what is both ancient and innovative, the emergent trend of restorative leadership offers breakthrough insight on how to mobilize the collective will to sustain and thrive at this time in our evolutionary history.

Manifesting a future that thrives in balance requires that we bring out the best of our diverse humanity. Restorative leadership guides us in doing just that as we remember what we have forgotten, balancing modernity's progress with a return to wisdom ways of knowing and being part of the interconnected web of life. As a leadership heart-mindset, restorative leadership's underlying principles that leadership is an innate and universal capacity, that the world is an interdependent and integrated whole, that genius, goodness, and generosity abound, and that everything is possible – along with their aligned collection of practices – yield globally resonant impact. Restorative leadership elevates leadership engagement to transcendent levels, understanding that with the power to shape the world comes the responsibility to do so with noble intention.

It is time to reawaken to the interconnectedness of all life and act for the highest benefit to all. Striving to do no harm and to heal the Earth, our communities, and ourselves, there exists a unique opportunity before us: To restore humanity's sense of interdependent wholeness and to ignite the collective will to fulfill humanity's potential. Each of us is in a unique position to play a distinct coevolutionary role in charting the future of life itself. It is time that we activate our individual and collective power in service to future generations of all life.

References

Araujo Freire, A. M., & Macedo, D. (Eds) (1998). *The Paulo Freire Reader.* New York: Continuum.

Bell, B., Gaventa, J., & Peters, J. (1990). *We Make the Road by Walking: Conversations on education and social change: Myles Horton and Paulo Freire.* Philadelphia, PA: Temple University Press.

Benyus, J. (1997). *Biomimicry: Innovation inspired by nature.* New York: Harper Collins.

Benyus, J. (2009). Janine Benyus: Biomimicry in action. TED Talk. Available at: www.ted.com/talks/janine_benyus_biomimicry_in_action/transcript?language=en.

Biomimicry Institute. (2017). Janine Benyus: Co-founder, Biomimcry Institute. Retrieved from: https://biomimicry.org/janine-benyus/.

Bordas, J. (2007). *Salsa, Soul and Spirit: Leadership for a multicultural age.* San Francisco, CA: Berrett-Koehler.

Burns, J.M. (1978). *Leadership.* New York: Harper & Row.

Capra, F. (1996). *The Web of Life.* New York: Anchor Books.

Chief Seattle. (2015). First people. Retrieved from: www.firstpeople.us/FP-Html-Wisdom/ChiefSeattle.html.

Collinson, D. (2011). *Critical Leadership Studies.* In A. Bryman, D. Collinson, K. Grint, B. Jackson & M. Uhl-Bien (Eds), *The Sage Handbook of Leadership* (pp. 181–194). Thousand Oaks, CA: Sage Publications, Inc.

Dell'Amore, C. (2009). New Google Ocean Takes Google Earth Beyond the "Dirt". *National Geographic News*, February 2. Retrieved from: http://news.nationalgeographic.com/news/2009/02/090202-google-oceans-missions_2.html.

Downton, J.V. (1973). *Rebel Leadership: Commitment and charisma in the revolutionary process.* New York: Free Press.

Fox, T.J. (2013). *Green Town USA: The handbook for America's sustainable future.* New York: Hatherleigh Press.

Gardiner, J.J. (2006). Transactional, Transformational, and Transcendent Leadership: Metaphors mapping the evolution of the theory and practice of governance. *Kravis Leadership Institute Leadership Review*, 6(Spring), 62–76.

Greenleaf, R.K. (1977). *Servant Leadership: A journey into the nature of legitimate power and greatness.* Mahwah, NJ: Paulist Press.

Greensburg. (2017). Rebuilding Stronger, Better, Greener. Retrieved from: www.greensburgks.org/.

Haudenosaunee. (2017). Haudenosaunee Confederacy. Retrieved from: www.haude nosauneeconfederacy.com/values.html.

Hawken, P. (2017). *Drawdown: The most comprehensive plan ever proposed to reverse global warming.* New York: Penguin Books.

Heifetz, R.A., Grashow, A., & Linsky, M. (2009). *The Practice of Adaptive Leadership: Tools and tactics for changing your organization and the world.* Boston, MA: Harvard Business Press.

Horkheimer, M. (1972). *Critical Theory: Selected essays.* New York: Continuum.

Lake, O.O. (2017). Indigenous Women of Standing Rock Resistance Movement Speak Out on Divestment. Retrieved from: www.ecowatch.com/women-standin g-rock-divestment-2359104248.html.

Lappe, F.M. (2011). *EcoMind: Changing the way we think, to create the world we want.* New York: Nation Books.

Lovelock, J. (1979). *Gaia: A new look at life on earth.* Oxford: Oxford University Press.

Lovelock, J. (2003). Gaia: The living earth. *Nature,* 426(6968), 769–770. doi:10.1038/ 426769a.

Macy, J., & Johnstone, C. (2012). *Active Hope: How to face the mess we're in without going crazy.* Novato, CA: New World Library.

Meadows, D.H. (2008). *Thinking in Systems: A primer.* White River Junction, VT: Chelsea Green.

Morelle, R. (2016). World wildlife "falls by 58% in 40 years." *BBC News,* October 27. Retrieved from: www.bbc.com/news/science-environment-37775622.

National Geographic. (2017). Explorers bios. Retrieved from: www.nationalgeograp hic.com/explorers/bios/sylvia-earle/.

OED. (2017). *Oxford English Dictionary.* Retrieved from: www.oed.com/.

Senge, P., Hamilton, H., & Kania, J. (2015). The Dawn of System Leadership. *Stanford Social Innovation Review,* 13(1), 27–33.

Steffen, S.L. (2012). Beyond Environmental Leadership to Restorative Leadership: An emerging framework for cultivating resilient communities in the 21st century. In D.R. Gallagher (Ed.), *Environmental Leadership: A reference handbook* (pp. 273– 281). Thousand Oaks, CA: Sage Publications, Inc.

Steffen, S.L. (2016). Earth Day is Ocean Day. Retrieved from: www.restorative-lea dership.org/blog/earth-day-is-ocean-day.

United Nations. (2015). Transforming our World: The 2030 agenda for sustainable development. Retrieved from: www.un.org/ga/search/view_doc.asp?symbol=A/ RES/70/1&Lang=E.

WCED. (1987). *Brundtland Report: Our common future.* Oxford: Oxford University Press.

WECAN. (2013). Women's Earth & Climate Action Network: A Declaration. Retrieved from: http://wecaninternational.org/pages/declaration#.WVV3KRPyuHp.

Western, S. (2013). *Leadership: A critical text.* Thousand Oaks, CA: Sage Publications, Inc.

Wheatley, M. (2006). *Leadership and the New Science: Discovering order in a chaotic world.* San Francisco, CA: Berrett-Koehler.

Conclusion

Benjamin W. Redekop, Deborah Rigling Gallagher and Rian Satterwhite

A critical perspective on leadership requires us to examine *what is*, to uncover hidden biases and tired explanations, so that we can work toward *what can be*. Accordingly, a critical perspective is not one bound by critique alone, but with an eye toward change. This approach is perhaps best described by the philosopher Michel Foucault, who stated, "I don't construct my analyses in order to say, 'This is the way things are, you are trapped.' I say these things only insofar as I believe it enables us to transform them. Everything I do is done with the conviction that it may be of use" (Foucault, 2002, pp. 294–295). In a time of existential crisis in the natural world, critical analysis – analysis that seeks to upend ineffectual dogma and liberate us from orthodox thinking – is not only useful, but *required*. To that end, our work here centered on gathering leadership thinkers and leadership doers from a variety of perspectives to critically examine existing leadership theories and practices, offer hopeful innovations, and inspire future work.

What have we learned from this diverse examination of innovations in environmental leadership?

First, we understand that mainstream approaches to thinking about leadership, which consider leadership position equal to leadership behavior and celebrate the individual leader's charisma while ignoring cultural context, are unhelpful (Bendell, Little, & Sutherland, Chapter 1). This critique is especially insightful as we face the shared dilemmas of sustainability including, but not limited to, climate change. A critical perspective on environmental leadership asks us to unlearn old ways of thinking that identify problems and challenges to be conquered by hierarchical leaders. Outmoded understandings and practices of leadership both reflect and perpetuate the unsustainable world-system that has emerged in the past few centuries and as such can be seen as part of the problem. Instead we must reconfigure our understanding of leadership in a way that embraces the vibrant ecosystem in which environmental leadership operates, and learn to accept and celebrate our connectedness.

Fortified with a critique of conventional leadership theories, we understand that to make progress we must build a new set of theories and practices. Our exploration here offers a number of paths forward. We explore the use of a critical constructivist lens (Satterwhite, Chapter 2) on leadership for sustainability, which implores us to knit together contexts of biosphere, systems, and justice. Linking these universal and shared contexts offers opportunities to discover leadership that connects humans and nature, emphasizes positive change in the world, and seeks to eliminate oppression. Use of such a lens acknowledges that we are both embodied (physical) and moral (spiritual) beings who are part of larger natural and social systems that we did not create, which indeed created us. For too long leadership scholars have bought into the notion that leaders are free agents operating without constraints – outside of, rather than embedded within, the natural and social systems that organize the world. One of the great strengths of an ecological perspective on leadership is that it decenters positional leadership and helps us to see it as an important but partial representation of ways in which leadership may be enacted. We are all embedded in larger contexts that condition and shape our behavior and thinking.

So, too, we ponder the eco-leadership paradox (Western, Chapter 3). Eco-leadership is motivated by a need to incorporate ethical concepts and notions of connectivity into our understanding of leadership. A paradox arises when we are driven to employ increasingly outdated leadership discourses to bring eco-leadership into being. Western suggests eco-leadership is a meta-discourse that prods us to move beyond individualized and organization-bound conceptions of leadership and make connections between society, technology, and nature. It is not so much a matter of "solving" the paradox as of engaging it in a productive manner, which can mean not simply rejecting outdated forms of leadership entirely, but rather employing those elements in limited ways as needed moving forward. Such an approach recognizes that we are situated in time and that lasting change usually happens slowly and incrementally.

We also understand that to truly make progress we must locate considerations of purpose and place (Evans, Chapter 4) in our leadership theories going forward. If we forget that sustainability is a normative concept that rejects hegemony, is tightly linked to social justice, and depends on collaboration and equal access to opportunities to serve, we will have missed an opportunity to address key environmental and socio-ethical challenges.

A critical examination of innovative approaches to environmental leadership must also consider how theory is anchored in the natural world and how descriptions of exemplary leadership practice can amplify lessons initiated through critique. We've shown that leadership is a complex system and therefore concepts from complexity science such as open systems, feedback loops, and interdependence can be applied to increase our understanding of how organizations effectively implement principles of eco-leadership to confront environmental challenges (Cletzer & Kaufman, Chapter 5). Armed with this knowledge, we set out into the field with an indigenous mentor to learn how the natural world can be incorporated as the sixth component of a widely held leadership model to make that model more synthetic and integrative (McManus, Chapter 6). This new understanding helps us to posit that leadership both functions within the natural world and is regulated by it – a critical perspective far outside of traditional theories that are anchored in charisma and power. We see how innovative, collaborative, and non-positional environmental leadership operates in often overlooked majority world settings, such as the tropical biosphere (Kosempel, Olson, & Penados, Chapter 7), where the impacts of climate change and environmental degradation are close at hand.

Climate change, perhaps the supreme existential challenge of environmental leadership, plays a significant role in helping us to connect our critical exploration of environmental leadership with the materiality of living in the Anthropocene. Examining environmental leadership innovation at the level of global politics (Gallagher, Chapter 8), we see how an international governance system can serve as a platform for collaborative leadership, which untethers members from organization-bound entitlements to form leadership collectives for the common good. We find that climate change increasingly calls people to act not as heroic, positional leaders, but to acknowledge leadership's connecting role in our societal ecosystem. Climate change leaders are more likely to find success in catalyzing followers' action through exposure to inspiration and hope rather than frightening scenarios (Redekop & Thomas, Chapter 9). Here, as in other settings, we see that bottom-up leadership at the grassroots is a promising way forward. Calling attention to local impacts of climate change, attending to local concerns and interests, and involving local communities in discussion and action on climate change are approaches being used by grassroots climate leaders worldwide. Engaging others via personal narrative and storytelling, and the establishment of emotional connection and vulnerability are also prevalent behaviors exhibited by second-generation climate leaders.

Followers' responses to climate change are thus impacted by a variety of contextual factors, and those wishing to show leadership on this issue must be aware of and respond to them (Brown & McManus, Chapter 10). We find again and again that leaders must be locally grounded and understand that economic and social conditions offer unique challenges. Such conditions create both barriers and opportunities for enacting environmental leadership even in the face of visible, urgent impacts of climate change, as we see in our study of Ethiopian environmental leadership (Mengistu, Shimelis, & Miller, Chapter 11).

In many such contexts (including in the "first world"), reliance on top-down governmental leadership can be disempowering and the solutions proposed inappropriate to local conditions. One of the many paradoxes of leadership on climate change is the apparent need for coordinated global action – due to the severity and urgency of the problem – in the face of the well-documented human tendency to think and act locally. Given such paradoxes, traditional mainstream approaches to leadership provide at best a partial answer and at worst (as argued in Chapters 1 and 4) exacerbate the problem. Perhaps Western's treatment of the "eco-leadership paradox" is helpful here: eco-leadership functions as a "meta-discourse" that deploys traditional leadership behaviors in a provisional and productive manner as we move into a new era of global connection and change.

Lastly, our examination of innovation in environmental leadership leads us to acknowledge that environmental leadership is in the end a personal endeavor. Personal environmental leadership practice calls on leaders to turn from charisma and heroism to rely on openness and introspection, and to apply long-term thinking, rather than a focus on short-term victories (Allen, Chapter 13). We know that we can improve environmental leadership practice – with its related social-justice dimensions – by learning important lessons from indigenous leaders who have long fostered connections to followers through storytelling (Andrews, Chapter 12).

Innovative environmental leadership practice at its best offers leaders and followers opportunities to mount a noble cause and in so doing seek restoration, both of the earth and of themselves (Steffen, Chapter 14). Here, we are again reminded of the connection-building role of leadership. Seen from this vantage point, environmental leaders are more like "connectors" than directors (whether of orchestras or organizations or the body politic). Indeed, one of the guiding themes of this book has been the importance of connection.

Foucault noted that critique "should be an instrument for those who fight, those who resist and refuse what is" (1991, p. 84). The existential challenges of environmental leadership detailed in this volume call on us to critically revise theory and update our practice. We must move away from leadership theory and practice that operate in myopic ignorance of the larger natural and social systems of which we are a part; that disrupt communities, celebrate position over impact, and serve harmful power dynamics by generating limited narratives of heroism and charisma. Instead, we must commit to developing critical, reflective, and connective practices with one another. The theories that guide us should be grounded in empiricism and intuition, in pragmatism and justice, in lived and inherited wisdom. As responsible inhabitants of the biosphere, we must relentlessly pursue connectedness, collaboration, and justice; in doing so we will develop leadership practices that better serve people *and* the planet.

The Editors

References

Foucault, M. (1991). Questions of Method. In G. Burchell et al. (Eds), *The Foucault Effect: Studies in governmentality with two lectures by and an interview with Michel Foucault* (pp. 73–86). Chicago, IL: University of Chicago Press.

Foucault, M. (2002). Interview with Michel Foucault. In J. Faubion (Ed.), *Michel Foucault: Power, essential works of Foucault 1954–1984* (pp. 239–297). London: Penguin Books.

Index

For Product Safety Concerns and Information please contact our EU
representative GPSR@taylorandfrancis.com
Taylor & Francis Verlag GmbH, Kaufingerstraße 24, 80331 München, Germany

www.ingramcontent.com/pod-product-compliance
Ingram Content Group UK Ltd.
Pitfield, Milton Keynes, MK11 3LW, UK
UKHW020939180425
457613UK00019B/462